THE NEW URBAN HISTORY

FORTHCOMING VOLUMES IN THE MSSB SERIES *Quantitative Studies in History:*

PUBLISHED:

The New Urban History

Quantitative Explorations by
American Historians

EDITED BY

Leo F. Schnore

WITH A FOREWORD BY

Eric E. Lampard

CONTRIBUTORS

Martyn J. Bowden - Kathleen Neils Conzen
Claudia Dale Goldin - Robert Higgs - Kenneth T. Jackson
Zane L. Miller - Allan R. Pred - Gregory H. Singleton
Joseph A. Swanson - Jeffrey G. Williamson

PRINCETON UNIVERSITY PRESS

LCC: 73-2474
ISBN: 0-691-04624-7 (Hardcover Edition)
ISBN: 0-691-04624-7 (Limited Paperback Edition)

Library of Congress Cataloging in Publication Data will
be found on the last printed page of this book

Publication of this book has been aided by
the Whitney Darrow Publication Reserve Fund of
Princeton University Press

Chapter 1, "Large-City Interdependence and the Pre-electronic Diffusion
of Innovations in the United States," by Allan R. Pred, is reprinted from
Geographical Analysis, Vol. 3 (April, 1971), pp. 165–181. Copyright © 1971
by the Ohio State University Press. All Rights Reserved.

An abbreviated version of Chapter 8, "Urbanization and Inventiveness
in the United States, 1870-1920," by Robert Higgs, appeared in the
Journal of Political Economy, Vol. 79 (May-June, 1971), pp. 661–667.
Copyright © 1971 by the University of Chicago Press. All Rights Reserved.
Still another short version of the Higgs essay appeared in
Cities in American History, edited by Kenneth T. Jackson and
Stanley K. Schultz, pp. 16–22.
Copyright © 1972 by Alfred A. Knopf, Inc. All Rights Reserved.

Printed in the United States of America
by Princeton University Press, Princeton, New Jersey

FOR Our Parents

Series Preface

THIS third volume of the MSSB series, *Quantitative Studies in History*, deals with the process of urbanization in the United States. The focus is primarily on the experiences of the nineteenth century, but some attention is given to the experiences of the early decades of the twentieth century, and there are a few glances backward to developments prior to 1800. The main substantive problems are the delineation of the forces which promoted the growth of cities, and the analysis of the effects of such growth on the economic, social, and political life of the inhabitants. The quantitative techniques which are employed to probe these issues are, for the most part, fairly simple. As several of the essays demonstrate, "mere" counting can yield quite important insights. Still, for some problems more complex techniques, such as regression analysis, were required.

The Mathematical Social Science Board (MSSB) was established in 1964 under the aegis of the Center for Advanced Study in the Behavioral Sciences "to foster advanced research and training in the application of mathematical methods in the social sciences." The following fields are each represented on MSSB by one member: anthropology, economics, history, geography, linguistics, political science, psychology, and sociology. The three methodological disciplines of mathematics, statistics, and computer science are also represented. Members of MSSB are appointed, subject to the approval of the Board of Trustees of the Center, for a term of four years. At the present time the members of MSSB are:

Allen Newell, Department of Computer Science, Carnegie-Mellon
University

Stanley Peters, Department of Linguistics, University of Texas

Roy Radner, Departments of Economics and Statistics, University
of California (Berkeley)

William H. Riker, Department of Political Science, University of
Rochester

Herbert A. Simon, Department of Industrial Relations, Carnegie-
Mellon University

Charles Tilly, Departments of History and Sociology, University of
Michigan

MSSB has established advisory committees to plan its activities in
the various substantive fields with which it is concerned. The current
members of the History Advisory Committee are listed on page ii
above.

Supported by grants from the National Science Foundation,[1] MSSB
has organized five major classes of activities.

(1) Training Programs, which last from two to eight weeks during
the summer, are designed to provide young pre- and post-Ph.D.'s with
intensive training in some of the mathematics pertinent to their substantive fields and with examples of applications to specific problems.

(2) Research and Training Seminars, which last from four to six
weeks, are composed of both senior scientists and younger people
who have already received some training in mathematical applications. The focus is on recent research, on the intensive exploration of
new ideas, and on the generation of new research. The training is
less formal than in (1); it has the apprentice nature of advanced
graduate work.

(3) Advanced Research Workshops last from four to six weeks, but
are almost exclusively restricted to senior scientists and are devoted
to fostering advanced research. They afford the possibility of extensive
and penetrating contact over a prolonged period, which would otherwise probably not be possible, of men deeply steeped in research.

(4) Preparation of Teaching Materials. In some areas, the absence
of effective teaching materials—even of suitable research papers—is
a very limiting factor in the development of research and teaching
activities within the university framework. The Board has, therefore,

[1] This volume was prepared with the support of National Science Foundation
Grant number GS3256. Any opinions, findings, conclusions, or recommendations
expressed below are those of the authors and do not necessarily reflect the views
of NSF or MSSB.

viii

felt that it could accelerate the development of such materials, in part by financial support, and in part by help in organizing their preparation.

(5) Special Conferences. Short conferences, lasting a few days, are organized to explore the possibilities of the successful development of mathematical theory and training in some particular area that has not previously been represented in the programs, or to review the progress of research in particular areas when such a review seems warranted.

Robert William Fogel, for the
History Advisory Committee, MSSB

Cambridge, Massachusetts
May, 1974

Contents

THE NEW URBAN HISTORY

Further Reflections on the "New" Urban History: A Prefatory Note

LEO F. SCHNORE

I

THE PAPERS gathered in this volume are representative products of a three-day conference held in Madison, Wisconsin, in June 1970. The conference was entitled "The New Urban History: Quantitative Explorations" and was jointly supported by the Mathematical Social Science Board and the University of Wisconsin. It is appropriate at this time to take a retrospective view of the aims and actual products of the conference, especially with respect to the question of whether or not they constitute a "new" urban history.

The original aims were quite simple: to bring together a group of younger American scholars who were using quantitative methods on urban-historical problems—at whatever level of statistical or mathematical sophistication, and regardless of disciplinary background or affiliation or period of interest, remote in time or more modern. To this end, a small group of "urbanists" at Madison—the editor and Stanley K. Schultz (Department of History), David Ward (Department of Geography), and Jeffrey G. Williamson (Department of Economics)—formed an ad hoc committee to consider who might be invited, and in what capacity these individuals might serve, as authors, discussants, or panel members. Papers were prepared in advance, oral summary presentations were made, and the entire proceedings were taped. A final session devoted to a panel discussion was arranged in which some "old" historians, more traditionally oriented scholars, were asked to react to the preceding five three-hour sessions, the papers themselves, and the foregoing formal and informal discussions.[1]

II

To the editor's knowledge, the very first use of the phrase "the new urban history" appeared as the subtitle in a book edited by Stephan Thernstrom and Richard Sennett—*Nineteenth-Century Cities: Essays*

---

[1] A roughly edited transcript of this taped panel discussion is available upon request to the editor, in care of the Center for Demography and Ecology, 3220 Social Science Building, University of Wisconsin, Madison, Wisconsin 53706.

in the New Urban History.[2] In the preface to that work, the editors explicitly characterized the "new" urban history as having three related traits: (1) an interest in linking sociological theory to historical data, moving back and forth across the boundaries separating the traditional disciplines; (2) an understanding of the uses of quantitative materials; (3) an eagerness to broaden the scope of urban studies to embrace the social experience of ordinary, unexceptional people.[3]

Except for the matter of quantification and special attention to sociology, this characterization of the field is strikingly reminiscent of "the new history" advocated at Columbia University by James Harvey Robinson shortly after World War I. As the late Richard Hofstadter put it, "Robinson appealed to his colleagues to make history increasingly relevant to the present and its problems, to look at political events in their social and economic environment, to write history which took account of the experiences of the common man, and to cooperate with the social sciences."[4] Our efforts in the Madison conference were clearly oriented in this direction, as the following pages will amply demonstrate.

The only real consensus achieved at the Madison conference, however, was that an "old-new" distinction was insufficient to embrace much of the urban-historical work that was going on in the 1960s. More than a simple dichotomy is required. A trichotomy makes more sense. In addition to (1) the traditional or "old" narrative historian, it was argued, one must recognize (2) the enumerator, or one who merely counts and presents findings in simple percentage distributions or uncomplicated cross-tabulations, and (3) the model-builder, or one who constructs a formal theory in statistical or mathematical terms, and who tests hypotheses derived therefrom. Indeed, this third class must be understood to cover such work as the last chapter in this book—by the economists Swanson and Williamson—wherein empirical data are not confronted at all.

In any event, the new urban historians sometimes seem preoccupied with a very limited range of problems. Chief among these are questions of urban stratification and social mobility (once thought to be the private preserve of sociologists and a few economists) and spatial patterns in cities (heretofore the sole concern of "social ecologists"

---

[2] New Haven: Yale University Press, 1969. This volume was the product of a conference held at Yale University in November 1968.

[3] Thernstrom and Sennett, *ibid.*, Preface, p. vii.

[4] Richard Hofstadter, "History and Sociology in the United States," in Hofstadter and Seymour Martin Lipset (editors), *Sociology and History: Methods* (New York: Basic Books, Inc., 1968), p. 8.

and geographers). As some of the participants pointed out, issues of urban leadership and broader questions concerning the evolving institutional structure of the American city have not been pointedly addressed by quantitative means. Perhaps that is because psychologizing at a distance—whether through time or across cultures—is a hazardous and frustrating business.[5]

In an attempt to gain consensus, the editor confronted the panel and the other participants with a schematic summary of certain central tendencies in the works of "old" versus "new" urban historians. It was set out as follows:

"OLD"	"NEW"
1) *Narrative* in style	1) *Quantitative* in emphasis
2) More clearly *substantive* interest in intellectual problems, with eclectic dependence on documentary evidence	2) *Methodological* emphases; "how to" answer questions of more concern than the questions themselves
3) *Traditional periodization,* with presidential terms (or such categories as "the antebellum period" or "the Progressive era") used as the time frame for study	3) *Urban-relevant periodization,* such as those based on forms of intra- and interurban transportation
4) *Synthetic,* in the sense of efforts to encompass the story whole	4) *Analytic,* in the sense of focussing on specific hypotheses
5) Given to *localistic* case studies, or "urban biography"	5) *Comparative* in orientation, with regional and even national coverage; many cities studied

This scheme was flatly rejected all around. Instances were cited, for example, in which "old" urban historians (such as Carl Bridenbaugh and Blake McKelvey) had used quantitative materials. Equally persuasive was the point that some "new" urban historians (including some of those represented in this volume) were not averse to case studies; another example is the controversial work of Peter R. Knights,

---

[5] See the priorities for quantitative urban-historical research set out in Leo F. Schnore, "Problems in the Quantitative Study of Urban History," In Harold James Dyos (editor), *The Study of Urban History* (London: Edward Arnold, Ltd., 1968), pp. 189-208. The Dyos volume is also the product of a conference, this one held at the University of Leicester in September 1966.

exclusively focussed on Boston.[6] The only consensus achieved was that (1) there is a limited range of substantive questions and problems that can be addressed by quantitative methods, and (2) we should clearly identify those that are more *and* less amenable to statistical or mathematical treatment.

III

SOME of the problems that can be and are being analyzed with quantitative approaches have recently been suggested. Since our Madison conference was held, one of the acknowledged leaders in the field—Stephan Thernstrom—has published some "Reflections on the New Urban History."[7] He actually displays considerable uneasiness in putting forth the rubric itself. He opines that the very label "the new urban history" may have been somewhat misleading in three respects.

> First, the image it conveyed of a monolithic "old" urban history was obviously oversimplified. . . .[8] A second possibly misleading feature of the phrase, "the new urban history," lies with the term "urban," which seems to imply that this is a distinctive specialized field of historical inquiry. I am doubtful about that. . . .[9]
> A final comment on the label "the new urban history" is that although it consciously echoes "the new economic history," the analogy should not be pressed too far. Quantitative evidence plays a greater role in both types of literature than in their traditional counterparts. In both there is less sheer description, and more use of theory. But the differences are important.[10]

To find one of the exemplars of the field displaying such hesitancy in using the term should serve as a caution to us all.

Actually, however, one need not build up unrealizable hopes of fulfillment by simply pointing to some commonalities in a body of work that is now being fashioned day by day. It is not presently possible to offer a comprehensive and synthetic statement of what is transpiring under the rubric "the new urban history." Topically,

[6] Peter R. Knights, *The Plain People of Boston, 1830-1860: A Study in City Growth* (New York: Oxford University Press, 1971).

[7] Stephan Thernstrom, "Reflections on the New Urban History," *Daedalus*, 100 (Spring 1971), pp. 359-375.

[8] *Ibid.*, p. 360.

[9] *Ibid.*, p. 361.

[10] *Ibid.*, p. 362.

the field is extremely diverse, as these nine essays demonstrate. There is no unitary subject matter, nor problem, nor method. One cannot fashion an agenda for a field that is so new and subject to radical innovations. One hesitates, for example, to suggest the full implications of the computerization of a great deal of urban-historical data that seems to lie just around the corner.

Actually, there is much to be gained by a more modest perspective on the field. And this takes us back to the question of the very motivation of the conference organizers. It was the purpose of the organizers of the conference to bring together younger American scholars who were working in a variety of disciplines with quantitative methods on urban-historical problems. What the conference revealed most clearly was that there is wide variation in levels of quantitative sophistication in use. In part, at least, this variation is attributable to the fact that the various social science disciplines have reached different levels of methodological sophistication. Thus we find the work of the historical economists (represented in this volume by Goldin, Higgs, and Swanson and Williamson) tends to be heavily mathematical or statistical. The historical geographers (here including Bowden and Pred) occupy an intermediate ground. In the main, the papers by the historians (Conzen, Jackson, Miller, and Singleton) tend to require much less mathematical or statistical facility on the part of the reader. In this respect, then, the papers collected here reflect the differing methodological statuses of the three fields. Many of the papers presented here are the products of rather simple enumerations of data. Others involve the construction of fairly difficult mathematical models. The last paper, by Swanson and Williamson, is of this latter character; it is devoid of actual data, and represents a logical exercise of considerable sophistication.

Actually, the entire field of urban history may itself be regarded as relatively "new," at least if one considers the recent availability of courses and books with such a title. It would be rather presumptuous, then, to single out only a fraction of the work carried out under the "urban" rubric as distinctively "new." Scholars in every age seem to work with the available tools, and much of today's urban history is probably quantitative on this account; the field itself emerged in a time when students of history in general were being urged by many older scholars to include some mathematics and/or statistics in their training. (Witness the emergence of "cliometrics" since World War II. Quantitative treatments of topics other than those traditionally encompassed by economic history may now be found in relative abundance.)

Thernstrom, himself, has identified five major problems that seem most amenable to quantitative study: (1) "Urban population fluidity," or studies of "physical mobility" or migration;[11] (2) "Class and ethnic differences in spatial mobility," or migration differentials;[12] (3) "Rates and trends in social mobility."[13] (One of the important tentative conclusions set out by Thernstrom is as follows: "It is also noteworthy that, despite the old tradition of social criticism which sees the class system becoming more rigid as a result of the spread of factory production, the close of the frontier, the shrinking of class differentials in birth rates, and various other causes, there seems to have been astonishing uniformity in mobility rates over a long span of time;"[14]) (4) "Immigration and differential opportunity," or the study of particular ethnic groups and their experience with the opportunity structure in the United States;[15] (5) "Negro migrants and European immigrants," stressing the particular disadvantages of the black in gaining a foothold on what has been conceived of as the peculiarly American "ladder of opportunity."[16]

Other areas of investigation that Thernstrom sees as opening up include (1) family structure of black and other groups in nineteenth- and early twentieth-century cities, (2) the "texture" of neighborhood life and "the flow of people between socially distinct sections of the city,"[17] (3) urban institutions like schools, churches, and voluntary associations, and (4) "the interaction between urban environments and the social organization of work."[18] Thernstrom concludes:

> The emphasis of research in the new urban history thus far has been heavily quantitative. The sources which had been most neglected by previous investigators were peculiarly well-suited to quantitative treatment and seemed to offer a quick pay-off to those willing to attempt it. This was salutary on the whole, I think, because there was a great deal to be learned from even the most

[11] *Ibid.*, pp. 366-367. The editor has had other thoughts about the "new" label, too. See Leo F. Schnore, review of Scott Greer, et al. (editors), *The New Urbanization* (New York: St. Martin's Press, 1968), in *Urban Affairs Quarterly*, 4 (December 1968), pp. 257-261.

[12] Thernstrom, *op. cit.*, pp. 367-368.

[13] *Ibid.*, pp. 368-369.

[14] *Ibid.*, p. 369. This area has been of special interest to sociologists and some economists. See Leo F. Schnore, "Social Mobility in Demographic Perspective," *American Sociological Review*, 26 (June 1961), pp. 407-423.

[15] Thernstrom, *op. cit.*, p. 369.

[16] *Ibid.*, pp. 369-370.

[17] *Ibid.*

[18] *Ibid.*

simple-minded efforts to measure phenomena which in the past had been discussed on the basis of colorful examples and casual impressions.[19]

In all these works, it would appear that "pure" rather than "applied" research interests prevail. The remoteness in time of much of the effort is one stumbling block to ready application of research findings to current social and political concerns. This has always plagued the socially conscious historian. But the search for relevance goes on. None would deny that Thernstrom's five key topics are of contemporary concern to policy makers and the politically involved sector of the public at large. One need not agree with Staughton Lynd, who has held that "the historian's first duty, I believe, is the sensitive chronicling in depth of the important events of his own lifetime."[20] Such a time frame seems too restrictive. Moreover, the nonspecialist and the lay public can gain much from the kinds of work cited by Thernstrom and some of the scholarly effort represented in this volume. To take a cliché and give it fresh nuances, the reader can achieve that most valuable of intellectual commodities: historical perspective on contemporary urban social, economic, and political problems. The current interest in occupational mobility, for example, is part of a larger concern over the fulfillment of the American dream of an "open" society that dates at least from the egalitarian rhetoric of our Constitution.[21]

IV

ALL told, some two dozen scholars participated in the Madison conference as contributors of papers, discussants, session chairmen, or panelists. Listed alphabetically, they were: Martyn J. Bowden (Graduate School of Geography, Clark University), A. Theodore Brown (Department of History, University of Wisconsin [Milwaukee]), Kathleen Neils Conzen (Department of History, Wellesley College), Reynolds Farley (Department of Sociology, University of Michigan), Charles N. Glaab (Department of History, University of Toledo), Peter G.

---

[19] *Ibid.*, p. 370.

[20] Staughton Lynd, "Historical Past and Existential Present," in Theodore Roszak (editor), *The Dissenting Academy* (New York: Pantheon Books, 1968), p. 103.

[21] For sociological perspective on the recent past, see Peter M. Blau and Otis Dudley Duncan (with the collaboration of Andrea Tyree), *The American Occupational Structure* (New York: John Wiley & Sons, Inc., 1967). That sociologists are quite capable of writing history is amply demonstrated in Beverly Duncan and Stanley Lieberson, *Metropolis and Region in Transition* (Beverly Hills: Sage Publications, 1970), especially Parts I-III.

Goheen (Department of Geography, University of Chicago), Claudia Dale Goldin (Department of Economics, University of Wisconsin [Madison]), Lawrence J. Golicz (Department of History, University of Maine), Herbert G. Gutman (Department of History, City College University of New York), Robert Higgs (Department of Economics, University of Washington), Richard J. Hopkins (Department of History, Ohio State University), Kenneth T. Jackson (Department of History, Columbia University), David J. Loschky (Department of Economics, University of Missouri [Columbia]), Blake McKelvey (City Historian, Rochester, New York), Zane L. Miller (Department of History, University of Cincinnati), Allan R. Pred (Department of Geography, University of California [Berkeley]), Leo F. Schnore (Department of Sociology, University of Wisconsin [Madison]), Stanley K. Schultz (Department of History, University of Wisconsin [Madison]), Gregory H. Singleton (Department of History, Northeastern Illinois University), Eugene Smolensky (Department of Economics, University of Wisconsin [Madison]), Joseph A. Swanson (Department of Economics, University of Iowa), Richard C. Wade (Department of History, City University of New York), Thomas J. Weiss (Department of Economics, University of Kansas [Lawrence]), Jeffrey G. Williamson (Department of Economics, University of Wisconsin [Madison]), and Halliman H. Winsborough (Department of Sociology, University of Wisconsin [Madison]). Much of Eric E. Lampard's argument in the Foreword to this book—*ad verecundiam*—depends on "authoritative" books and articles from *all* of the social sciences.

In order to save the reader the trouble of totting up this list according to discipline, there were a dozen historians, barely outnumbered by a baker's dozen from other fields—seven economists, three geographers, and three sociologists. In any case, the editor is grateful to all these colleagues for their contributions, large or small, to the success of this entire enterprise. Thanks must also go to Ms. Irene Bickenbach, at the Center for Advanced Study in the Behavioral Sciences, where most of the basic editorial work was accomplished. Ms. Patsy J. Blair, Ms. Marge Crowley, and Ms. Donna S. Taylor also worked on the arduous task of proofreading. Their patience with the editor and his many foibles is greatly appreciated. The encouragement of Robert W. Fogel (Department of Economics, Harvard University) and Preston S. Cutler (Center for Advanced Study in the Behavioral Sciences) was also invaluable.

Taken together, these nine chapters illustrate the wide variety of concepts and methods now used in studying urban history. It is our hope that these essays, with their varying approaches, will provide useful models for subsequent work in the area by the next generation of students of the American city. If this should prove to be the case, our conference efforts will have been fully repaid.

Center for Advanced Study in the Behavioral Sciences
March, 1972

Revised, Madison, Wisconsin
April, 1974

Two Cheers for Quantitative History:
An Agnostic Foreword

ERIC E. LAMPARD

I

URBAN history is currently among the most flourishing fields of historical study in the United States. Its popularity stems, in part, from the growth of professional historiographical interests and, in still larger part, from a heightened public interest in the character and quality of contemporary urban life. The increasing scale of the historiographical enterprise since the Second World War has been marked not only by the rise of exotic fields of foreign-area specialization but also by a disintegration of the older inherited structure of United States history itself. So-called urban history has become one of the principal beneficiaries of this progressive differentiation and specialization of interests at home. It is now hard to believe that, as recently as 1957, a distinguished historian of "the middle period" could have declared to this writer: "Urban history? Why I cover the city in my postbellum course!" At that time, the number of urban history courses around the country could probably have been counted on the fingers of two hands. Should this anecdote seem unduly idiographic and qualitative to appear in a volume such as this, let us introduce some hard survey data. By 1967-1968 about fifty major colleges and universities in the United States were offering courses in urban history and "in nearly 150 of the responding institutions provisions existed or were in prospect for the study of the history of the American city."[1] In the ensuing five years the number of courses regularly offered has almost doubled and, despite the recent slump in the market for Ph.D.'s in American history, the demand for urban "specialists" has held up remarkably well.

The vogue of urban history is not, however, a consequence of the quantity or quality of its specialized literature but of the "Urban Crisis" as represented by the mass media during the 1960s. College and university departments of history, like their counterparts in social sciences, jumped aboard the urban bandwagon which offered both rapid transit to larger enrollments and a much-needed transport of

[1] Bayrd Still and Diana Klebanow, "The Teaching of American Urban History," *Journal of American History*, 55 (March 1969), pp. 843-847.

"relevance" to the undergraduate curriculum. The complaisant graduate departments responded by marketing some of their newly minted Ph.D.'s—whose dissertations happened to relate to reform movements, immigrants, political machines, social mobility, or one or another social problem—as *urban* historians. The Negro and student uprisings of the years 1964-1968 were further grist for the graduate mills under such fashionable heads as "the ghetto," "violence," "poverty," "the third world," each of which could be furnished with an instant history. Insofar as younger scholars subsequently fraternized with sociologists, geographers, economists, or planners in the schools where they found themselves teaching urban history, or began reading more widely than their graduate history curricula had ever allowed, they were able to adapt their dissertations for publication as *urban* history. Thus a more self-consciously "urban" monographic literature did emerge in the later 1960s to supplement the older city biographies and case studies which had appeared more randomly over the previous 40 years.[2]

If present discontents in American society have prompted the demand for urban history, a more persistent disquiet within the company of professional historians has quickened the supply of historical accountants. Doubts have arisen concerning the adequacy of the discipline's essentially *letristic* method of treating the evidence.[3] The point

[2] Eric E. Lampard, "The Dimensions of Urban History: A Footnote to the 'Urban Crisis'," *Pacific Historical Review*, 39 (August 1970), pp. 261-278. Also Charles N. Glaab, "The Historian and the American City," in Philip M. Hauser and Leo F. Schnore (editors), *The Study of Urbanization* (New York: John Wiley & Sons, Inc., 1965), pp. 53-80, a bibliographic survey. For current bibliography, see regular issues of the Urban History Group *Newsletter* published at the Department of History, University of Wisconsin-Milwaukee, and edited by A. Theodore Brown.

[3] The term "letristic" is used throughout this essay rather than the term "qualitative" not only because the activity of writing history, or historiography in the proper sense, has always been considered a branch of letters but because this writer has never been able to understand what "qualitative methods" are. Perhaps they yield what Karl Polanyi called "tacit knowledge" as distinct from knowledge obtained by explicit theory or method. Certainly much historical writing scarcely warrants the classification "nonfiction." To my tacit knowledge, the term "qualitative method" was not used before some historians began using the term "quantitative method." Statisticians, however, have long made a distinction between quantitative and qualitative variables (see note 7 below). Louis Chevalier, "A Reactionary View of Urban History," *Times Literary Supplement* (London, September 8, 1966), pp. 796-797, is a considered rejection of social science methods applied to the study of the past by a distinguished demographic historian, lover of Balzac, and *piéton de Paris*. He calls for a return to "a qualitative tradition of scholarship . . . wide reading and wide learning or, more simply still, a sound dose of common sense." On the question of appropriate methods for treating historical "mass events" and "particular events," see Folke Dovring, *History as a Social Science: An Essay on the Nature and Purpose of Historical Studies* (The Hague: M. Nijhoff, 1960), pp. 37-71.

13

is not that historians, like journalists or lawyers, communicate their findings in ordinary prose language, that they have personal biases, that they often plead causes, or that they are lax in gathering their sources, but rather: how do they know what they say they know?

One line of criticism has its root in recent developments in the science of linguistics and seeks to refine the ways in which historians use language. Another has its origins in efforts to employ the "language" of mathematics and techniques of statistics. The latter so-called quantitative methods are increasingly recognized as providing workaday answers to questions of knowledge in some fields of historical inquiry, not least in the study of urbanization. It is not that they offer the sure efficiency of numbers in place of the occasional elegance of letters; quantitative methods have been most rewarding when used in the analysis of mass events. Unless we view all of the past as chaos or history as *histoire événementielle,* a chronicle of discrete events, then it is possible to see that some uncertain processes of human experience may be simulated in the processes of mathematical models, with particular regard to the amounts of "uncertainty" involved. When it comes to re-creating the ambience and atmosphere of people or places from the past, however, numbers can only render their petty sums and small dividends in common with others, much as do epigraphy, paleography, bibliography, and all such instruments. They are no substitutes for empathy, imagination, and literary art. There will always be a story to tell, and it may sometimes contain a moral.

Doubtless many historians are too busy writing histories to bother much with mathematics and statistics. Others will vehemently deny their suitability on the ground that history is "different." Some may think the question "how do I know?" unimportant enough to leave to philosophers. A growing number already care enough to count.

Counting operations have constituted a minor branch of modern historiographical technique, in fact, almost from the beginning. Just as individual scholars were writing urban histories decades before the "Urban Crisis" of the 1960s, others had pioneered in the quantitative approach only decades after the emergence of historiography as a distinctive branch of modern letters in the mid-nineteenth century. Like most pioneering endeavors, to be sure, the early ventures were tentative and crude; they involved little more than arraying the data in tabular form and suggesting the relations among them by the simple method of inspection. It was as if well-authenticated and chronologically ordered "facts," whether given in words or in numbers, could speak for themselves. No formal operations or statistical methods were required. The early economic historians, for example, seldom went beyond percentaging or averaging; their numbers were used to illustrate points in the narrative rather than to test the reliability of an interpretation. Perhaps the nearest approach to a "quantitative school" in the United States was, significantly, that which briefly developed around Frederick Jackson Turner at the University of Wisconsin in considering the master's celebrated "frontier" thesis. But, for all the professional historians' identification with the critical and scientific spirit of the late nineteenth century, quantification was not one of the distinguishing features of the "new"—more interpretatively inclined—history which emerged after 1900. If the student of modern history, for example, wanted to know more about the growth of population and cities than appeared in the United States Census, he would have had to turn to early social scientists such as Richmond Mayo-Smith, Charles Horton Cooley, Adna F. Weber, or Walter F. Willcox. As late as 1932 Abbott Payson Usher could argue that the possibilities and limitations of "the Quantitative Method" were not properly understood even by some of the most expert economic historians.[4]

In recent decades younger-minded historians, regardless of age, have awakened to the fact that they have been speaking "quantitatively" all their professional and private lives. Terms such as "relationship," "factor," "significance," "structure," "system," "function," "depends," "change," and "continuity" are to be found in almost any historical narrative where generalizations are involved. Mathematical ideas occur in the vernacular not simply as numerical statements but in countless expressions indicating place and direction, shape or form, size and comparison. No historian can dispense altogether with words and phrases such as "several," "a great deal," "by and large," "nearly," "partly," "group," "within limits," "vary with," "one after another," or "scattered." Not all these notions are strictly quantitative; some are simply relational like many of the theorems of plane geometry; but they are alike mathematical in character. Dates, for example, designate quantities and directions of time intervals. Even to say that "Theodore Roosevelt succeeded William McKinley as president" is to specify a function, "the successor of," and allow its values

---

[4] A. P. Usher, "The Application of the Quantitative Method of Economic History," *Journal of Political Economy*, 40 (April 1932), p. 209. Usher later suggested that, unlike those who wrote history from a nonempirical standpoint, the modern empiricist need not treat "ideals" or "values" as "ends in themselves; they are means to the continuing realization of organic relations between individuals and various social groupings which are the setting for his [*sic*] life." "The Significance of Modern Empiricism for History and Economics," *Journal of Economic History*, 9 (1949), pp. 137-155.

to be "presidents of the United States." There is no need to document the obvious *ad infinitum*, although a mathematician can tell us a short way to get even that far out.

There are perhaps six or seven basic mathematical and logical ideas potentially helpful to the historian in describing and comprehending what happens, how, and for what proximate cause.[5] Doubtless there are many others but the following have a great appeal for this "innumerate" writer and are used by a few contributors to this volume. (1) The notion of variables (different values or quantities of x, y, etc.) and the formulae which embody their prescribed or "cookbook" interrelations. (2) Functions and their graphs which show corresponding changes of dependence between variables where, say, $y = f(x)$. (3) Various estimating procedures which can range from more or less reasonable guessing to the most abstruse calculations. Two standard operations from the *infinitesimal* calculus, (4) derivation and integration, have great relevance for studying the rates and magnitudes of change. The derivative measures the instantaneous rate of change of any continuous variable y as a function of time, x, by letting the incremental time interval, Δx, become smaller and smaller more or less indefinitely; the integral is the sum, Σ, of changes in the variable y as the intervals of x become smaller between given limits but as the number of small intervals becomes correspondingly larger and larger. The derivative of a function f of x is written $D_x f$ or df/dx, while the integral, from initial limit a to b, of f with respect to x can be written $\int_a^b f\,dx$. Suppose milk to be flowing from a tank truck into a vat at a given rate of one gallon every ten seconds, then the rate of change of the volume of milk in the vat is the derivative, in this case a constant rate, 360 gallons an hour, six gallons a minute, 1/10th of a gallon per second, etc., but the volume of milk in the vat at any moment is the integral from the initial moment, or cumulative consequence, of the rate of flow.

Certain propositions from logic, such as (5) properties and relations,

---

[5] There are many introductory books written for the nonmathematician as well as useful primers of statistical methods. This writer likes: Denning Miller, *Popular Mathematics* (New York: Coward-McCann, 1942); Richard Courant and Herbert Robbins, *What is Mathematics? An Elementary Approach to Ideas and Methods*, 4th ed. (New York: Oxford University Press, 1948); and E. C. Berkeley, *A Guide to Mathematics for the Intelligent Nonmathematician* (New York: Simon and Schuster, 1966). See also, P. J. McCarthy, *Introduction to Statistical Reasoning* (New York: McGraw-Hill, 1957), and Edward Shorter, *The Historian and the Computer: A Practical Guide* (Englewood Cliffs, New Jersey: Prentice-Hall, 1971). More generally, see W. H. Kruskal (editor), *Mathematical Sciences and Social Sciences* (Englewood Cliffs: Prentice-Hall, 1970).

are very helpful. The properties or attributes of a determine what class or kind of thing a is, while the relation or association between a, b, and c can be shown, in light of other properties, to be true or false. Finally, two statistical concepts, (6) probability and frequency distribution, are extremely powerful analytical tools. Probability is an estimate of the chances of some event's happening or not happening—the odds—based on the outcomes or experience of (a given number of) repeated and essentially like events in the past. A frequency distribution is an array of items or events which shows how a total number of observations are classified or distributed among various classes. For instance, a so-called *normal* distribution is one which shows many events or scores clustered around the midpoint, or "central tendency," and fewer and fewer to either side. Graphically, it looks like a "bell" curve. American cities ranked by size at every census since 1790 conform roughly to a rank-size rule or general frequency function, now identified as a "Yule distribution," which is highly skewed in the form of a "reversed-J" and, in the language of statisticians, yields "the steady state of a stochastic growth process."[6]

Clearly, most applications of such ideas to historical cases will be valid or invalid as relevant properties of events or forces, and their interrelations, are judged to be more or less like and comparable. Since most historical events and situations are not strictly repeatable, and may in some instances be characterized as unique, much critical effort must go into the task of establishing the grounds on which some events and sequences of events are judged to have the common attributes of a "class."[7] Otherwise, quantitative historical analysis

[6] A Yule distribution is a frequency function named after a statistician, and not a charitable handout at the winter solstice. In this case, if the smallest class of cities is being continuously enlarged by new entrants achieving a given threshold size, then the steady state of the universe of cities in question has a frequency function of the form $f(i) = ai - {}^cb^i$. Several distinctive patterns of city-size distributions have been observed empirically, but we have no better explanation for the range of these distributions among countries than the fact that it rests on the random "number and complexity" of forces affecting the urban structure" in each case. See Brian J. L. Berry, "City Size Distributions and Economic Development," *Economic Development and Cultural Change*, 9 (July 1961), pp. 573-588.

[7] To confuse matters, it is necessary to point out that statisticians would call the attributes of some of these events and situations "qualitative" rather than "quantitative." Qualitative variables are those which have recognizable properties of a *non-numerical* kind. Some of the qualitative variables are dichotomous, having a set of only two classes, e.g., male-female, heads-tails, city-country, although this last set is possibly a compression of many different types of residential attributes into a dichotomous set. The variable "current marital status" allows five classes: single, married, separated, divorced, widowed; "social status" may have an arbitrarily defined or conventional set of occupational categories. Time,

would prove to be merely a more systematic way of going wrong with confidence.

But none of the logical problems connected with generalization are very new to historians. For generations they have been arguing over "particulars" *versus* "generalities," "facts" and "trends," patterns in the past, or merely "one d—d thing after another." The difference between the *letristic* and quantitative styles in this regard is that the accountant must always be *explicit* either by reference to theoretical principles or by ruminating in his immediate text. The quantifier must, as it were, put all his 3-x-5 cards on the table, and much of his printout, too; he cannot bury them in footnotes with the implication that documentation is demonstration. Hence the tedium of quantitative briefing procedures and operational specifications, the thickets of algebra, and the intermittent lapses into turgid prose only to come up with something that was "obvious" to others all the time. While these features of the quantitative genre are certainly defensive, they are not designed to cover the tracks. They *are* the tracks, and any competent critic can follow with his knife at the ready. Needless to say, the resultant text may only provide bedtime reading for the chronic insomniac.

The heart of the quantitative matter, however, is not style but rather the attempt to make the logical truths embodied in theory conform to the factual truths of experience; to devise a *model* that "works." For it is only in the degree to which theoretical reasoning is sustained by experience that theory can ever be said to have *explained* what is observed to have happened.[8] Theories are coherent

---

although a continuous quantitative variable, can sometimes be operationalized as a dichotomous variable when, for example, relationships among other variables are hypothesized to be different at different periods: before and after the American Revolution, introduction of the automobile, railroads, and so forth. See chapter 8 below by Robert Higgs for the treatment of southern and non-southern states. Methods of *manipulating* qualitative variables are nonetheless quantitative.

[8] Herbert A. Simon, *Models of Man* (New York: John Wiley & Sons, Inc., 1957). The matter of historical explanation by statistical methods is critical. Functional relations between variables x and y are mutual in that the values of either can usually be determined by the other; the function is *implicit*. The y variable becomes an *explicit* function of x when the values of y depend, in some defined way, upon the value arbitrarily allotted to x. However, given the implicit function, y as an explicit function of x also makes x an explicit function of y; they are said to be inverse to each other. When y is the variable to be "explained" and x is the explanatory variable, y is called the *dependent* and x the *independent* variable. "Explanation" in this context is not, however, identical with "causal explanation." Even if it is convenient to designate one independent and the other dependent, the function does not thereby become "causal" by any mathematical logic. As R. G. D. Allen affirms, "Causal relations

groups of general propositions used as principles of explanation for a class of phenomena. But the logical truths of theory "exist" independently of the events and outcomes of the real world. They are deduced from initial conditions or premises which are given a priori; logical truths do not admit of exceptions or errors. If the reasoning is correct, they are incontrovertible. The "pure" theorist, the mathematical economist, for example, has little or no professional interest in the factual experience of the marketplace.

Factual or experiential truths, on the other hand, are general statements obtained by methods of induction. They embody observations made in the real world up to some point in time which may be generalized to the future. But they are never more than contingent truths, probabilities of something's happening, based on accumulated experience of the past, since the very next observation of the same phenomenon may indeed controvert them: *exceptio probat regulam.* Yet the exceptional case somehow does not "prove" the empirical rule to be false.[9]

The kind of conclusion or generalization that is drawn from cases, instances, or observations is at most a statistical summary. It has no explanatory power *of itself,* any more than does the mathematical logic of an explicit function. Whether the rule is worth keeping, whether it continues to provide a guide to practical behavior, depends on the further test of experience and whether human beings learn anything from experience.

It is precisely the role of theory to offer an explanation of future experience by *predicting* what an outcome will be. To be sure, the proposed explanation will be no more than a conjecture but, if future observations conform to the theoretically based "expectation," so the power or strength of the theory is enhanced. A model is simply an application of theoretical principles by means of mathematical logic to classes of actual events which can be summarized and manipulated in the form of statistics. Depending on the quantity of future experience the model predicts, so it is judged good or bad. Experience cannot disprove theory but it can test operationally the validity of a particular

---

occur only between quantities of actual phenomena and, when such a relation is *interpreted* by a function, it merely happens that one view of the function is dominant and the other neglected." *Mathematical Analysis for Economists* (London and New York: Macmillan & Co., 1967), pp. 28–30.

[9] This old Latin tag is frequently misunderstood. *Probat* is ordinarily rendered as "proves" in English. A better translation is "The exception *tests* the rule." We should understand "proves" in the sense of "proving ground," and not as a "demonstration" or "proof" in the logical sense.

model which is based on theory. Assuming the accuracy of the observations or evidence, changes can sometimes be introduced in the internal logic of the model to make it predict an even greater amount of the experience summarized by the data. Thus my understanding of the quantitative approach is that it is a hypothetical-deductive system of model-building—usually a system of mathematical equations—which is used to predict the as yet "unknown" events of the real world when, and if, the latter become "knowable." In short, the quantitative method must employ theory as well as statistical methods of handling data.

Fine for economists, demographers, or psychologists, says the skeptical historian; they presume to foretell the future and we do not. Our task is to recover the past which is "known," so to speak, but which has been distorted or forgotten and is, in greater or lesser degree, irretrievably lost. Our predicament is different. Their theories and methods do not work for us. Yes, we can gather statistics from the past up to a point, we almost literally dig up all manner of bits and pieces of evidence, and we try to fit together as many as we can in order to tell what happened. With the proper "feel" for places and periods we can even reach more or less agreed conclusions—a consensus—about why things happened in the way we think they did. We tell it "like it was"; our method has no need for hypothetical-deductive models or equations.

On the contrary, rejoins the eager quantifier, your description of the historiographical predicament is good but your conclusion that it is altogether different from ours is unwarranted. If we can build models to predict this or that future course of events, we can do the same thing for past outcomes and sequences of events. Why should the unfolding of the future be any different from the unfolding of the past? The years 1972-1973 will be "history" by 1980, the evidence will be in, just as by 1880 the evidence of 1872-1873 was in; we probably know less about 1980 today than was known about 1872-1873 in 1880. All our models do, in effect, is to link up a subsequent event or prognosis to a given set of prior conditions. We employ some generalized theoretical statement, which often embodies a lot of previous experience, to forge the link between the present or accumulated past and the future. In this light, prediction is simply a "prior" or tentative explanation of what will happen.

In making short-run predictions we assume that "other things will be equal." We anticipate that factors and forces not included in our model will not impinge upon the outcome sufficiently to render it wholly or immeasurably different from our "expected" outcome. If it appears that they do, and if such factors seem to have some regular or systematic kind of influence on the outcome, then we try to incorporate them as other independent variables in the model since the included variables are logically designed to determine the outcome as closely as possible. If we are unable to include them for logical reasons, then we have to scrap the model.

As long as the influence of such factors does not appear to be systematically affecting the average behavior of the included variables, however, all is not lost. Some factors in the external environment may be acting upon the properties of variables in the model because of changes which are unrelated to the working of the model itself. Such factors and influences are called *exogenous* variables in that changes in their values are given outside the workings of the *endogenous* variables of the model. Exogenous variables greatly complicate the design of realistic long-term models, but short-term models, which may also have historical application, usually indicate that changes in tastes, in knowledge, in population, or "institutions" are wholly exogenous. Where possible, however, the prevailing tastes, knowledge, etc., are included in the model as "givens" or "constants" having fixed numbers or coefficients that are called *parameters*. Parameters closely resemble exogenous variables except that they do not change; they build in the continuity of the accumulated past. They are chiefly behavioral, technological, or identity constants and where, in fact, they are not already known from past experience, they may sometimes be estimated from relevant sample data. In the equation $Y = a + bX$, for example, a change of X values predicts changes in Y values via the parameters a and b which are the known behavioral constants and constitute the "invariant" or unchanging link between the model's system variables Y and X. The parameters, in effect, tie in the variables' endogenous components to the model; they define the functional relationships of the system and make the model "go."[10]

In designing a model, the investigator not only tries to build in logical and functional relationships or structures among his included variables, he also tries to eliminate all unsystematic and inconsequential details. But since many of the models employed in social sciences are not "exact" models such as the equation given above,

[10] This model-building discussion is the effort made by the quantifier to meet the mathematical distinction between "explanation" and "causation." It is the attempt to restate a mathematical function $Y = f(X)$ in terms of quantities of actual or observed phenomena which inhere in the parameters, a, b, such that variable amounts of the X phenomenon will "work" variable amounts of change in the Y phenomenon. The functional relation is thus given *by experience* as irreversible and probably invariant.

21

attention must also be given to contingent effects of unanticipated or sporadic events. By including a so-called error term in the equation, the "exact" model is converted into a "stochastic" model which tries to make allowance for random or unsystematic influences on resulting values of Y. Thus the equation becomes: $Y = a + bX + e$, where e takes account of unsystematic influences, even of random errors and inaccuracies in the data. Some purists among theoreticians may insist that any and all significant variables and proper functions ought to be in the equations and they sometimes imply that what the econometrician, for example, attributes to randomness may well represent a "systematic lack of system" in what he is doing.[11] The skeptical historian may yet find an ally among the theorists who deplore the compromises which fanatical quantifiers are prepared to make with the world of experience. But insofar as a historian attempts to fall back upon his stock arguments for the "unique" causes of particular events, even a theorist might inquire why the historian usually assumes that random elements or fortuitous events dominate the conjunctions of the past, whether simultaneous or in sequence. Why, moreover, do some historians assume that such random elements are differently distributed at moments in the past from the way they would be at moments in the present or future?

Thus a historical model is in essence no different in form from a present model of the future. The logic of historical explanation is identical with the logic of predictive explanation. It is simply the formal estimation of the transition from one conjunction or state to another succeeding conjunction or state, given the initial conditions and a hypothesized "causal" relation or generalization. To be considered a causal relation in a formal sense, the relation between simultaneous or sequential events must have (1) a high probability of being invariant, and (2) be irreversible or asymmetric with respect to time.[12] If these conditions are fulfilled, then the model can offer a formal explanation of why the particular realization did in fact occur. The outcomes of 1880 are deemed to be predictions based upon initial conditions relating to such events as they obtained, say, in 1872-1873, or any other prior date. When the historian is aware of what happened in 1880, he can set up the initial conditions of earlier years and identify the intervening sequence of events that would have sufficed to bring

[11] A. H. Conrad and J. R. Meyer, "Economic Theory, Statistical Inference and Economic History," *Journal of Economic History*, 27 (December 1957), pp. 524-544, for the treatment of the "error" term and the reactions of economic theorists summarized by Simon Kuznets.

[12] Conrad and Meyer, *loc. cit.*

about the observed outcomes of 1880. Here again the logic of prediction has been transformed into a logic of historical explanation or *postdiction*.[13] Given the time that econometricians spend quarterbacking on Monday mornings in order to explain why their Friday-afternoon predictions went wrong—or turned out to be contrafactual —over the weekend, the skeptical historian may perhaps now concede that postdiction is a more highly developed skill than prediction.

But instead of limiting the historian's freedom of inquiry, such a method greatly enlarges the scope of historical investigation. If time and money permit, he can test out a number of possible and plausible explanations for 1880 simply by altering his initial estimates of prior conditions and then tracing through the events which would have followed logically had any given program of conditions been operative. If models can thus specify contrafactual worlds which were never observed by anybody, and methods are available to simulate or implement the observations which should have followed *mutatis mutandis*, then we are indeed acquiring a novel and most powerful method of studying certain kinds of historical problems. To be sure, at almost every stage of the preceding argument, epistemological, linguistic, and aesthetic queries may arise.[14] Certainly it is an incomplete and simplified version of the already impossible world. Perhaps, like the legendary Yankee, we have only been "whittling a lot of unsalable shoepegs into melon seeds."

A final problem with the quantitative approach is the historical accountant himself. This is certainly a difficulty for those who design graduate training programs in history departments, particularly if the quantitative method comes to be as widely used in political, social,

---

[13] Nicholas Rashevsky, *Looking at History Through Mathematics* (Cambridge, Mass.: M.I.T. Press, 1968), pp. 10-11, likens postdiction in historiography to the activity of the cosmogonist predicting events in the history of the universe which happened billions of years ago.

[14] See, for example, Haskell Fain, *Between Philosophy and History* (Princeton, New Jersey: Princeton University Press, 1970). Elias H. Tuma, *Economic History and the Social Sciences: Problems of Methodology* (Berkeley: University of California Press, 1971), is scarcely less critical of the "new" economic historians than he is of the "old." He is particularly skeptical about the hypothetical-deductive approach discussed above; it has led "new" historians to oversimplify problems "and to be quite selective and often arbitrary in their interpretations." Though "less precise," the findings of traditional historians "are more comprehensive and realistic" (p. 242). Peter Temin has drawn attention to the almost insuperable problems of index numbers used over long periods; they are "objective" and "subjective" at the same time. "In Pursuit of the Exact," *Times Literary Supplement* (London, July 28, 1966), pp. 652-653. Harry G. Johnson, "The Keynesian Revolution and the Monetarist Counter Revolution," *American Economic Review*, 61 (May 1971), insists that econometric testing is often "a euphemism for obtaining plausible numbers to provide ceremonial adequacy."

23

and "intellectual" research as well or as much as in economic and demographic studies. But the problem is also one of the public relations and politics of history departments. The quantifier is usually a missionary or a convert and he tends to come on a trifle strong. If the increasing scale of the historiographical enterprise can now support this degree of specialization, if the career chances of the quantitative historian have lately been improved, this is only after a rather long period of his being treated as a heretical novice, a worshipper—in the words of one prominent urban historian—"at the shrine of the Bitch-goddess Quantification."[15] He has tended to make orthodox devotees of Clio uneasy in their faith, and they already have much to be uneasy about without someone preaching that there is no salvation outside the Book of Numbers. His iconoclastic boorishness has often brought out the fretfulness, clownishness, and downright ugliness that is latent among members of every priestly class, and historians have been no exception in this regard. But, however they may represent themselves to strangers, most quantifiers know that there is neither certitude nor shelter in the arcana of the numbers

[15] Carl Bridenbaugh in his prickly article, "The Great Mutation," *American Historical Review,* 68 (January 1963), pp. 326-327. Bridenbaugh eventually concedes that "we need to know about such matters." Even Frederick Jackson Turner objected to the positivistic and condescending tone of the more confident economists such as John Bates Clark, who thought they understood "the full relation of economic theory, statistics, and history." Turner argued that "the pathway of history is strewn with the wrecks of the 'known and acknowledged truths of economic law'." Nevertheless, he welcomes the new materials, tools, points of view, hypotheses, and emphases of the social scientists in unraveling the historical complexities of time and place. He indicated that historians would have to learn to use the findings of social scientists "and in some reasonable degree master the essential tools of their trade." He also suggested that others would find something to learn in the "work and methods of historians." "Social Forces in American History," *American Historical Review,* 16 (January 1911), pp. 232-233. Turner was reacting to Clark's statement that "a principle is formulated by *a priori* reasoning concerning facts of common experience; it is then tested by statistics and promoted to the rank of a known and acknowledged truth; illustrations of its action are then found in narrative history and . . . the economic law becomes the interpreter of records that would otherwise be confusing and comparatively valueless; the law itself derives its final confirmation from the illustrations of its working which the records afford; but what is at least of equal importance is the parallel fact that the law affords the decisive test of the correctness of those assertions concerning the causes and the effects of past events which it is second nature to make and which historians almost invariably do make in connection with their narrations." If we update the meaning of terms such as "law" and "cause," this is not a bad statement for the 1970s; it had appeared in John R. Commons, et al. (editors), *Documentary History of American Industrial Society* (Cleveland: The Arthur H. Clark Company, 1910), I, pp. 43-44. Epistemological disputes among philosophers of science concerning "projectability" and "confirmation" have relevance, of course, for all attempts at rational justification of belief, in natural as well as social sciences.

game. If economic historians are among the most accomplished and best established of the historical accountants, any passing reference to their hieratic journals will disclose how vulnerable their "new" theology has become.[16] Their findings are regularly and promptly denounced as incomplete, inaccurate, incompetent, and—most cruel, perhaps—inelegant. But the critics, at least the ones they harken to, are worshippers at the same shrine, and many a cliometrician has learned to his psychic cost that the surest way to perish is to publish. Perhaps the quantifier comes on so strong among the Gentiles only because he comes out so weak from ritual encounters with those who observe the Numerical Law. All this will surely pass and, as in the social sciences where yesterday's oppressed Philistines now sit among the Sanhedrin and oppress, in turn, scholars of every persuasion are ultimately to be known by their fruits.

II

THIS conference volume is part of the "new" consciousness concerning the history of the American city. The authors include not only younger members of history departments but geographers and economists as well. Clio's house may have many mansions but the approach of these scholars is confidently quantitative: *ex fide fortis*. Their book ranges in time and topic over the entire field, although it properly makes no pretense at "full" coverage. It is a collection of different kinds of quantitative exploration, some more innovative than others, at least in the field of urban history. Even the least novel also serves when it reports findings from a place or a period which has not hitherto yielded much of quantitative account. None of its chapters realizes the full promise of quantitative studies suggested in this foreword. The models are quite limited, not strictly operationalized, or wholly theoretical and somewhat "overtooled." Nevertheless, they are always suggestive and indicate the shape of things to come. Some

---

[16] *Journal of Economic History; Explorations in Economic History;* and *Economic History Review.* See also the stinging review by Leo F. Schnore of Seymour Martin Lipset and Richard Hofstadter (editors), *Sociology and History: Methods* (New York: Basic Books, 1968) in *American Journal of Sociology,* 75 (November 1969), pp. 418-422. Quantifiers' critiques of quantifying also appear regularly in *Historical Methods Newsletter,* published by the Department of History, University of Pittsburgh. Margaret Walsh, for example, provides a searching examination of the MS and printed census returns for mid-19th century manufacturing: *HMN,* September 1970 and March 1971. More generally, see Amitai Etzioni and E. W. Lehman, "Some Dangers in 'Valid' Social Measurement," *Annals of the American Academy of Political and Social Science,* 373 (September 1967), pp. 1-15.

authors make generalizations which occasionally go beyond their reported findings. But in the field of United States urban history, quantitative explorations are still in the pioneer stage. We might easily refer to applications in the urban history of other countries or continents which go beyond pioneering but they would be of correspondingly lesser interest to students of United States history.[17] Let us rather accentuate the positive and stress what has already been accomplished rather than emphasize what remains to be done.

For all the apparent diversity of periods and themes treated in this volume, its contents bear on two of the central problems of modern urban history: (1) the growth and function of cities in society, and (2) the effects of growth on the internal organization and related social order of cities. Indeed, if the reader is not put off by the polite pedantries of quantification, he could scarcely find a more convenient collection wherein such disparate topics as slavery, the social accommodation of freedmen and the foreign-born, technological innovation and diffusion, and the extension and utilization of urban space are tied, directly or indirectly, into the fundamental process of urbanization.

The first three chapters deal with the growth and functions of cities, their internal differentiation and peripheral spread. The second set of three treats the accommodations which different socioeconomic, ethnic, racial, and sectarian elements in the urban population make to their changing environments. The last three chapters use economic theory to explore some of the same themes: the movement of slaves

[17] See Stephan Thernstrom, "Reflections on the New Urban History," *Daedalus*, 100 (Spring 1971), pp. 359-375; also Allan G. Bogue, "United States: The 'New' Political History," *Journal of Contemporary History*, 3 (January 1968), pp. 5-27. For Great Britain, Harold J. Dyos (editor), *The Study of Urban History* (London: Edward Arnold, Ltd., 1968), which also contains an article by François Bedarida on the status of urban history in France. Recent quantitative historical work in France is reviewed by F. Furet and E. LeRoy Ladurie, "L'historien et l'ordinateur: Compte-rendu provisoire d'enquête," *Editions "Naouka,"* Direction de la littérature orientale, Moscow, 1970. U.S. history has also seen a boom in demographic studies: see D. S. Smith, "The Demographic History of Colonial New England," *Journal of Economic History*, 32 (March 1972), pp. 165-183; Maris A. Vinovskis, "Mortality Rates and Trends in Massachusetts before 1860," *ibid.*, pp. 184-213; and J. E. Eblen, "Growth of the Black Population in *Ante-bellum* America, 1820-1860," *Population Studies*, 26 (July 1972), pp. 273-289. Michael P. Conzen, *Frontier Farming in an Urban Shadow* (Madison, Wisconsin: State Historical Society for the Department of History, 1971) is an excellent quantitative study of urban influence upon a rural township by an historical geographer. Also, John Modell, "The Peopling of a Working-Class Ward: Reading, Pennsylvania, 1850," *Journal of Social History*, 5 (Fall 1971), pp. 71-95, is a unique study of the contribution of native white rural migrants to the urban proletariat.

in and out of cities, the comparative inventiveness of urbanized populations, and relations between the location of firms and the growth of the urban work force and population. Each chapter in this last set treats its problem in terms of the "maximizing" paradigm which formally governs rational micro-economic choice.

In Chapter 1, Allan R. Pred shows how urban centers grow up and serve the larger social system. Under the conditions of transport and communications prevailing down through the early nineteenth century, interactions among North American cities were closely circumscribed by certain spatial biases in the interurban flows of commodities, persons, and information which gave some localities—partcularly at the termini of main travelled routes—a positional advantage over others. Thus, he argues, the time requirements for physical movement among centers, together with the volume and frequency of contacts, largely governed which places would grow in size and influence. The time-space convergence which followed the introduction of steamboat services on coastal and inland waterways tended to reinforce the hierarchical structure of city sites and sizes along the northeastern seaboard, Ohio Valley, and eastern Great Lakes axes of communication.[18] No comparable intraregional system appears to have developed among southern centers, although each of the major ports along the South Atlantic and Gulf coasts maintained its own commercial connections with New York, Boston, and one or two other northeastern entrepôts.

Meanwhile the cities served as foci for innovation and the diffusion of certain mechanical and institutional inventions, financial panics, and infectious disease. Pred's model of diffusion is not put to any stringent test but, since it is designed to account for some of the phenomena which do not conform with received theories of central-place interaction and dependence, it is not surprising that his evidence often controverts the "strictly hierarchical mode." Even a historical geographer unfamiliar with city-system theory might object to the specification that "P_i, P_j, and d_{ij}^b carry their familiar gravity model connotations" and also to the unexplained "$K = 3$" in Figure 1-1. In this case, perhaps, unfamiliarity may breed contempt.

Martyn J. Bowden's Chapter 2 assumes the development of the greater Atlantic trading system during the sixteenth and seventeenth

[18] A robust contemporary description of this process is given by J. W. Scott, "Commercial Cities and Towns of the United States. xii. Our Cities—Atlantic and Interior," *Hunt's Merchants' Magazine*, 19 (October 1848), pp. 383-386, and *idem.*, "The Growth of Towns in the United States," *ibid.*, 25 (November 1851), pp. 359-365. Scott "deduces" a "law of growth" from the average time of population duplication. Needless to add, his prophecies go awry and his "law" serves as a caution against percentaging.

centuries in order to focus on the gradual formation of several specialized trading, financial, and manufacturing nuclei within the central
areas of the London metropolis and its small outports on the eastern
seaboard of North America. With subsequent growth of this system,
seaboard centers such as New York, Philadelphia, and Boston experienced an *accelerated* process of inner nucleation in their business
districts based on a similar concentration of functions which had
"complementary or competitive linkages." By the third quarter of
the nineteenth century, the accretion and differentiation of functional
areas within the comparatively young and small west-coast center
of San Francisco was very rapid indeed. After a lengthy dissertation
on the shortcomings of previous studies, Bowden does provide striking
evidence of a lowering of the thresholds for the emergence of Central
Business Districts. The skeptic might wonder whether the existence
of so many subordinate patterns does not tend to overwhelm the underlying theory. It is historically significant, nevertheless, that both Pred's
urban hierarchy and Bowden's polynuclear Central Business Districts
preserved much of their earlier structure and manner of growth long
after the communication and transport revolutions brought about by
the magnetic telegraph, the railroad, the telephone, and even the
automobile.[19]

The enlargement of the Central Business Districts was a major
pressure behind the remarkable peripheral extension of the nineteenth-century cities. In Chapter 3, Kenneth T. Jackson argues that
many scholars, particularly in the social sciences, have greatly exaggerated the extent and character of differences between nineteenth-
and twentieth-century "suburban" spread. Quantitative differences in
urban densities, length of journey to work, and the spatial distribution
of socioeconomic classes do not signify any qualitative difference between the cities of the mid-nineteenth century, extending over a few
dozen square miles, and twentieth-century metropolitan areas covering
many hundreds, even thousands, of square miles. The only significant
distinction between deconcentration before and after *circa* 1890, Jackson affirms, is *political*, the failure of municipal boundaries to keep
pace with the accelerated drift to the periphery made possible by
the streetcar and the automobile. The only unique feature of today's

[19] More generally, see Eric E. Lampard, "The Evolving System of Cities in
the U.S.: Urbanization and Economic Development," in Harvey S. Perloff and
Lowden Wingo, Jr. (editors), *Issues in Urban Economics* (Baltimore: The
Johns Hopkins Press, 1968), pp. 81-139; and Beverly D. Duncan and Stanley
Lieberson, *Metropolis and Region in Transition* (Beverly Hills: Sage Publications,
1969). Also, Edgar M. Hoover, "The Evolving Form and Organization of the
Metropolis," in Perloff and Wingo, *op. cit.*, pp. 237-284.

dispersal patterns is said to be abandonment: "the desertion of apartments, buildings, and even whole blocks."[20]

This perspective on city sprawl, if not a blockbuster, is a very useful corrective to many popular and census-based notions of peripheral growth. But acts of annexation or consolidation were always political and there is no more reason for describing their diminution as political than for ascribing their earlier profusion to nonpolitical causes. Again, we cannot conclude that all or more of the population found in annexed areas resulted from an exodus from the inner city, nor that the social composition of "suburbs" has remained uniform and unchanged since the mid-nineteenth century. The author is of course aware that simple percentages of growth are somewhat misleading when increments are virtually from scratch.[21]

[20] Annexations have not altogether ceased even among some of the older and larger cities of the northeast and midwest. In recent decades central cities of the far west, southwest, and mountain states annex most frequently; but the larger the central city, the less likely to annex, although "age" (date when central city first reached 50,000 residents) is the most critical variable. "Age" here, of course, is not altogether independent of size. See Leo F. Schnore, *The Urban Scene: Human Ecology and Demography* New York: The Free Press, 1965), pp. 114-133. Between 1950 and 1960, fully 75 per cent of central cities of census metropolitan areas (212) experienced some annexation. In the inter-war years Milwaukee, for example, enlarged its corporate area by nearly 100 per cent and its population by 30 per cent. Over the decade 1950-1960, the city almost doubled its territory again but it contained a smaller share of its census metropolitan population in 1960 (58 per cent) than in 1950 (65 per cent).

[21] H. H. Winsborough provided the conference with an interesting footnote on the question of the automobile and deconcentration (in Cleveland and some sixty-four other cities during the period 1934-1960, "Changes in Mode of Travel to Work, 1934-1960"). Most of a 32-percentage-point increase in journey to work by private automobile was at the expense of shoe-leather rather than public transportation, which declined by only 6 percentage points over the quarter-century span for this particular group of cities. Furthermore, the overall density of the city populations *increased* with population growth during the period but "was diminished in 1960 in those cities demonstrating greater reliance on the use of the automobile." This latter diminution of densities was the outcome of a flattening of the density-distance relationship. Increased resort to automobile commutation increased tract density locally, but increased automobile use was directly related to distance from the city center. Winsborough's use of diagrammatic path analysis was highly illuminating, but his implicit model of change which relates average density simply to population size and use of the automobile without any reference to incremental changes in housing stock, per capita incomes, or net residential density presents an unduly simplified picture of the ways in which changes in journey to work affected metropolitan structure. See the somewhat different focus of D. Hansen, Jr. and J. F. Kain, "An Historical Model of Urban Form," Inter-University Committee on Urban Economics, *Proceedings of 2nd Research Conference,* Chicago, September 1970, pp. 1-53, which emphasizes "the cumulative nature of urban development" and treats the extent to which "the present structure of cities is determined by past circumstances."

29

III

THE three following chapters are variously concerned with ethnic, racial, occupational, and "religious" aspects of American city morphogeny. In Chapter 4, Kathleen Neils Conzen treats patterns of residence in early Milwaukee, a rapidly growing "frontier" city, in the period 1836-1860. Milwaukee's population differed from those in the stereotypical cities of the northeast in that the foreign-born elements settled there at roughly the same time as and in similar proportion to the native-born; they were alike migrants. Thus the city was a "new town" with no established neighborhoods and no stock of older housing to hand down to newcomers. In what is perhaps the most sophisticated and careful analysis of nineteenth-century social areas to date, Mrs. Conzen tests some of the conventional sociological and ecological wisdom grounded in twentieth-century conditions. Her analysis of distance gradients broadly confirms the "hypothetical pattern of central high-status settlement and low-status periphery" commonly attributed to pre-industrial cities, but her factor analysis and mapping technique enable her to delineate early neighborhoods in terms of variables which include dimensions of family status (age, sex, married/single, family size, etc.) as well as the more commonplace indicators of national origin and socioeconomic (usually occupational) class.[22] She also shows a high degree of "congregation" and "clustering"—better terms than "segregation"—by different nationalities as well as a central mixed residential area oriented toward the needs of a mercantile city. The close association of nationality and occupational class clarifies the emergence of distinctive social areas which then grow out along sectoral lines, "unless stopped by entrenched groups or physical obstacles, and set the spatial framework within which the city has evolved." The ethnic grouping appears to be a kind of subsocial environment which eases its members' accommodation to an American urban way.

Implicit in Mrs. Conzen's study of early growth is a high degree of residential mobility among newcomers as they pass through successive stages of their individual life-cycles, find new employments, and experience changes in their status. A paper by Richard J. Hopkins,

---

[22] Factor analysis is a technique for studying a set of data from their intercorrelations—a matrix of intercorrelations—such that different portions of the variance may be assigned to particular factors. The patterning of social space in a pre-industrial city is also given, by less exacting methods, in Allan Kulikoff, "The Progress of Inequality in Revolutionary Boston," *William and Mary Quarterly,* 28 (July 1971), pp. 375-412. Boston's case reveals what happens when a city population grows without at least commensurate growth in its economy.

given at the Madison conference but published elsewhere, offered confirmation of the association between changing job status and residential movement in the case of Atlanta, a city which grew up in post-bellum decades almost as rapidly as Milwaukee before the war.[23] Hopkins found that native-born whites in his sample improved their occupational status from unskilled manual to skilled or nonmanual jobs with greater frequency than the unskilled manual foreign-born but, by 1900, the latter were doing as well as native whites. In contrast, status improvement among Negro unskilled manual workers was comparatively minor, while competition from whites was probably felt most strongly by those blacks who did upgrade their job status. Among white-collar workers (clerks, bookkeepers, salesmen, etc.), the native-white and foreign-born elements had a more varied experience. By the mid-1890s over half the sample members in this category had accomplished the difficult leap to petty-business proprietorships but roughly 10 and 17 per cent of native and foreign-born white-collar workers respectively appear to have lost job status over each decade from the 1870s to the 1890s.

Hopkins' study also confirmed some of the pioneering work of Peter R. Knights on persistence of residence in U.S. cities.[24] Less than half of 1870 sample heads of household remained in Atlanta in 1880 and under a quarter by 1896 (no special account is taken of the intervening deaths). Contrary to popular belief, Negro persistence—especially among the unskilled—was higher than for foreign-born whites of equivalent job status and much higher than for native whites. Persis-

[23] Hopkins, "Status, Mobility, and the Dimensions of Change in a Southern City: Atlanta, 1870-1910," in Kenneth T. Jackson and Stanley K. Schultz (editors), *Cities in American History* (New York: Alfred A. Knopf, 1972) pp. 216-231.

[24] See Peter R. Knights, "Population Turnover, Persistence, and Residential Mobility in Boston, 1830-1860," in Stephan Thernstrom and Richard Sennett (editors), *Nineteenth-Century Cities* (New Haven: Yale University Press, 1969), and Knights, *The Plain People of Boston, 1830-1860: A Study in City Growth* (New York: Oxford University Press, 1971), pp. 48-77. Blake McKelvey also treated the turnover phenomenon in *Rochester, The Flower City, 1855-1890* (Cambridge, Mass.: Harvard University Press, 1949), p. 3, and James C. Malin did it for farm population: "The Turnover of Farm Population in Kansas," *Kansas Historical Quarterly,* 4 (1935), pp. 339-372. See also Merle Curti et al., *The Making of an American Community* (Stanford: Stanford University Press, 1959); Allan G. Bogue, *From Prairie to Corn Belt* (Chicago: University of Chicago Press, 1963); and Peter J. Coleman, "Restless Grant County: Americans on the Move," *Wisconsin Magazine of History,* 45 (1962), pp. 16-20; and W. G. Robbins, "Opportunity and Persistence in the Pacific Northwest: A Quantitative Study of Early Roseburg, Oregon," *Pacific Historical Review,* 39 (August 1970), pp. 279-296. More generally, see Stephan Thernstrom and Peter R. Knights, "Men in Motion: Some Data and Speculations About Urban Population Mobility in 19th Century America," *Journal of Interdisciplinary History,* 1 (Autumn 1970), pp. 7-35.

31

tence among white-collar business and professional groups, however, was much higher for natives than among manual workers of either nativity or racial grouping and, in the long term, higher than for immigrants in the business and professional class. Thus, the most persistent residents, in occupational terms, appear to have been the highest native-white and the lowest black elements in the population.

In an analysis of residential movements, Hopkins focused on a socially heterogeneous area on the city's near south side. There he found that individuals at the top of the occupational tree did not shift their dwelling as frequently as those on lower branches. Skilled blue-collar workers were the most mobile but, whereas white movement was progressively outward, that of the blacks was toward two well-defined Negro sections on the east and west sides of the downtown area. Like early Milwaukeans, these residents of Atlanta were evidently using their personal resources to "control" their physical environments; the blacks, of course, had smaller resources and hence fewer options than other segments of the population. Hopkins found that by 1900 these differentiated environments ranged "outward from the lowest at the center to the highest on the periphery."

While Atlanta of "the new south" was still a comparatively small city, its role as a regional transportation center does not seem to have impinged much on its residential pattern. But, with a population growing from around 20,000 to 85,000, one might have expected—from Bowden's explanation of lower thresholds for polynuclear CBDs—the physical expansion of the business district to have been a potent factor in the relocation of its residents. One wonders, moreover, whether the social-spatial pattern of "the modern city"—the core-periphery upward class gradient—is quite as uniform as Hopkins suggests. He is aware, for example, of Schnore's analysis of several distinctive types of residential structure in metropolitan areas during the period 1940-1960. These variants, to be sure, were mostly found among newer medium-sized metropolitan areas of the far west and southwest; nevertheless, giants such as Los Angeles, Tucson, Memphis, and, in certain respects, Miami were deviants from the typically "modern" structure as recently as 1960.[25]

The careful delineation of neighborhoods in ante-bellum Milwaukee by Kathleen Conzen suggested the limits of the "preindustrial" stereo-

[25] Schnore, *The Urban Scene*, pp. 203-293. Also, H. J. Gans, "Urbanism and Suburbanism as Ways of Life: A Re-evaluation of Definitions," in Arnold Rose (editor), *Human Behavior and Social Processes* (Boston: Houghton Mifflin, 1962), pp. 625-648. More generally, Melvin M. Webber, "The Urban Place and the Nonplace Urban Realm," in Webber et al., *Explorations into Urban Structure* (Philadelphia: University of Pennsylvania Press, 1964), pp. 79-153.

type as nothing more than a summary view of that city's social-spatial order. But the rapid growth of Milwaukee as a manufacturing and transport center later in the century did not bring its pattern of land use and residence into conformity with the "modern" stereotype either. Topographical features as well as transportation axes closely affected the reorganization of the city's plan. Milwaukee witnessed not only the development of a high-class residential section on its far north side along the lakeshore, but also new working-class and moderate-income suburbs to the northwest and south of the old built-up core. These latter areas—all within the city limits—were occupied by younger families and recent arrivals from Europe. The resulting residential structure was still much more variegated in terms of socioeconomic class than the "modern" or "industrial" city stereotype would suggest. Nevertheless, the tendency to ethnic congregation persisted—among Germans and Poles, for example—across the expanses of the enlarged city as it had in the more constricted spaces of the old "frontier" city. By the turn of the century, when Milwaukee's population exceeded 285,000, housing in parts of the old German and Irish wards, adjacent to spreading commercial and manufacturing sectors, was being "handed down" to some of the most recent arrivals. In the early 1900s newcomers from southern Italy and the Russian Pale were situated in core enclaves where the familiar succession of poverty, crowding, and environmental deterioration had become more widespread.[26]

The question of whether particular cities conform to typical patterns is of no great moment. Although construction of "types" may be a useful exercise in some social sciences, it is doubtful if the practice has much heuristic merit in historiography, however convenient as a pedagogic or literary device. Historical interests are probably better served when abstraction illuminates the *processes* of change, development, or transformation; for, on closer examination, most periods and places in history turn out to be "transitional." Accordingly, the sociological notions of status change and mobility have exercised a strong attraction for "new" urban historians since they appear to combine measurable elements of both social structure and process. Yet, insofar as studies of social mobility derive their empirical content almost

[26] Based on Roger D. Simon, "The Expansion of an Industrial City: Milwaukee, 1880-1910," unpublished Ph.D. dissertation, University of Wisconsin, 1971, which treats the development of peripheral suburbs within the city limits by different socioeconomic and ethnic groupings. Simon shows (1) why different groups either settled or moved where they did, and (2) the quality of the different physical environments in terms of housing, transport, street improvement, sewers, and water mains.

wholly from occupational categories of the industrial labor force, some historians may wonder what precisely is being quantified; where comparative studies are involved, doubts multiply as the number of cities increases.

Surely the "status" which enters in as a determinant of behavior in particular communities is ascribed in a far more intricate and circumscribed social system than is reflected by half a dozen or so rankings in a national occupational "prestige hierarchy." To collapse an ever-widening spectrum of urban jobs—without regard to establishment, industry, organization, or local labor markets—into a highly aggregated set of statuses, and manipulate redistributions of a sample population among such statuses even to one decimal place, is perhaps to pursue metrics to the point of self-deception. The issue here is not whether some subset of a sample does better, on average, in up-grading its job status than others, nor whether the lower orders achieve some of the material and psychological gains of upward mobility, but rather what are the resulting frequencies supposed to have measured? Leaving aside technical questions involved in the use of sample subsets, to take little or no account of variables such as income, wealth, schooling, family size, and age (not to mention numerous less quantifiable attributes of sample members) is to adumbrate a very thin society indeed. Finally, to compare changes of status among different groups on the gross areal basis of political wards, or to ascribe statuses to blocks of dwellings based on the same occupational-status scale as their residents, serves alike to obscure any possible significance of neighborhood.[27]

Zane Miller's Chapter 5 is concerned with Negro migration and offers a comparative study of the black populations of five southern cities—Richmond, Savannah, New Orleans, Louisville, and Birmingham—over roughly the same period as Hopkins' study of Atlanta. A general pattern of social discrimination, job disadvantage, and heightened segregation of residence occurs in each of the cities notwithstanding certain differences rooted in their historical and economic contexts. Yet Miller affirms some residential betterment, modest

[27] Quite apart from conceptual problems, the question of measuring change of status has not received adequate attention from social scientists; see Otis Dudley Duncan, "Methodological Issues in the Analysis of Social Mobility," in Neil J. Smelser and S. M. Lipset (editors), *Social Structure and Mobility in Economic Development* (Chicago: Aldine Publishing Company, 1966), pp. 51-97. On problems of a "labor market" interpretation of aggregate and comparative social mobility during industrialization, see Eric E. Lampard, "Historical Contours of Contemporary Urban Society: A Comparative View," *Journal of Contemporary History,* 4 (July 1969), especially pp. 18-25.

attainments in schooling, the emergence of a black bourgeoisie, and the attraction of rural blacks on a selective basis. These developments contribute, in turn, to the appearance of the race pride and civic betterment movement during the early twentieth century. The findings give some support to the contemporary opinions of Cable and DuBois regarding the Negro's stake in urbanization.[28] They also underline Hopkins' point concerning the attitudes and behavior of people who have undergone constant alteration in their urban lives; such experiences were far more personal and immediate for the many thousands of persons involved than were the more general national trends. We are in dire need of some kind of phenomenological sociology. There could scarcely be a more pressing methodological issue for those social scientists who presume to be "policy scientists"—and modify the attitudes or behavior of human beings—than to explore the possibilities that must lie somewhere between the approach of the "objective" observer counting his subjects' behaviors and the approach of the social surveyor tallying "subjective" responses to his "objective" questionnaire.

Given the inferior living conditions of and discrimination against Negroes in southern cities, Miller confesses it "difficult" to see why blacks would abandon the countryside. By 1910 some of the young and talented were doubtless moving to the north, but surely the rele-

[28] L. B. DeGraaf, "The City of Black Angels: Emergence of the Los Angeles Ghetto, 1890-1930," *Pacific Historical Review*, 39 (August 1970), pp. 323-352, argues that social discrimination and residential segregation were also accompanied by relative socioeconomic betterment when compared with such places of origin as rural Texas. By 1930 more than one-third of black families in Los Angeles owned their own homes; conditions were generally more favorable than in the black ghettos of major eastern cities. He also asserts that immigrants of European origin did not face a comparably hostile environment in Los Angeles. Theodore Hershberg, "Free Blacks in Ante-bellum Philadelphia: A Study of Ex-slaves, Freeborn, and Socio-economic Decline," *Journal of Social History*, 5 (Winter 1971), pp. 183-209, indicates a deterioration in the social environment of all Philadelphia Negroes between 1830 and 1860 but argues that slave-born freedmen were relatively more successful than the free-born blacks in coping with this situation. He suggests that the "destructive" nature of the anti-bellum northern city was intensified for blacks in postwar decades owing to heightened "racism" and not to "the legacy of slavery." As of 1880, he concludes that black families were generally more stable in southern cities than in northern cities. On persistent barriers against Negroes compared with other ethnic and "culturally deprived" elements generally, see Peter M. Blau and Otis Dudley Duncan, *The American Occupational Structure* (New York: John Wiley & Sons, Inc., 1967), especially pp. 404-407. Also, Sam B. Warner, Jr., and C. B. Burke, "Cultural Change and the Ghetto," *Journal of Contemporary History*, 4 (October 1969), pp. 173-187, and Timothy L. Smith, "New Approaches to the History of Immigration in 20th-Century America," *American Historical Review*, 71 (July 1966), pp. 1265-1279.

vant condition affecting Negro migration to the cities was *their* relative condition in the countryside, no matter what the conditions of whites in town or country. Similarly, the relevant condition for moving northward would be the relative characteristics of urban destinations, north and south. Is not this what DuBois understood? The age structure of the rural black population would also be pertinent in comparing the changing age structures of blacks in southern cities before and after 1900. One also wonders whether the age structures of blacks in cities north of the Ohio after 1900 would show a bulge in the under-25's complementing the "void" in the 15-24 age group in southern cities, 1900-1920.

Miller contends that the urbanization of blacks resulted in a beneficial heightening of "group consciousness" as well as some individual betterment. In what is, for one reader at least, the most original, if rather unfinished, exploration, Gregory H. Singleton's Chapter 6 on Protestant fundamentalism exposes some of the possible psychic "costs" of urbanization paid by migrants of native birth and ancestry. The heightening of group consciousness in this case does not seem to be associated with any sense of betterment. In the decade or so after the first trial Armageddon, 1914-1918, something like a third of the adherents of fundamentalist and sympathetically related sects ended up in the nation's cities, with perhaps the heaviest *relative* concentrations in four western states: California, Oregon, Nevada, and Arizona. Negro migrants are thought to have made up "one-third of the membership of the 'Sympathetic' denominations." The author's admittedly unrepresentative Los Angeles sample is gleaned from a harvest of surviving church directories of the downtown and southeastern sections for the years 1919-1926.

Membership in such congregations was overwhelmingly among unskilled and semi-skilled workers. But there were doubtless many other lower-class Protestants around Los Angeles at the time who were neither fundamentalists nor sympathizers, not even church-goers, perhaps. It is not clear, therefore, whether Singleton is asserting that fundamentalist membership was a function of church location. The matter of appropriate controls is clearly critical in treating such a fortuitous population. But Singleton is surely wise to insist "that to be classified as semi-skilled means more than stating that one is empolyed as a semi-skilled laborer." The residences of sample members, for example, proved to be even more transient than the locations of their churches; their level of voter registration was lower than that of the more stable (less migratory?) membership of established denominations, yet registration did rise somewhat among the members of the attenuated sample who continued to reside in the same areas (reached by the organizations?). The arrest-rates of fundamentalists for misdemeanors and of sympathizers for felonies were always above average for the city population as a whole. Arrest-rates in both categories of offense for members of established denominations were negligible.

Singleton asserts that his subjects were as "alienated" from the fragmented modern metropolis as they were from the "modernist" tendencies evinced by establishment denominations. The evidence for "alienation," however, is not made manifest. By the early 1930s, nevertheless, there are portents of greater accommodation. Clearly, fundamentalist and sympathetic Angelenos—with the exception of archangels like Milton and Lyman Stewart—were rich and powerful only in their expectation of betterment in Christ's Kingdom. Perhaps the Depression was their sign.

IV

UNDERLYING the growth and differentiation of cities across North America from Jamestown to Los Angeles of the Anglo-period was the evolution of commercial and industrial systems of production and consumption within a broadly liberal set of political-social institutions. Although even an Anglo-society is always more than a marketplace, the economist's idealized notion of "the price system" has come to furnish a potent intellectual framework—a theology of original scarcity—for justifying the order of this world where everything has a price. Nowadays economists "explain" the growth and redistribution of population, the development of technology and applied arts, as well as the transformation of social institutions. The "new" economic interpretation of history has again raised the godhead of Mammon, with an appealingly plasticized face. Properly construed, his market paradigm offers the optimum possible world and, with the refinement of cliometric technique, a quantitative estimate of the degree to which mankind at any time persists in the error of an irrational sub-optimal state. The last three chapters of this new urban testament exhibit the powers of positivist thinking in the solution of historiographical problems.

In Chapter 7, for example, Claudia Dale Goldin proffers an explanation for the relative decline of slavery in southern cities almost entirely in terms of well-specified price conditions and the logic of market behavior. There is evidence that the rate of *increase* in urban slave numbers reported by the census had slackened and, in some instances, turned negative during the pre-Civil War decade. By 1860 the slave population of the cities included a greater proportion of females, fewer children under ten years, and more adults over 55, together with a greater relative concentration of skilled workers, than at any previous census back at least to 1820. Meanwhile, slave prices continued to rise overall in both country *and* town.

Miss Goldin is able to make economic sense of these paradoxical tendencies—and cast doubt on earlier ad hoc judgments regarding the incompatibility of slavery and urban life—by considering the differential impacts of price increases on the demand for field hands and for city slaves. She postulates that the effect of a given price increase on the demand for slaves (the elasticity of demand) would be smaller in the agricultural sector, where there were fewer alternative sources of labor, than in the more competitive urban sector, where slaves were coming to be in short physical supply and where "free" labor might be substituted. Rising agricultural demand would thus tend to bid up slave prices with the result that owners of unskilled urban males could realize a capital gain by selling them off to the country.[29] Meanwhile, urban demand might still make it worthwhile, despite rising costs of maintenance and control, for owners to retain certain skilled hands and females in cities.

Miss Goldin's tentative conclusion is that slaves were pulled out of the urban south, not pushed. Either way, ownership supplied the momentum and, to ply an old medieval saw: in America *Stadtluft macht nur die Unternehmung frei.* Miss Goldin's chapter represents a nice exercise in the normative logic of markets but it does not proceed to the operational test. It does not, for example, derive specific demand schedules from historical data although it employs historical data—as Schumpeter put it—"in order to know precisely what there is to be explained."

Robert Higgs' Chapter 8 uses the market logic of the "production function" to account for the well-known association of inventive activity with city life. He treats the production of inventions much like the production of any other market good: essentially a relation between costs and revenues which determines the rate of return. If inventive capacities are randomly distributed through the entire population, then the costs of producing the revenues earned by the invention should alone determine whether it is profitable to invent. The aspiring inventor will need information concerning (1) the market potential for his product (the expected flow of revenue), and (2)

[29] See the interesting commentary of Archer Jones and Robert J. Carlsson, "Slavery and Saving," *American Journal of Economics and Sociology,* 30 (April 1971), pp. 171-177.

whatever has to go into the invention (his initial input cost). Higgs asserts that, prior to modern mass communications, both kinds of knowledge would be more readily available (cheaper) within the informal information networks of cities than among the spatially dispersed populations of the countryside. According to Higgs's theory, inventiveness in a population should always increase *ceteris paribus* in direct proportion to its level of urban concentration; i.e., the functional relation between urbanization and inventiveness is linear.

Proceeding to operations, differences in levels of urbanized population (u/p) are hypothesized as the "explanation" of variations in a population's inventiveness (i/p), or $i = f(u)$, such that inventiveness is made an explicit function of urbanization. (Higgs is not responsible for this particular notation.) The amount of inventiveness is uniquely determined *at a time* by a given level of urbanization, as might easily be read off along the coordinate axes of a simple graph plotting i along the vertical and u along the horizontal. Note that time itself is not included as a variable in this expression. Thus Higgs's treatment of the hypothesized relation is no more than a "cross-sectional" observation at a particular point in time and not a time-series of observations. But the values given are a cross-section for the several states of the Union at successive, albeit discrete, points in time— namely, the dates of the federal censuses between 1870 and 1920. At each census we get the proportion of each state's population resident in "cities" (places of at least 2,500 population) and the average number of U.S. patents per 100,000 of state populations for three years centered on the census year in question; these are the values of u and i respectively. Insofar as such decadal observations are interpreted in the census time-frame, the operation is an exercise in "comparative statics" where functional conditions are assumed to be unchanged and no explicit reference is made to the time-path of intervening adjustments.

Higgs also offers another possible "explanation" of variations in inventiveness by reading Adam Smith's division-of-labor hypothesis to imply a similarly linear relation between a population's inventiveness (i/p), and the proportion of its work force involved in manufacturing (m/w), such that $i = f(m)$. Finally, he recognizes the possibility that certain "social-structural" peculiarities may have limited the inventiveness of populations in *southern* states which otherwise exhibit similar employment structures and levels of urbanization to non-southern states.[30] This hypothesized peculiarity of southern states, how-

[30] A. W. Niemi, Jr., "Structural Shifts in Southern Manufacturing, 1849–1899," *Business History Review,* 45 (Spring 1971), suggests that the capital-supply

ever, does not have a numerical value, such as u or m above; hence the difference that a southern milieu might make to a population's inventiveness is included in his operation, not as a continuous function, but by a qualitative "dummy," yes/no, variable which simply registers whether or not a given state population is situated in the south. Operationally this is a restriction of a function to the southern subset of the domain "states."

The regression analysis shows that, at every date, the inventiveness of state populations is correlated far more positively and significantly with urbanization than with manufacturing employment or a southern/nonsouthern milieu. Thus Higgs confirms the difference in urban and rural inventiveness but it is *not* clear that he has explained it. The earlier theorizing about information cost advantage remains no more than one of several possible ad hoc explanations since he failed to operationalize such costs in any of his equations. Moreover, if urbanization has been displaced by mass communications and institutionalized "R & D" (research and development) as the stimulus to invention in the present century, why is this change not reflected in a weakening of the association predicted by the urbanization hypothesis? By 1920 either urban-rural information cost differentials had not narrowed sufficiently or perhaps the city simply had greater need for patented inventions than did the countryside.[31] Indeed, population concentration might be viewed as a societal process which generates "externalities" and fosters innovation on an unprecedented *scale.* Under liberal legal and accounting conventions, many externalities can be appropriated by individuals and firms while others remain, as Alfred Marshall put it, in "the industrial atmosphere" of localities and regions. No doubt, as Higgs adds, urbanization, technical progress, and economic

problem and uneducated labor force kept southern manufactures heavily resource-oriented in the later nineteenth century, whereas the structure of the region's manufacturing output in the ante-bellum period had been converging on that of regions outside the south. The "New South" was thus "maximizing" its wealth of natural resources along lines of comparative advantage. Niemi does not, however, test this last hypothesis.

[31] Irwin Feller, "The Urban Location of U.S. Invention, 1860-1910," *Explorations in Economic History,* 8 (Spring 1971), shows that from 30 to 40 per cent of all U.S. patents in those years were taken out by residents of 35 larger industrial cities (falling off over time) whose populations rose meanwhile from 10 to 19 per cent of all U.S. population. His regression suggests that the more a city's labor force was committed to manufactures, the fewer the city's patents. Differences in the inventiveness of city populations were, nevertheless, related to city size and employment structure, and to the "everyday nature" of most patents before 1910. The inventiveness of the 35 large-city populations had no discernible effect on their subsequent population growth.

growth may be represented in a "time series formulation" as a *self-sustaining* process, a ramifying response to changes in relative rates of return on agricultural and nonagricultural activities which accompany rising average incomes and urbanized consumer patterns. This problem has elsewhere been treated cybernetically as a "learning" system or *self-transforming* process.[32] But the identification of industrial cities as foci of a social system creating opportunities and forcing innovation—as well as social and environmental "problems"—will not rank among the major findings of the "new" urban history.

Finally, in Chapter 9, Joseph A. Swanson and Jeffrey G. Williamson pursue the logic of the market in order to construct a wholly symbolic model of most efficient plant location. Their exercise is projected against the kinds of institutional background prevailing in the United States between the Civil War and World War I. They employ recent developments in the investment of capital theory of the firm to define the most efficient or equilibrium solution as one in which the entrepreneur determines among several possible sites which will afford him maximum net receipts on his investment in new plant or, more precisely, will maximize the present value of discounted future cash flows. They further indicate that alternative locations will differ in this regard owing to *differential factor prices* over some indefinite span of time. The production function which relates these variable factor prices to the expected return on the product will include labor, capital in the form of machinery, and certain public services such as police and fire protection, sewage treatment, and purchased power supply. Thus a maximizing entrepreneur should take into account the money wages paid to workers (the purchasing power of which is assumed to be equal at alternative sites), the costs of borrowing and servicing capital, and outlays (especially property taxes) of an assortment of public services.

Insofar as firms locate new plants according to these specifications, the authors postulate a *systematic* relation of factor input prices to characteristics of particular sites, notably population density, which

---

[32] Magoroh Maruyama, "The Second Cybernetics: Deviation Amplifying Mutual Causal Processes," *American Scientist*, 51 (1963), reprinted in *General Systems*, 8 (1963), pp. 231-241. Also, Lampard, "Evolving System of Cities," in Perloff and Wingo, *op. cit.*, pp. 96-100. The common historical conception of "process" intimates merely a succession of events in time. R. F. Berkhofer, *A Behavioral Approach to Historical Analysis* (New York: Free Press, 1969), pp. 243-245, for example, treats "process" as a recurrent sequence of events or actions. Such a view neglects the relations of process to innovation and change and ignores the larger problems of the development and transformation of patterns or "structures" in human activities. The cybernetic or information systems approach is, of course, only one way of treating this issue.

they say approximates city size. Hence price changes outside the control of the firm will determine its location decisions since the *directions* (vectors) of factor price changes at a time are given by differences in urban environments, for which city sizes serve as proxies. The directions are as follows. (1) Prices of goods and services in workers' household budgets or wage-goods *increase* with city size. For example, prices of western farm products consumed by workers rise because of transport and distribution costs, but, as outlays on farm foods and fibers come to absorb a smaller share of workers' expenditures, the rising costs of labor-intensive services such as education or medical care absorb a correspondingly large share. (No comparably remote material inputs are indicated for the plant which for this period is assumed to be "footloose" in the northeast.) On the other hand, (2) borrowing costs of firms *decrease* with city size since the network of banks and other financial intermediaries tends to concentrate its lending resources in the largest cities. The long-term trend of interest rates in a developing economic system, however, will be downward. Finally, (3) the average cost of public services at first tends to *decrease* with scale but will eventually tend to rise again in the largest cities (a U-shaped cost function).

Given rising real wages, Swanson and Williamson then derive the combined impacts of falling economy-wide interest rates and rising costs of public services on the optimal equilibrium site at any time. They conclude that both variables "should contribute to a lowering of optimal city sizes." Allowing for lags in adjustment, they predict "greater relative growth rates in cities of intermediate size, not unlike recent twentieth-century American experience."

Notwithstanding the authors' attempt to conjure up "empirical premises" with respect to hypothetical input-price patterns, the historian may find the entire exploration lacking in concreteness. Even if he can appreciate the sharp breach with the tradition of location economics and concedes the superiority of an optimal capital accumulation approach, the historian is likely to ask what possible relevance all this can have to the tasks of writing urban history. An affirmative, if not altogether straightforward, answer might go like this. The authors propose an approach to the creation of new industrial facilities in the form of a theory of "urban" investment in which the enterprise adjusts its stocks of factor inputs to changing optimal conditions which occur in the business environment. To the extent that plant creation necessarily involves a decision as to location, this highly abstract calculus has a very concrete outcome for the site where the investment is ultimately made. Jobs are generated: hence also households, families, and population—with all the ramifications that such accretions entail.

Those places which attract new plants require a larger labor force, and the rate of growth of the nation's labor force is, in effect, a weighted average of the growth rates of particular places where such plants are located. Thus the pattern of city growth which we observe historically can be viewed as the aggregate of individual firms' attempts to adjust their stocks of inputs to a new vector of input prices.

This formal model, notwithstanding the indeterminacies involved, enables Swanson and Williamson to characterize sites of "particular population density" as optimal with respect to new plant locations and hence most likely to succeed in generating population growth. If it were possible to link a model of city growth, in terms of capital formation, to the more familiar multiplier and agglomerative type analysis, such as that offered by Wilbur R. Thompson,[33] we should have what is virtually a complete description of urban growth. Could any contribution by economists to the study of urban history be more germane? Meanwhile, Swanson and Williamson furnish a carefully considered research agenda—not another laundry list of things t'would be nice to know—which can keep economists and cliometricians usefully in full employment over the course of the next business cycle. They might even uncover a case of a highly rational entrepreneur who once made a location decision along the lines specified in this model.

V

Such are some of the fruits of these historical accountants offered at the close of a decade of "urban crisis." They have dealt with jobs, residences, neighborhoods, adjustment, status, accommodation, innovation, and location. They have conjectured and measured some of the attitudes and behavior of capitalists, workers, immigrants, and freedmen, and have speculated upon the varieties and amounts of resources with which households, firms, and assorted social groupings cope with their changing environments, physical and social.[34] No

---

[33] Wilbur R. Thompson, "Internal and External Factors in the Development of Urban Economies," with an econometric model of urban economic development by Thompson and J. M. Matilla, in Perloff and Wingo, *op. cit.*, pp. 43-62, 63-78. Also, E. S. Mills and D. M. de Ferranti, "Market Choice and Optimum City Size," *American Economic Review*, 61 (May 1971) treat distortions in the provision and financing of local public services, pollution, and congestion, which are said to be a function of city size.

[34] Two of the chapters touch upon changing patterns of consumption, including the demand for municipal services. M. H. Frisch, "L'histoire urbaine américaine. Réflexion sur les tendances récentes," *Annales: E.S.C.*, 25 (Juillet-Août, 1970), pp. 880-896, might still regard these diverse fruits of historical accounting as too "austere," too divorced from the concerns of mainstream historiography.

prizes are offered to those who can indicate other urban topics worthy of exploration. But except as one paper deals with innovations and their diffusion, and another adds an afterthought concerning economic growth as a self-sustaining process, none attempts to describe the dynamics of the "urban system" as a whole.

To be sure, an association between rising per capita incomes, the shift into nonagricultural employments, and the growth and redistribution of population across the continent has long been recognized. Similarly, the concentration of population and secondary, tertiary, and quarternary occupations in and around the cities. Students of the primary trend of industrialization have also noted that the experience has been characterized by periodic instabilities. The most obvious pattern felt in our quotidian lives by entrepreneurs, workers, and human beings is the alternating sequence of good and bad times known as the business cycle. These comparatively short and occasionally sharp fluctuations reflect, in essence, the changing intensity with which existing productive resources are utilized. Until recently it was not known whether there was any other kind of patterning of aggregate movement around the primary trend, although there were intimations in both theory and experience that capitalist industrial development in the United States and elsewhere had proceeded in "surges," "long waves," and "secular movements" at least down into the 1920s. There were notable swings, for example, in population growth, in volumes of significant outputs, and in price series which established empirically a rough periodicity for this "trend cycle" in several important sectors. Periods of relatively rapid urbanization of population alternated with periods of slower urbanization and from around 1890 the rate of overall urban increase appeared to slacken with each successive wave. Statistical economists in the years after World War II designated the phenomenon as "Kuznets' cycles"—after the master.[35]

He argues, for example, that "the more basic question . . . is . . . not the use of quantification, but the place and purpose of such usage in urban history; not the employment of social science concepts and techniques, but rather which social science concepts, what techniques, and—most importantly—to what explanatory end they are to be employed."

[35] Moses Abramovitz, "The Passing of the Kuznets Cycle," *Economica*, 35 (November 1968), pp. 349-369. Also, Hope T. Eldridge and Dorothy S. Thomas, *Population Redistribution and Economic Growth, United States 1870–1950*, III, *Demographic Analyses*, with an introduction by Simon Kuznets (Philadelphia: The American Philosophical Society, 1964); and Harvey S. Perloff, Edgar S. Dunn, Eric E. Lampard, and Richard F. Muth, *Regions, Resources, and Economic Growth* (Baltimore: Johns Hopkins Press, 1960), pp. 122-129, 222-232. L. E. Galloway and R. K. Vedder, "The Mobility of Native Americans," *Journal of Economic History*, 31 (September 1971), pp. 613-649.

Of special interest to "new" social historians is the fact that marked variations of from 15 to 25 years' duration do seem to occur in rates of growth of U.S. population, labor force, and household numbers from the first half of the last century. Various models have been proposed to account for the possible existence and mode of sustained movements in economic and demographic activity in the United States. The most interesting, perhaps, from the viewpoint of social historians, is that proposed by Richard A. Easterlin, according to which the "working" of the model is registered by demographic variables in their interaction with critical variables in the economic environment.[36] Changes in the population (migration, fertility, labor-force participation, and proportions of given age and sex groups who function as heads of household) are viewed as short-period responses in behavior to variations in economic conditions (notably income and employment opportunities). Whereas the business cycle can be interpreted as variations in aggregate demand for existing resources, Kuznets' cycles or long swings can be seen as variations in the supply of incremental resources.

Easterlin's model proceeds in three stages: (1) the impact of total demand on labor-market conditions; (2) the effect of labor-market conditions on the number and spending behavior of households; and (3) feedbacks of the latter on total demand. An assumed increase in the rate of growth of private investment leads to a spurt in aggregate demand which is transmitted to the labor market and is met by the existing unemployed and/or new participants in the work force. Rising demand for labor is increasingly centered in the nonfarm urban sectors. If the demand for labor is sustained, it will lead to an increased rate of rural-to-urban migration as well as immigration by foreigners and higher participation rates among almost all segments of the population. The enhanced employment opportunities in cities generate a demand for more housing, urban facilities, and services. All the latter outlays for households and services are fed back by multiplier effects on the market so as to engender *upswings* in business activity, new construction, new firms, public utilities, and other population-sensitive types of capital formation. Thus responses to changes in the economic environment lead to what Easterlin calls "long-term commitments" by households and firms which can maintain expenditures over periods much longer than the short-term business cycle. Unless they continue to be reinforced, however, the petering out of

[36] Richard A. Easterlin, *Population, Labor Force and Long Swings in Economic Growth: The American Experience* (New York: Columbia University Press, 1968) also contains an excellent guide to the literature. The model is described, p. 49.

these time-lagged expansive commitments leads to a long *downswing* in rates of growth with similar interactions among the variables except that declining rates of increase are substituted for rising rates.

This model does not offer an explanation for the transition from rising rates of increase to falling rates (or vice versa). Hence it does not demonstrate a "self-generating" or "self-explanatory" swing. But insofar as the primary trend of industrialization reflects the workings of technical progress and improvements in the quality of human resources and institutional management (which are embodied in long swings in productivity ratios) there is no reason yet to exclude the possibility of such a formally endogenous model.[37] In any event, the effects of these and other (still exogenous) forces do tend to modify the course of long-swing movements, notably by their effects on successive urban development booms and associated changes in life-styles.

Although there are complex theoretical and metrical issues connected with the long-swing analysis of socioeconomic change, the historian should not dismiss the phenomenon as just another statistical stunt. Marked surges in the development of new resources are given empirically: waves of migration and immigration, the opening of new lands and development of material resources in successive "wests," the growth of cities, etc. They are a part of the primary stuff out of which the history of "the American dream" is made, well down into the present century when the visible hand of government is made more manifest. Thus the long-swing framework offers a potentially important framework for social history.

We might begin and end close to home. With a little help from such background, random(?), eventualities as war, public policy decisions, and Sputnik, the long swing clarifies why so many of us who came of economic and military age in the 1940s and 1950s have, partly as a result of earlier immigration curbs, lower family fertility, and the spread of secondary education in the inter-war years,

---

[37] W. W. McCormick and C. M. Franks, "A Self-Generating Model of Long Swings for the American Economy, 1860-1940," *Journal of Economic History*, 32 (June 1971), affirm that the core variables (income, population, capital formation, and general level of business) are "enhanced in explanatory value" by the addition to the model of variables representing money supply and technical change. The authors judge their model's predictive power to be good but "not good enough to rule out either a more complex model or the influence of exogenous forces." Also, B. W. Poulson and J. M. Dowling, "Background Conditions and the Spectral Analysis Test of the Long Swings Hypothesis," *Explorations in Economic History*, 8 (Spring 1971), pp. 343-351. Their findings uphold the hypothesis but do not provide a basis for accepting or rejecting the existence of swings in the U.S. data.

"enjoyed" a rapid growth in relative incomes, unusually rapid upward mobility on the occupational ladder (for women and blacks, too), opportunities for earlier marriage, separate households, a baby boom, and, if Kenneth T. Jackson will allow, consumption of suburban bliss on an unprecedented scale. This long swing, notwithstanding ups and downs of business, had important income effects in the labor market on the demand for young people—not least those with the kinds of worldly expertise now taught in multiversities. There was correspondingly less response from rural-to-urban or foreign migration than was possible in the past. With the end of the "100 month" business boom in the late 1960s, the long swing (if indeed still operative) may itself have petered out, and it is unlikely that cohorts coming of age in the 1970s—the products of our lagged baby boom—will have it quite as good, any more than those who were unwise enough to enter in the 1920s and early 1930s. The rapid growth of the younger labor force in the 1960s (supplemented more by immigration again than was immediately realized) has led to a deterioration of their relative income position, to deferment of marriage, later household formation, and much lower fertility, all of which may or may not add up to a new life-style. Their ultimate fate as cohorts may well turn on what happens in the further urbanization of the metropolitan "outer cities" and on a growing awareness that we are part of a human ecosystem, what Kenneth Boulding has dubbed the spaceship Earth.

At the outset the matter of a slump in demand for new Ph.D.'s in American history was mentioned. The implication of a long-swing model, modified by government decisions, should not be overlooked. The demand for, and greater participation of, urban specialists is holding up well, and one guess would be that the demand for, and greater participation by, quantitative urban specialists in the still-growing historiographical enterprise will hold up even better. But these are prophecies and divinations, not predictions, although they may be comforting to some among the graduate students who read this book.

Clio's house has many mansions and can accommodate her ardent metricians as well as her steadfast letrists. Indeed she welcomes them, for her art, ἱστορία, was originally the quest for knowledge in the fullest sense: inquiry, investigation, research, and not narrative as such. Two hundred years or so elapsed before *historikos*, the storyteller, superseded *historeōn*, the knowledge-seeker. Although Herodotus indicated the new usage, his immortal gift was as *historiē*, and it was not before Aristotle, a mere philosopher, that the word was applied to the literary outcome rather than to the process of inquiry which went into it.

Clio's only condition for entry to her precinct is that the scholarly enterprise remain humane. As Charles Horton Cooley, no mean student of cities, put it:

> Use diagrams, by all means, use classification, use maps, curves, statistics—and forget them! These are methods of manipulating the material, as they are in botany or zoology. But the materials themselves are living wholes which can only be apprehended by a trained sympathy in contact with them. And when you have reached your conclusions, no presentation of them is adequate that does not restore the facts to their human reality.[38]

Cooley was not an historian, but this is what Louis Chevalier also meant when he offered his "reactionary view of urban history." It is probably what Hugh Trevor-Roper implied when he suggested that historians "need professional methods but always for the pursuit of lay ends." Surely this issue no longer divides us. So, an end to quantifying, and back to our notes and data tapes, remembering only that all historians best serve their Muse by serving best her readers.

[38] Charles Horton Cooley, *Life and the Student* (New York: Alfred A. Knopf, 1927), p. 156, as quoted in Leo F. Schnore, "Cooley as a Territorial Demographer," in Albert J. Reiss, Jr. (editor), *Cooley and Sociological Analysis* (Ann Arbor: University of Michigan Press, 1968), pp. 13-31.

PART ONE
THE GROWTH AND FUNCTION
OF CITIES

1

Large-City Interdependence and the
Pre-Electronic Diffusion of Innovations
in the United States

ALLAN R. PRED

I

Modelers of the diffusion of innovations over space, from Häger-strand[1] to Hudson,[2] have focused on the processes by which relevant information spreads from person to person or place to place. When approaching such processes in an historical context, whether one is concerned with information merely relating to the existence of an innovation or with messages pertaining to the positive or negative experiences of those who have already adopted an innovation, it is important to realize that spatial biases in the availability of public and private information in pre-electronic environments were very pro-nounced by modern standards. Consequently, although a depiction of the general characteristics of pre-electronic information circulation over long distances is not the principal objective of this paper, the topic must be briefly touched upon in order later to consider the relationships between high-order urban interdependencies and pre-electronic innovation diffusion. Those wishing more elaborate details on spatial biases in the availability of information during the U.S. pre-electronic era, which began its termination in 1844 with the open-ing of an electromagnetic telegraph line between Baltimore and Wash-ington, are referred to other of my work.[3]

[1] Torsten Hägerstrand, *The Propagation of Innovation Waves* (Lund: Lund Studies in Geography, Series B, Number 4, 1952); Hägerstrand, *Innovation Diffusion as a Spatial Process* (Chicago: University of Chicago Press, 1967); originally published as *Innovationsforloppet ur korlogisk synpunkt* (Lund: G.W.K. Gleerup, 1953).

[2] John C. Hudson, "Diffusion in a Central Place System," *Geographical Analysis,* 1 (1969), pp. 45-58.

[3] Allan R. Pred, "Urban System Growth and the Long-Distance Flow of Informa-tion Through Pre-electronic U.S. Newspapers," *Economic Geography,* 47 (1971), pp. 488-524; and *idem, Urban Growth and the Circulation of Information: The United States System of Cities, 1790-1840* (Cambridge: Harvard University Press, 1973).

II

By definition, in a pre-electronic context public as well as private information could circulate over long distances only as an accompaniment to human spatial interaction. That is, newspapers, journals, and other printed matter—which are the only forms that public information could take so long as electronic message transmission was not technically feasible—could be moved from place to place only if personally carried by foot or horse, or shipped in humanly controlled vehicles or vessels. Therefore, in the U.S. and elsewhere, the speed of nonlocal private and public information transmission during any specific period was limited by the current state of transportation technology. This meant that, even under the best of conditions, information moved at a pace that was sluggish to a degree not easy for the modern imagination to comprehend. Examination of pre-electronic conditions in a single city, Philadelphia, should be adequate to bring home this point.

Were some major event to occur today in either a European metropolis or a domestic point as distant as San Francisco, a Philadelphian would be able to hear of it within minutes or hours on radio or television, or within a day in the press. In contrast, in 1790 the average time-lag between occurrence of events in London and Paris and publication of news regarding them in Philadelphia was, respectively, 67.5 and 80.8 days. Similarly, the 1790 Philadelphia newspaper reader found, on the average, that his news from such a relatively nearby city as Baltimore was 6.0 days old, and that from more distant cities such as Boston (12.0 days) and Savannah (33.6 days) was much older. (These foreign and domestic time-lags were both based on a seasonally stratified sample of 48 issues of the *Journal* and the *Packet*, two Philadelphia newspapers.) In 1841, the Philadelphia newspaper reader still found himself at a considerable temporal as well as spatial remove from most nonlocal events, despite improvements in the rapidity of information circulation brought about during the intervening fifty-one years by extensions and improvements in the postal network, the widespread adoption of the steamboat, and a few railroad openings. True, European news was now weeks rather than months old, and the mean time-lag between nonlocal occurrence and Philadelphia publication had been diminished to 1.1 days for Baltimore events and 2.7 days for Boston events. However, European news was almost invariably printed only after being plagiarized from the New York press[4] and mean public information time-lags for places outside of the Northeast still remained sizeable, e.g., 13.0 days for Mobile, 11.0 days for St. Louis, and 8.0 days for Detroit. (All 1841 time-lags were based on a seasonally stratified sample of 48 issues of the *Philadelphia Public Ledger.*)

TABLE 1-1   NEWSPAPER AND POSTAL CONSUMPTION PER CAPITA
IN THE U.S.: 1790 AND 1840

	1790	*1840*	*1840/1700*
Total population (1,000's)	3,929	17,120	4.4
Postage revenues ($1,000's)	37.9	4,543.0	119.9
Annual postage revenues per capita ($)	0.01	0.27	27.0
Newspapers published	92	1,404	15.3
Newspaper editions per week[a]	147	2,281	15.5
Estimated total annual circulation (1,000's)	3,975[b]	147,500[c]	37.1
Annual number of newspaper copies per capita	1.0	8.6	8.6

SOURCES: U.S. Bureau of the Census, *Historical Statistics of the U.S., Colonial Times to 1957* (Washington: U.S. Government Printing Office, 1960), pp. 7 and 497; W. E. Rich, *The History of the U.S. Post Office in the Year 1829* (Cambridge, Mass.: Harvard University Press, 1924), p. 184; A. M. Lee, *The Daily Newspaper in America* (New York: Macmillan, 1937), pp. 16 and 718; *The American Almanac and Repository of Useful Knowledge* (Boston: David H. Williams, 1840), p. 69; F. Hudson, *Journalism in the U.S., from 1690 to 1872* (New York: Harper, 1873), p. 772.

[a] Obtained by assigning values of six to dailies, three to tri-weeklies, two to semi-weeklies, and one to weeklies.

[b] Datum actually for 1789.

[c] This represents a very crude estimate based on a compromise between a conservative estimate of annual circulation put at 100,000,000, and an estimate of 195,838,673 which was inflated by including the annual sales of 227 periodicals not classified as newspapers by the 1840 U.S. Census.

Not only did nonlocal public and private information move slowly throughout pre-electronic times, but, despite steady increases that outstripped the rate of population growth, the volume that was acquired and moved per capita was very low by present-day standards (Table 1-1). The technology of newspaper printing, illiteracy,[5] and

[4] *Ibid.*

[5] In 1840 the census authorities reported that 22.0 per cent of the population twenty years old and over was illiterate. Moreover, since "the head of the family was asked for the total number of illiterates in each family . . . [the method] undoubtedly led to some understatement." U.S. Bureau of the Census, *Historical Statistics of the U.S., Colonial Times to 1957* (Washington: U.S. Government Printing Office, 1960), p. 206.

other factors were surely in part responsible for a situation where, as the pre-electronic period entered its twilight years, the volume of mail was sufficient to provide each adult inhabitant with little more than one piece of correspondence every third month,[6] and the number of newspapers sold amounted to just over one per month per person over nineteen years old.[7] However, what almost certainly lies at the heart of the matter is the fact that both the consumption of nonlocal information through the press and the exchange of information through the mails were evidently income-elastic. Except for the so-called penny press, which appeared in a few of the nation's larger cities during the mid- and late-1830s, newspapers sold for 6 to 12.5 cents per copy and dailies from $6.00 to $10.00 per annum.[8] The postal charges, which remained unchanged from 1816 to 1845, differed little from those in effect during the preceding years of confederation. They were graduated by distance zones, ranging from six cents for the first 30 miles to twenty-five cents for distances exceeding 400 miles. Double rates were assessed for two-sheet letters, triple rates for three-sheet letters, and quadruple rates for "packets" containing four or more sheets.[9] That these newspaper costs and postal rates were probably perceived as expensive by the vast majority of the population should be apparent from the following income statistics. (1) *Daily* wage rates for nonfarm labor in the United States as a whole stood at approximately $1.00 in 1800, $0.75 in 1818, and $0.85 in 1840. (2) *Monthly* wage rates for nonslave agricultural labor were roughly $10.00 in 1800, $9.30 in 1818, and $10.40 in 1840. (3) Total *annual* income per capita in 1840, exclusive of persons employed in commerce and their dependents, varied from a low of $32 in Iowa to a high of $102 in Rhode Island, with the national mean being roughly $55.[10] If, then, the direct acquisition and dispatch of informa-

[6] Based on an estimate, presented in an annual report of the Postmaster General, of the total number of letters carried by the U.S. Post Office during 1837 (*Niles' Weekly Register,* Jan. 13, 1838) and an 1837 population estimate (U.S. Bureau of the Census, *op. cit.,* p. 7).

[7] Actually 14.3 copies per annum for each person twenty or older. Obtained by using the circulation estimate given in Table 1, and deducting the total of all those nineteen or younger (U.S. Bureau of the Census, *op. cit.,* p. 10) from the national population total.

[8] Alfred McClung Lee, *The Daily Newspaper in America: The Evolution of a Social Instrument* (New York: Macmillan, 1937), pp. 467, 259. See also Daniel Hewett, "Daniel Hewett's List of Newspapers and Periodicals in the U.S. in 1828," *Proceedings of the American Antiquarian Society,* 44 (1934), pp. 365-396.

[9] Wesley E. Rich, *The History of the U.S. Post Office to the Year 1829* (Cambridge, Mass.: Harvard University Press, 1924), pp. 137-140; see also U.S. Bureau of the Census, *op. cit.,* p. 498.

[10] Stanley Lebergott, "Wage Trends, 1800-1900," in *Trends in the American*

tion from and over long distances was largely confined to the economic elite, it may be conjectured that in pre-electronic days the "two-step flow of communications" hypothesis was of even greater validity than it is today. That is, newspapers and other nonlocal information became widely known locally as a result of its having flowed as private information from "influentials," or opinion leaders, to less wealthy individuals, or "influencees."[11]

In view of the above observations on the volume and slowness of long-distance pre-electronic information circulation, we can speak of two varieties of spatial biases in the availability of pre-electronic information: (1) time-lag spatial biases and (2) contact-array spatial biases.

Since long-distance pre-electronic information transmission could not occur more or less instantaneously, it was by definition time-consuming. Hence, at a specific point in time (t_r) after an event which occurred at time t_e, public or private word of it could have been potentially available only to individuals dwelling within the area around the source node to which it was feasible to move (travel or transport) during the interval $t_r - t_e$. Thus, the subset of places where individuals could obtain news of the event more quickly than the average length of time required for all places in the circulation system could be said to have had a positive bias in potential information availability for that news, as well as for any other messages of identical locational origin. By the same token, that subset of places where receipt absorbed a greater than average length of time could be described as having had a negative bias in potential information availability.

The unique contract-array biases of each rural community and city in the U.S. during the eighteenth and early nineteenth centuries were usually defined by the economic activities and, to a lesser degree, by the family ties of its inhabitants. In most instances the "mean information field," or total array of nonlocal contacts, of each individual place was such that its residents were more likely to encounter nonredundant or new information from those places, normally nearby, with which contact frequency was high, and less likely to acquire previously unencountered information from those places, normally relatively distant, with which contact frequency was low. Hence, for any particular place, positive biases in information availability would have existed for that set of other places with which it had an above-

---

Economy in the Nineteenth Century (Princeton: Princeton University Press, 1960), pp. 449-499; see especially pp. 462, 471-473, 482-484.

[11] Elihu Katz, "The Two-Step Flow of Communications: An Up-to-Date Report on an Hypothesis," *Public Opinion Quarterly*, 21 (1957), pp. 61-78.

average frequency, or probability, of contact. Similarly, for any particular place, negative biases in information availability would have existed for that set of other places with which it had a below-average or zero direct contact probability.

Except where pre-electronic messages could move by a coastal shipping or inland waterway route, and thus bypass intermediate points, there was an intimate connection between time-lag and contact-array spatial biases in information availability. More specifically, time was consumed as information progressed from one place to another through a series of dyadic linkages, or *contact-array elements*. Or, the time-lag between information origin in one place and receipt in another was related to the contact-array of both places as well as that of a number of intervening places. To state it somewhat differently, pre-electronic information circulated via networks containing distance and other biases by successively flowing from nodes or origin, or places already possessing the information in question at a specified time interval, to nodes of destination, or places experiencing initial receipt of the information in the subsequent time interval.[12] This latter terminology is consistent with Brown's "conceptual framework of spatial diffusion,"[13] since, if so desired, it permits pre-electronic long-distance information circulation to be interpreted as a directed linear graph in which the pattern of internodal linkages is altered with the passage of time.

III

PRE-ELECTRONIC COMMODITY FLOWS BETWEEN LARGE CITIES

Through the construction of a series of time-lag surface maps for individual cities,[14] and an unpublished analysis of a variety of data concerning pre-electronic information circulation, the author has reached two interrelated conclusions regarding such circulation within three urban subsystems, or regional urban systems: (1) the area to the east of the Alleghenies, and to the north of the Potomac; (2) the Ohio Valley; and (3) the Eastern Great Lakes. One is that the vast bulk of the most pronounced time-lag and contact-array spatial biases were quite apparently the consequence of interurban economic relationships. The second is that "information often moved at greater speeds and/or with greater frequency between the highest-

[12] Pred, *Urban Growth and the Circulation of Information* . . . , *op. cit.*

[13] Lawrence Brown, *Diffusion Processes and Location: A Conceptual Framework and Bibliography* (Philadelphia: Regional Science Research Institute, 1968).

[14] *Urban Growth and the Circulation of Information* . . . , *op. cit.*

order places in a given subsystem (e.g., Baltimore, Philadelphia, New York, and Boston) than between each one of those places and most, if not all, subservient lower-order centers in their respective hinterlands."[15] Inasmuch as the exact nature of these pre-electronic interurban economic relationships is unfamiliar to most readers, and inasmuch as some acquaintance with them is crucial to the diffusion-theory arguments to be subsequently made, this section will examine one set of such relationships, those for Baltimore, Boston, New York and Philadelphia in 1820 and 1840.

TABLE 1-2   POPULATION OF FOUR
HIGH-ORDER CITIES: 1820 AND 1840

	1820	1840
New York[a]	130,881	348,943
Philadelphia[b]	108,809	220,423
Boston[c]	54,024	118,857
Baltimore	62,738	102,313

SOURCE: G. R. Taylor, "Comment," in D. T. Gilchrist, *The Growth of the Seaport Cities, 1790-1825* (Charlottesville: The University Press of Virginia, 1937), p. 39.

[a] Including Brooklyn. As with Philadelphia and Boston, "suburban" population is included because, in each case, the adjacent "suburbs," if not as yet legally wedded, were physically and functionally integrated with their respective compact central cities.

[b] Including Kensington, Moyamensing, Northern Liberties, Spring Garden, and Southwark.

[c] Including Cambridge, Charlestown, Roxbury, and Dorchester.

In both 1820 and 1840 the four cities in question were the largest in the country as well as the largest centers in the Northeast (Table 1-2). Contrary to central-place theory, which would permit goods flows only from New York to each of the other centers immediately below it in the hierarchy, and from Philadelphia to the roughly equal-sized Boston and Baltimore, coastal shipping interaction occurred in both directions between every possible pair of ports (Tables 1-3 and 1-4). Moreover, this interaction was relatively as well as absolutely great in volume, despite the fact that the two dates in question are

[15] *Ibid.*

those of depression years.[16] In 1820 and 1840 New York and Boston both provided more arrivals for Philadelphia than did any other port inside or outside the Northeast. In those same two years, New York and Boston also each accounted for more arrivals in Baltimore than did any other port in the country, although in 1840 New Orleans was

TABLE 1-3   COASTAL SHIPPING ARRIVAL MATRIX FOR
FOUR HIGH-ORDER CITIES: 1820

Arrivals at[b]	Arrivals From in Number of Vessels[a]			
	New York	Philadelphia	Boston	Baltimore
New York	X	100	101	54
Philadelphia	68	X	72	12[c]
Boston	91	43	X	72
Baltimore	38	13[c]	56	X

SOURCE: Compiled from all 104 editions issued in 1820 of the *New York Shipping and Commercial List*.

[a] The source data did not distinguish among ships, brigs, schooners, and sloops. Given the variations in carrying capacity of these different vessel-types, the arrival totals must be regarded as only crude estimates of the volume of shipping interaction between the four ports (cf. footnote a in Table 1-4).

[b] The number of arrivals recorded for any pair of ports is not equal at both termini (e.g., 100 at New York from Philadelphia, but only 68 at Philadelphia from New York) for several reasons. Probably most important is the fact that vessels were generally recorded as arriving from their last port of call rather than from their port of origin. Thus, a vessel from New York which stopped at Wilmington, Delaware, before continuing on to Philadelphia, would most likely have been recorded in the Quaker City as a Wilmington arrival.

[c] See footnote 22.

very close on the heels of Boston. Likewise, in 1820 and 1840 New York, Philadelphia, and Baltimore were three of Boston's four most important arrival origins (in both years New Orleans was the country's fifth city). In 1840 Baltimore, though less important than Boston and Philadelphia in New York's coastal trade, still ranked fifth among the latter's domestic-arrival origins. (New Orleans and Mobile both occupied a more prominent place in the New York picture due to the scale of the cotton trade.) Only between Philadelphia and Balti-

[16] The impact of the 1840 depression on coastal shipping between these major ports is suggested by the following. In 1835, a pre-depression year, Boston arrivals in New York totalled 404 (751 as weighted in Table 1-4), or almost half again as many as in 1840. See Robert G. Albion, *The Rise of New York Port, 1815-1860* (New York: Scribner's, 1939), p. 397.

more, separated by an extremely roundabout route to the south of Cape Charles, was the volume of through coastal shipping interaction relatively small.

The composition of coastal commodity flows crisscrossing among New York, Baltimore, Boston, and Philadelphia was of three basic

TABLE 1-4 COASTAL SHIPPING ARRIVAL MATRIX FOR
FOUR HIGH-ORDER CITIES: 1840

Arrivals at[b]	Arrivals From in Number of Vessels (Weighted Arrivals in Parentheses)[a]			
	New York	Philadelphia	Boston	Baltimore
New York	X	210 (333)	335 (577)	175 (290)
Philadelphia	233 (370)	X	90 (172)	5 (9)[c]
Boston	245 (388)	191 (320)	X	107 (178)
Baltimore	144 (250)	4 (6)[c]	67 (124)	X

SOURCE: Compiled from all 104 editions in 1840 of the *New York Shipping and Commercial List.*

[a] Most of the vessels employed on major U.S. coastal shipping routes at this date fell into one of four general categories of progressively larger average size and carrying capacity. "The sloop, which was generally the smallest type, had a single mast, supporting a large fore-and-aft sail. The schooner likewise had fore-and-aft sails, generally with two masts but occasionally, . . . with three. The brig had two masts but was square-rigged; that is, each mast supported several sails which crossed from side to side of the vessel instead of lying fore-and-aft. Finally, the full-rigged ship had three masts, all of which were square-rigged." (See R. G. Albion, *Square-Riggers on Schedule* (Princeton: Princeton University Press, 1938), p. 13.) Based on the tonnage data and discussion presented by Albion, arrivals (all of which were specified by vessel-type in the source material), were weighted as follows: ships 4.0; brigs 2.0; schooners 1.5; and sloops 1.0. Note that even the weighted arrivals must be regarded as crude estimates of shipping interaction among the four ports, inasmuch as there was no practical way of taking into account vessel-to-vessel variations in value of cargo carried. See Albion, *The Rise of New York Port* (New York: Scribner's, 1939), pp. 303-307.

[b] See footnote b in Table 1-3.

[c] See footnote 22.

types: (1) agricultural or raw material production from the hinterland of the port of origin; (2) manufactures produced in the port of origin or its lower-order dependents; and (3) redistributive shipments. The last category subsumes goods originating at one port and sent to a second to be reshipped out of the region, as well as goods originating outside of the region and reshipped from one of the four ports to another. More specifically, during the two-decade period Boston receipts included: flour, corn, oats, and other grains for itself and the textile- and shoe-producing towns in its hinterland from Baltimore, Philadelphia, and New York (especially after completion of the Erie Canal); hides and leather for the boot and shoe industries about Lynn from Baltimore, Philadelphia, and New York (a considerable volume of hides brought to New York from the West and Latin America were moved coastwise to Boston only after being tanned); an increasing volume of Lehigh, Schuykill, and Lackawanna anthracite coals from Philadelphia; a variety of foreign imports from New York; and steam engines and miscellaneous manufactures from Philadelphia.[17] During the 1820s and 1830s, commodities arriving by coastal shipping at Philadelphia included: shoes for local and immediate hinterland consumption from Boston; textiles and shoes from Boston to be resold to Western merchants; and English dry goods and a diversity of other foreign imports from New York.[18] From 1820 to 1840, New York's coastal receipts included: shoes and textiles from Boston, the lion's share of which was forwarded either west or south by local merchants; mackerel and surplus foreign imports from Boston; diverse industrial commodities from Philadelphia, many of which were reshipped to Southern ports; mounting volumes of coal from Philadelphia; flour from Baltimore (of decreasing importance after the Erie Canal opened); and coffee and tobacco from Baltimore (the latter was both locally processed for domestic redistribution and transferred

[17] A more precise reflection of the role played by New York, Philadelphia, and Baltimore in Boston's trade is provided by the following data. Of the 1,607,492 bushels of corn which arrived in Boston in 1839, 475,236 were from Baltimore, 231,000 from New York and 201,701 from Philadelphia. Of the 487,764 bushels of oats and rye received that same year, 115,272 were from New York, 82,616 from Baltimore, and 79,627 from Philadelphia. Of Boston's 1839 flour imports of 451,667 barrels, 153,450 came from New York, 61,093 from Baltimore and 25,872 from Philadelphia. Of the 96,365 tons of domestic and foreign coal arriving in Boston in 1839, Philadelphia provided 72,488. Data from *Hazard's U.S. Commercial and Statistical Register* (Philadelphia), Feb. 12, 1840. Also see Edward Chase Kirkland, *Men, Cities, and Transportation: A Study in New England History, 1820-1900* (Cambridge, Mass.: Harvard University Press, 1948), Vol. I, pp. 11 and 14-15; Robert G. Albion, *Square-Riggers on Schedule* (Princeton: Princeton University Press, 1938), pp. 127 and 189; J. S. Buckingham, *America, Historical, Statistical, and Descriptive* (New York: Harper and Brothers, 1841), Vol. 1, p. 360.

[18] Julius Rubin, *Canal or Railroad? Imitation and Innovation in Response to the Erie Canal in Philadelphia, Baltimore, and Boston* (Philadelphia: Transactions of the American Philosophical Society, New Series, Vol. 51, Part 7, 1961), pp. 18-19; Robert G. Albion, *Square-Riggers on Schedule, op. cit.*, p. 134; *Niles' Weekly Register* (Baltimore), Dec. 8, 1832; Albert Fishlow, *American Railroads and the Transformation of the Ante-Bellum Economy* (Cambridge, Mass.: Harvard University Press, 1965), pp. 270-271.

to New York-owned vessels for export to Europe).[19] Finally, coastal acquisitions at Baltimore during this same period included: leather products from Boston, varied foreign imports from New York; and apparently, on occasion, manufactured goods from Philadelphia.

Although overland transport costs over any but very short distances were prohibitive in pre-electronic times (except where limited stretches of railroad appeared in the 1830s),[20] additional commodity flows occurred among Boston, New York, Philadelphia, and Baltimore by means other than coastal shipping. More importantly, the Delaware and Raritan Canal, completed in 1834 across the waist of New Jersey from New Brunswick to Bordentown, provided an important new commodity-exchange route between New York and Philadelphia. In 1840, 172,120 tons of merchandise were barged along this canal.[21] Another canal, the Chesapeake and Delaware completed in 1830, drastically reduced the water distance between Baltimore and Philadelphia. In 1838, 131,760 tons were carried along this route, at least 50 per cent of which moved between the two large cities, including coal, hardware, and dry goods westward from Philadelphia, and raw and manufactured tobacco eastward from Baltimore.[22] In addition, coastal arrivals in New York from Providence often contained merchan-

---

[19] Edward Chase Kirkland, *Men, Cities and Transportation, op. cit.,* Vol. 1, p. 14, Vol. 2, p. 229. See also Robert G. Albion, *The Rise of New York Port, op. cit.,* pp. 127 and 138-139.

[20] During the first two decades of the nineteenth century, freight charges for shipment by wagon varied from time to time and place to place between 30 and 70 cents per ton-mile. See George R. Taylor, *The Transportation Revolution, 1815-1860* (New York: Holt, Rinehart and Winston, 1962), p. 133. Overland transport charges fell thereafter, but in 1839 an engineer-economist still estimated costs were 15 to 20 cents per ton-mile by turnpike, 10 to 15 cents by macadam road, and 2.5 cents by railroad. *By contrast, 1839 canal rates, which were considerably higher than those imposed by coasting vessels, were on the average about 1.5 cents per ton-mile.* See Kent T. Healy, "Transportation as a Factor in Economic Growth," *Journal of Economic History,* 7 (December, 1947), pp. 72-88.

[21] *Hunt's Merchants' Magazine* (New York), April, 1848, p. 434. A good part of the traffic on this canal originated on the Lehigh Canal. See Kent T. Healy, *op. cit.,* p. 84.

[22] James W. Livingood, *The Philadelphia-Baltimore Trade Rivalry, 1780-1860* (Harrisburg: The Pennsylvania Historical and Museum Commission, 1947), pp. 96-98; *Hazard's Register, op. cit.,* June 22, 1842. The traffic on the Chesapeake and Delaware Canal doubtlessly accounts in part for the surprisingly small volume of coastal shipping shown between Philadelphia and Baltimore in Table 1-4. There are some indications that during the 1820s the volume of trade moving between the two ports by a route which included a land leg over the Delmarva Peninsula exceeded that moved by coastal shipping. This makes the small volume of Baltimore-Philadelphia interaction in Table 1-3 somewhat more understandable. See George Armroyd, *A Connected View of the Whole Internal Navigation of the United States* (Philadelphia: Lydia R. Bailey, 1830), pp. 160-161.

dise of high value per unit weight from Boston, for Boston merchants often used the forty-two-mile land route to Providence, served by railroad after 1835, so as to avoid the devious sea route around Cape Cod.[23]

IV

The meanings implicitly and explicitly attached to the term "urban system" are not always unambiguous or consistent with one another. Thus, to place the ensuing discussion of interurban diffusion, or diffusion in an *urban system,* in the clearest possible light, a definition will be specified. Here, an urban system is a set of cities which are interrelated or interdependent in such a way that any significant change in the occupational structure, total income, and/or population of one member city will bring about some alteration in the occupational structure, total income, and/or population of one or more other set members.[24]

To this date, theoretical statements regarding the interurban diffusion of innovations have been framed in the hierarchical terminology of Christallerian central place theory. Most such thinking can be traced to Hägerstrand's 1952 observation that "The urban hierarchy canalizes [channels] the course of diffusion,"[25] and to his later reformulation, made with respect to the diffusion of the Rotary movement in Europe: "A closer analysis shows that the spread along the initial 'frontier' is led through the urban hierarchy. The point of introduction in a new country is its primate city; sometimes some other metropolis. Then centers next in rank follow. Soon, however, this order is broken up and replaced by one where the neighborhood effect dominates over the pure size succession."[26]

Although Berry and others have frequently referred to the "filtering" of innovations downward through the urban hierarchy, the argument has been stated most formally by Hudson.[27] The key assumption to his stochastic model is as follows: "A message emanating from a single center of order m diffuses downward through the hierarchy

[23] George R. Taylor, *op. cit.,* p. 154.

[24] Olof Wärneryd, *Interdependence in Urban Systems* (Göteborg: Regionkonsult Aktiebolag, 1968), pp. 16-19.

[25] Hägerstrand, *The Propagation of Innovation Waves, op. cit.,* p. 8.

[26] Torsten Hägerstrand, "Aspects of the Spatial Structure of Social Communications and the Diffusion of Information," *Papers of the Regional Science Association,* 16 (1966), p. 40.

[27] John C. Hudson, *op. cit.*

such that in the first interval of time, Δt, after a center has heard the message, it in turn tells every place that it directly dominates. Thus, the message eventually reaches all q^{m-1} places." More specifically, as a result of his other definitions and assumptions: "Once a center has heard a message, it is equally likely to pass this in the next time period to any of the towns that it directly dominates."[28] The shortcomings of Hudson's otherwise excellent effort, as well as the basic weaknesses in the arguments of other proponents of the theory of hierarchical diffusion, are best summarized by referring to Figure 1-1, which depicts the hierarchical dominance structure

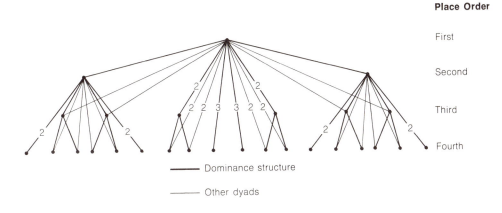

Place Order

First

Second

Third

Fourth

—— Dominance structure

——— Other dyads

FIG. 1-1 Dominance structure and other interaction dyads in a Christallerian urban system where $K = 3$. See text for additional dyads and clarification.

and some of the other direct linkages (*information flow paths*) for the four highest order places in a Christallerian central place system where $K = 3$. The only undiagrammed linkages, or flow paths, involve the procurement of highest- (first-) order goods from the single first-order place by the six left-most and six right-most fourth-order places. (Numbers in Figure 1-1 refer to the number of orders of goods procured by lower-order places from higher-order places. Unnumbered dyads involve only one order of goods.) The unsatisfactory features of this schema are three in number. (1) There is no lateral diffusion between second-order places, or between any pair of second-, third-, and fourth-order places when both are not members of the same nesting arrangement. That is, each nest culminating at the single first-order place is a closed diffusion system. And, in other words,

[28] *Ibid.*, pp. 51-52.

the next-to-largest places in an urban system cannot exchange information. (2) There is no lateral diffusion between places of the same
order in the same nesting arrangement, or subsystem. That is, under
no circumstances can an innovation diffuse from one place of a given
population to another place of roughly the same population. (3) Even
within the same nested subsystem, diffusion from a lower-order place
to a higher-order place is precluded. That is, even where the separating distance is small, it is impossible for an innovation to diffuse from
one place of a given population to another place of larger population.

All three of these criticisms are merely to say that in most urban
systems the interdependencies which govern the economy and size
of individual cities are not confined to central place activities, or the
tertiary sector. Rather than constituting the *entire set* of interdependencies within an urban system, hierarchically ordered tertiary activities (and related market-oriented industrial activities) are usually
responsible for a *major subset* of such interdependencies. Other interurban interaction and nonhierarchical interdependencies are generated
by the flow of inputs and outputs associated with other than market-
oriented manufacturing, and by the shipment of geographically specialized agricultural commodities. Noteworthily, it is evident from
the discussion of the preceding section that the pattern of interurban
commodity flows of a nonhierarchical character was relatively complex, even before both the U.S. economy as a whole and individual
urban economies became highly industrialized and thus capable of
generating much larger and more complex input and output flows.[29]

Since interurban commodity flows of any type may be regarded
as both outcomes and generators of information flows, it can be argued
that in both pre-electronic and electronic contexts nonhierarchical
economic interdependencies between cities should also contribute to
the probabilistic diffusion of innovations within an urban system. In
at least one sense, this should be even more true of pre-electronic
systems; for, it is to be recalled, the consumption and exchange of
information over long distances was income-elastic. In short, most
long-distance information flows, economic and noneconomic, came
about as a result of the information acquisition and exchange of the

[29] It is estimated that manufacturing accounted for only 17 per cent of the
value of all U.S. commodity output in 1839. See Robert E. Gallman, "Commodity
Output, 1839-1899," in *Trends in the American Economy in The Nineteenth
Century*, a report of the National Bureau of Economic Research (Princeton:
Princeton University Press, 1960), p. 26. On the relatively low level of manufactur-
ing in major U.S. cities during the pre-electronic era, see Allan R. Pred, *The
Spatial Dynamics of U.S. Urban-Industrial Growth, 1800-1914* (Cambridge, Mass.:
The M.I.T. Press, 1966), pp. 146 ff.

economic elite who were conducting or attempting to initiate nonlocal business.[30]

One way of removing some of the objections raised to hierarchical diffusion models is to propose that interurban message flows are channelled by the interdependencies existing in a Löschian central place system, where market-oriented industries as well as tertiary activities are present. (Here, in order to remain consistent with Hudson-like formulations, one would have to assume that once a given center received an innovation-relevant message, it could pass this message in the next time period to any city, regardless of size, which is dependent upon it for secondary or tertiary goods.) One possible set of conditions that could arise under these circumstances can be discerned from Figures 1-2 and 1-3 which, for the sake of maintaining comparability with Figure 1-1, are confined to twenty-seven places. Figure 1-2, which is derived from Stolper,[31] shows the location of seven orders of activity (designated by numbers) in cities (designated by letters) whose population is proportional to the number of other centers, or market areas (designated by sloping lines), served by each locally present activity.[32] Figure 1-3 indicates the interaction dyads (*information flow paths*) existing in the system. (Numbers in Figure 1-3 refer to the number of goods procured from one place by another. Unnumbered dyads involve only one good.) In a Löschian urban system, urban size does not automatically define the array of activities locally present; consequently, there can be lateral diffusion between places of roughly the same population. For the same reason, there can be diffusion from a center of given population to another city of larger population, although in the majority of cases Figure 1-3 would yield diffusion from a larger place to a smaller place. Nonetheless, this Löschian schema is still unsatisfactory insofar as it does not permit the exchange of information between the next-to-largest places in an urban system, or, for that matter, between any pair of places which do not belong to the same physically continuous

---

[30] In 1840 it could still be said: "By far the greater portion of postage is paid on business letters, and it is the increase or diminution of this branch of correspondence, which mainly occasions an augmentation or declension of the revenues of the [Post Office] department." See *Hazard's U.S. Commercial and Statistical Register*, Aug. 19, 1840.

[31] Wolfgang Stolper, "Spatial Order and the Economic Growth of Cities," *Economic Development and Cultural Change*, 3 (1954-1955), pp. 137-146.

[32] Stolper's modified Löschian schema, which diagrammatically is confined to centers located on a straight line passing through the system's largest metropolis (A), requires that it "be imagined that the distribution of production schematized . . . exists also in all directions."

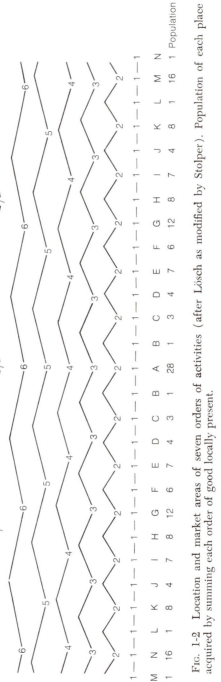

	M	N	L	K	J	H	G	F	E	D	C	B	A	B	C	D	E	F	G	H	I	J	K	L	M	N	
	1	16	1	8	4	7	8	12	6	7	4	3	1	28	1	3	4	7	6	12	8	7	4	8	1	16	1	Population

Fig. 1-2 Location and market areas of seven orders of activities (after Lösch as modified by Stolper). Population of each place acquired by summing each order of good locally present.

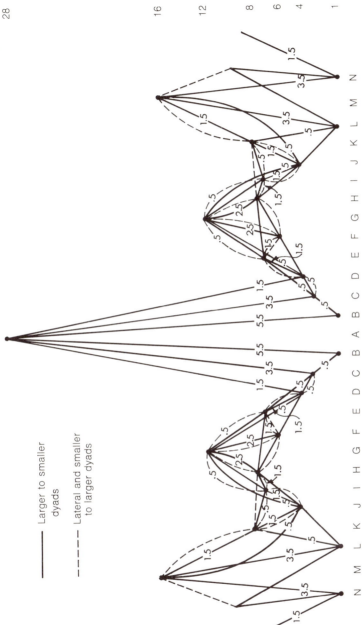

FIG. 1-3 Interaction dyads in Stolper's modified Löschian urban system.

subsystem. (Note the complete absence of contact between all places to the left and right of A in Figure 1-3).

It would seem that the most realistic descriptive model of diffusion within an urban system would be one that combined the Christallerian hierarchical spread of present models, the lateral and smaller-to-larger-place dissemination allowed by a Löschian schema, and a considerable degree of information exchange between very high-order places, or between places in the size class(es) just below the largest city in the system (Figure 1-4). Moreover, it would have to allow

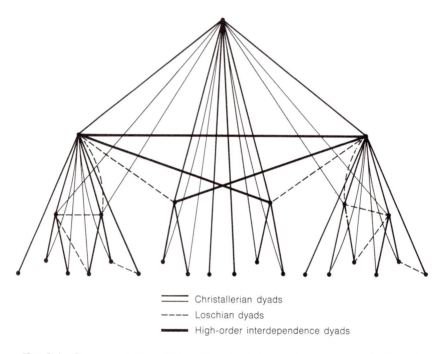

<table>
<tr><td>═══</td><td>Christallerian dyads</td></tr>
<tr><td>----</td><td>Loschian dyads</td></tr>
<tr><td>▬▬▬</td><td>High-order interdependence dyads</td></tr>
</table>

Fɪɢ. 1-4 One permutation of interaction dyads in an urban system with Christallerian and Löschian qualities, plus high-order interdependence. Undiagrammed are dyads connecting the largest place with the six left-most and six right-most places of the smallest size-class shown.

that information also flowed opposite to the direction of goods movement along any interaction dyad within the urban system either because information-bearing consumers had to go to the source of goods, or because order requests had to precede actual shipment to the consuming center. Taking this last point into consideration would mean that once a center (i) has received a message or adopted an innovation, it could pass it on in the next time period (Δt) to any city (j) to which it sent goods *or from which it received goods*. Thus, during Δt, the probability of receipt or adoption at the jth city (M_{ij}) could be expressed as follows:

$$M_{ij} = \frac{f\,(P_iG_{j \to i})(P_jG_{i \to j})}{d_{ij}^b}, \quad \text{where } P_i, \; P_j \text{ and } d_{ij}^b \text{ carry their familiar}$$

gravity model connotations, and G_{j-i} and G_{i-j} are whole or fractional goods moved from j to i and i to j. Under these circumstances, as time accumulated and diffusion occurred by passing through a series of overlapping urban information fields, larger places would tend to be early to receive or adopt, their contact probabilities being high with a number of other places as a result both of the sizes of their population and the variety of their goods origins and destinations. At the same time, small places, unless close to a major city, would tend to receive or adopt late because of their relatively limited populations and array of goods origins and destinations. Regardless of where diffusion in a system began, it would be very likely to jump quite quickly to the largest places. Note, however, that with some economic innovations cost and/or market-threshold characteristics can lead to spatially clustered or curtailed acceptance patterns within the urban system.[33]

V

PRE-ELECTRONIC DIFFUSION EVIDENCE

At least four previously made points merit a juxtaposed restatement at this juncture, in order to make clear what kind of empirical evidence one should anticipate finding on pre-electronic innovation diffusion.

(1) The pre-electronic circulation of public and private information over long distances was income-elastic. Most information acquisition and exchange was directly or indirectly associated with the conduct of nonlocal business.

(2) Because pre-electronic information circulation could not occur in the absence of human spatial interaction, there were considerable time-lag and contact-array spatial biases in the availability of information. Perhaps most importantly, information often moved with greater speed and frequency among the largest places in a given urban subsystem than between each such place and most, if not all, subservient lower-order places in its own hinterland.

[33] Allan R. Pred, *The Spatial Dynamics of U.S. Urban-Industrial Growth, op. cit.*, pp. 135-141.

(3) The economic interdependence of high-order pre-electronic cities was reflected in three basic types of commodity flows: (a) agricultural or raw material production from the hinterland of the city of origin; (b) manufactures produced in the city of origin or its lower-order dependents; and (c) redistributive shipments.

(4) On general grounds, it can be argued that usually diffusion within an urban system should not occur merely hierarchically, or in rank-size order from large to progressively smaller places. It also should occur laterally, especially between large or high-order places, and from smaller or larger places. *On the basis of Table 1-3, this should be particularly true of the pre-electronic U.S. urban system.*

Given space limitations, it is not feasible to reproduce a great amount of detail regarding any particular diffusion process. Instead, the strategy chosen is that of presenting synopsized evidence on a number of interurban diffusion processes. (More substantive evidence is available in book form. (See footnote 3.)

The first daily newspaper appeared in 1784 in Philadelphia, then the largest city in the country. By 1790 there were three dailies in New York, four in Philadelphia, and one in Charleston, then the nation's fourth-ranking city. There had also been an unsuccessful effort in Baltimore. By 1800 there were six dailies in Philadelphia, five in New York, three each in Charleston and Baltimore, and five or six in and around Washington, D.C., most of them founded in the year in which the city was made the capital. During the 1790-1800 interval, short-lived dailies had operated in Boston and Richmond. Although it is difficult to establish how many acceptances in New York, Charleston, and Baltimore were the result of lateral diffusion, and how many were the result of direct hierarchical diffusion from Philadelphia, it is known that there were at least two cases of diffusion from a large place to an even larger place—from New York to Philadelphia, and from Richmond to Charleston.[34] Moreover, it is striking that the innovation was essentially passed in one way or another between large centers, each of which (except Washington) presumably dominated its own hinterland hierarchically, with no adoptions in subservient lower-order centers where newspapers of less frequent appearance were published. Admittedly, there might have been some threshold effect; but the circulation necessary to sustain a daily with the limited printing technology of 1790-1800 was quite small, perhaps no more than 400.[35]

---

[34] G. F. Pyle, "The Diffusion of Cholera in the United States in the Nineteenth Century," *Geographical Analysis*, 1 (1969), pp. 59-75.

[35] Lee, *op. cit.*, pp. 728-730.

In a study of the locational sequence of bank diffusion in Massachusetts from 1784 to 1836,[36] it was found that adoption occurred in the largest city previously without the innovation in four of the first five cases, but in only five of the first eighteen cases. That is, there was not an orderly progression of acceptances downward through the urban-size hierarchy, which suggests both some lateral diffusion, and some diffusion from smaller to larger places. However, conceivably other factors, particularly rural market-area competition, also could have contributed to the "disorderly" pattern of acceptances.

The pre-electronic diffusion of the local passenger, or intra-urban, street railway was extremely limited. The New York and Harlem Railroad, which commenced operations in 1832, is usually acknowledged to have been the first street railway in the United States. However, in 1831 horse-drawn B&O railroad cars used the streets of Baltimore to provide access to terminals. The only other pre-1844 adoptions occurred in New Orleans in 1835, when the city ranked fifth in the country, and in Cleveland and Buffalo in 1834, where services ceased during the Panic of 1837.[37] Both Cleveland (interpolated 1834 population about 3,000) and Buffalo (interpolated 1834 population about 11,500) were much smaller than numerous other places which failed to adopt until the 1850s. Within the framework presented in the previous section, it may be speculated that Cleveland and Buffalo received intermediately valued probability "hits" from New York, based on their economic interdependencies with that city.

In his inquiry into the diffusion of the cholera epidemic of 1832, Pyle concluded that while "cholera struck larger cities and subsequently showed up in small cities immediately adjacent to the larger cities," spread occurred along three paths of movement, *with inter-urban distance being a more important diffusion determinant than city size.*[38] If person-to-person epidemical contacts are substituted for information in general, this may be regarded as a special case where time-lag spatial biases in the availability of information resulted in some pre-electronic diffusion between similarly sized cities, and from smaller to larger cities.

For most of the presented cases, as well as in almost every study of interurban diffusion, there is the implicit or explicit assumption

---

[36] Peter D. Girling, *The Diffusion of Banks in the United States from 1781 to 1861* (unpublished Master's thesis, Pennsylvania State University, Department of Geography, 1968), pp. 79-83.

[37] Arthur J. Krim, *The Innovation and Diffusion of the Street Railway in North America* (unpublished Master's thesis, University of Chicago, Department of Geography, 1967).

[38] Pyle, *op. cit.*

that the order of acceptances reflects the channels through which diffusion has occurred. This assumption often stands on shaky grounds, since there usually exist place-to-place variations in the time elapsed between initial information receipt, subsequent acquisition of adoption-experience and other innovation-relevant information, and final acceptance. This assumption can be put aside for much of the diffusion of the cessation of specie payments by banks during the Panic of 1837; for public resolutions in favor of cessation made by local businessmen and/or bankers often revealed the source(s) of diffusion influence.

Although in large measure ascribable to overspeculation in the purchase of public lands and a hasty expansion of trade debts to Britain, the roots of the 1837 panic are complex.[39] During the panic, banks did not close their doors, but merely refused to convert deposits and bank-notes into coin, in some instances because they lacked the specie to cover local demands made on them, in others to prevent the depletion of their reserves by nonlocals attempting to cash paper money issued by other banks. Here no attempt will be made to reconstruct the diffusion of specie payment cessation in total. Rather, the intent is only to show that there were numerous instances where information and diffusion influence flowed from smaller to larger cities.

New York banks suspended specie payment on May 10, 1837, and the stoppage of payments by banks in the rest of the country during the next few weeks is usually depicted as having spread from there.[40] For the most part this is true. In Providence, Boston, Albany, Rochester, Detroit, and a host of other cities, word of specie payment suspension in New York usually resulted in almost immediate local imitation. However, the New York decision apparently was partly attributable to reports "mentioned in some of the New York papers that the banks of Baltimore intended to suspend specie payment"; and, similarly, the Philadelphia decision of May 11 was partly influenced by the incorrect rumor that banks had already suspended payments in the smaller Baltimore, as well as in New York.[41] Moreover, specie suspension had begun independently in the South as early as May 4 in Natchez (1840 population, 3,612).[42] Events in Natchez had a clear

[39] Bray Hammond, *Bank and Politics in America from the Revolution to the Civil War* (Princeton: Princeton University Press, 1957), pp. 451-499; Reginald C. McGrane, *The Panic of 1837* (Chicago: University of Chicago Press, 1924).

[40] McGrane, *op. cit.*, p. 93.

[41] *Philadelphia Public Ledger*, May 11, 1837; *Baltimore Patriot*, May 10 and 11, 1837; *Richmond Enquirer*, May 10, 1837.

[42] *Boston Evening Transcript*, May 22, 1837.

influence on the stopping of coin payments on May 12 in New Orleans (1840 population, 102,193).[43] Banks in Mobile (1840 population 12,672) took action on May 12 after hearing of suspensions in Montgomery (1840 population, 2,179); the bankers of Charleston (1840 population, 29,261) who ceased paying specie on May 17, were evidently affected by rumors from the smaller Mobile,[44] as well as by knowledge of suspensions in New York, Philadelphia, and Baltimore.[45] No decision was reached in Richmond (1840 population, 20,153), despite awareness of events in the major cities of the Northeast, until it was known that sister banks in Norfolk (1840 population, 10,920) had also followed suit.[46] Specie cessation was decided upon in Augusta, Georgia (1840 population, 6,403) after word was received from numerous centers in the northeast and south, including the less populous city of Natchez.[47]

Finally, the locational pattern of inventive activity for any pre-electronic year suggests that, at least in the early stages of diffusion processes, spread frequently occurred between large cities and from smaller to larger places. For example, in 1820 the U.S. government issued 154 patents to domestic residents, of which twenty-one went to New York, eleven to Baltimore, six to Philadelphia, six to Boston, and the remaining 108 to lesser places.[48] Thus, if one assumes that each one of the subset of 154 inventions that actually became practically implemented eventually began its diffusion from the city of invention, it becomes quite obvious that only in the case of the New York inventions could the entire interurban diffusion sequence have been in full accord with a hierarchical diffusion model based upon Christallerian central place theory.

VI

CLOSING REMARKS

This paper has shown that nonhierarchical as well as hierarchical interdependencies existed within the pre-electronic U.S. urban system.

[43] *The Picayune* (New Orleans), May 12, 1837; *Richmond Whig and Public Advertiser,* May 23, 1837.

[44] *Annapolis Maryland Gazette,* May 18, 1837.

[45] *Charleston Mercury,* May 15 and 18, 1837; *Charleston Courier,* May 15, 1837.

[46] *Richmond Whig and Public Advertiser,* May 16, 1837; *Richmond Enquirer,* May 16, 1837.

[47] Milledgeville (Ga.) *Federal Union,* May 23, 1837.

[48] Henry Ellsworth, *A Digest of Patents issued by the United States from 1790 to January 1, 1839* (Washington: Peter Force, by Act of Congress, 1840).

Although not exhaustive, the evidence presented indicates that specific pre-electronic interurban diffusion processes were in conformity with what one would expect both from these economic interdependencies within the urban system and from intimately related time-lag and contact-array spatial biases in the availability of information. The evidence regarding both large-city economic interdependencies and interurban diffusion supports a model developed elsewhere[49] which describes how and why the top ranks of various regional urban systems in the United States stabilized by the mid-nineteenth century.

Although time-lag spatial biases in the availability of information became insignificant with the completion of the nation's telegraph network, it is further proposed that the $f \dfrac{(P_i G)_{j \to i},(P_j G_{i \to j})}{d_{ij}^b}$ formulation, which allows for lateral and smaller-to-larger diffusion dyads, often describes diffusion within an urban system of the electronic era better than any strictly hierarchical model. This argument rests on the fact that since the mid-nineteenth century the growth of manufacturing and relative declines in the cost of transportation have combined to bring about greater and more complex nonhierarchical urban interdependencies.

[49] *Pred, Urban Growth and the Circulation of Information* . . . , *op. cit.*

2

Growth of the Central Districts in Large Cities

MARTYN J. BOWDEN

I

SINCE the publication of Murphy and Vance's studies of the American Central Business District (CBD) in 1955[1] there has been a spate of descriptions of the present-day central business district.[2] These studies applied the methods of delimitation and analysis developed by Murphy and Vance, and answered their call for a testing and application of their methods in cities outside the United States and in the various regions of the United States. But in all this work there have been some notable omissions. First, the central district of the large city, particularly in America, has been neglected.[3] Second, and

[1] Raymond E. Murphy and J. E. Vance, Jr., "Delimiting the CBD," *Economic Geography*, 30, 1954, pp. 189-222; "A Comparative Study of Nine Central Business Districts," *Economic Geography*, 30, 1954, pp. 301-336; Raymond E. Murphy, J. E. Vance, Jr., and Bart Epstein, "Internal Structure of the CBD," *Economic Geography*, 31, 1955, pp. 21-46. These articles were published together as *Central Business District Studies* (Worcester, Mass: Clark University, 1955).

[2] Peter Scott, "The Australian CBD," *Economic Geography*, 35, 1959, pp. 290-314; D. Hywel Davies, "The Hard Core of Cape Town's Central Business District: An Attempt at Delimitation," *Economic Geography*, 36, 1960, pp. 53-69; D. Hywel Davies, "Boundary Study as a Tool in CBD Analysis: An Interpretation of Certain Aspects of the Boundary of Cape Town's Central Business District," *Economic Geography*, 35, 1959, pp. 322-345; Harm J. de Blij. "The Functional Structure and Central Business District of Lourenco Marques, Mozambique." *Economic Geography*, 38, 1962, pp. 56-77; D. R. Diamond, "The Central Business District of Glasgow," in Proceedings of the IGU Symposium in Urban Geography, Lund, 1960, *Lund Studies in Geography*, ser. B, Human Geography, 24, Royal University of Lund, Sweden, 1962, pp. 525-534. Many more studies can be found in Mary Vance (compiler), *Central Business Districts*, Exchange Bibliography No. 23, Oakland: Council of Planning Librarians, 1963; Shirley F. Weiss, *The Central Business District in Transition, Methodological Approaches to CBD Analysis and Forecasting Future Space Needs*, City and Regional Planning Studies, Research Paper No. 1, Chapel Hill: Department of City and Regional Planning, University of North Carolina, 1957, pp. 37-44; Brian J. L. Berry and Allan R. Pred, *Central Place Studies: A Bibliography of Theory and Applications*, Regional Science Research Institute, Bibliography Series: No. 1, 1961.

[3] An underlying assumption of the Murphy and Vance studies was that medium-sized and large central districts grew in the same way, with constituent establishments competing for proximity to the peak land-value intersection. There was thus no need for studies of large central districts.

more important, no attempt has been made, using the primary evidence of city directories and a consistent method of delimitation of the historical CBD, to show how central districts, large and small, have grown and shifted their location through time.[4] Surprisingly, Murphy and Vance's conceptions of the zones of assimilation and discard[5] were intuitive and not based on primary historical research, and the same is true of Griffin and Preston's conceptions of the changes in the character of the Transition Zone and the edges of the Central District since the early 1900s.[6] These studies and the large number of essentially static studies of the CBD in the last decade have contributed little or nothing toward a much-needed theory of central-district growth.

In essence there is no theory of central-district growth. Burgess, Hoyt, and Harris and Ullman[7] made general statements on the direction of CBD expansion and its causes. But only Harris and Ullman were particularly concerned with the CBD. And beyond recognizing internal differentiation within the large CBD they went no further than Burgess and Hoyt. These and most subsequent writers on the CBD appear to subscribe to the Ratcliffian schema with individual activities competing for proximity to the point of maximum accessibility, attempting to overcome the friction of distance, with each (depending on ability to pay rent) gravitating to a niche in the Central District.[8]

[4] David Ward's "The Industrial Revolution and the Emergence of Boston's Central Business District," *Economic Geography*, 42 (1966) pp. 152-171, used neither a consistent delimitation method nor city directories. And Anthony C. Hughes, *The Delimitation of the Central Business District of Washington, D.C., Over Time* (unpublished M.A. thesis, University of Maryland, 1966), delimited the central district at four points in time but was not concerned with using the results as a key to growth.

[5] Murphy, Vance, and Epstein, *op. cit.*, 42.

[6] D. W. Griffin and R. E. Preston, "A restatement of the Transition Zone Concept," *Annals, Association of American Geographers*, 56 (1966), pp. 341, 349.

[7] Ernest W. Burgess, "The Growth of the City," *The City*, Robert E. Park, et al., (editors), (Chicago: University of Chicago Press, 1925), pp. 50-58; Homer Hoyt and Arthur M. Weimer, *Principles of Urban Real Estate*. Rev. ed. (New York: Ronald Press, 1948), pp. 70-71; Chauncy Harris and Edward L. Ullman, "The Nature of Cities," *Annals of the American Academy of Political & Social Science*, 242 (1945), pp. 14-17.

[8] Richard U. Ratcliff, "The Dynamics of Efficiency in the Locational Distribution of Urban Activities," *The Metropolis in Modern Life*, R. M. Fisher, (editor), (New York: Doubleday & Co., 1955), pp. 125-148; Walter Firey, *Land Use in Central Boston* (Cambridge, Mass.: Harvard University Press, 1945), pp. 10-22.

Two theorists who approached the problem in a different way were Hurd and Haig,[9] both of whom saw the Central District as a collection of districts, each made up of competitive, complementary, and auxiliary activities.[10] Perhaps because they dealt in the main with New York City they thought of activities on two levels, as gravitating to a central *area* of high accessibility, but as specifically gravitating to districts within the central area rather than toward the peak land-value intersection or the point of maximum accessibility. Research for my dissertation, *The Dynamics of City Growth: An Historical Geography of the San Francisco Central District 1850-1931*,[11] which was based primarily on analyses of annual city directories, convinced me of the greater validity of the Hurd-Haig framework for central-district study, particularly the framework as elaborated by Mitchell and Rapkin[12] and Rannells.[13] Rannells' conception of the *Core of the City* as many systems of action made up of establishments and linkages that find expression in the central area as nucleations or concentrations of linked establishments, was used in large part throughout the study.[14] This conception provided the basis for the classification of all land uses enumerated in the city business directories into 67 groups based on their competitive and complementary linkages.[15]

Rannells' three-part statistical techniques for measurement of change were suggestive, but less successful than his conceptual framework, which he failed to use in his study of Philadelphia. After preliminary application of the techniques, it proved necessary to reject one, modify another—the index of concentration—by adopting a fine-grid system that divided the average city block into six parts, and in the case of the third—the center of gravity—to replace it by the orthogonal median, which is less responsive to extreme (peripheral)

[9] Richard M. Hurd, *The Principles of City Land Values*, New York: The Record and Guide, 1903, pp. 56-88; Robert M. Haig, *Major Economic Factors in Metropolitan Growth and Arrangement*, Vol. 1, Regional Survey, New York: Regional Plan of New York, 1927, pp. 19-44.

[10] The terms are those of John Rannells, *The Core of the City* (New York: Columbia University Press, 1956), pp. 17-20, 29-30, 51-61, but the ideas were expressed first in Hurd, *op. cit.*, pp. 78-85, and Haig, *op. cit.*, pp. 36-44.

[11] Martyn J. Bowden, *The Dynamics of City Growth: An Historical Geography of the San Francisco Central District 1850-1931* (unpublished Ph.D. dissertation, University of California, Berkeley, 1967).

[12] Robert B. Mitchell and Chester Rapkin, *Urban Traffic: A Function of Land Use* (New York: Columbia University Press, 1954) pp. 14, 60-133.

[13] Rannells, *loc. cit.*

[14] *Ibid.*

[15] Bowden, *op. cit.*, pp. 22-23.

cases as a summary measure of distributions.[16] Development and application of a method for delimiting the Central District through time[17] also made it possible to calculate a simple *central tendency index* (the percentage of establishments of a particular activity group in the Central District relative to those of the same group in the city as a whole).[18] These three simple measures were used, where the data allowed, throughout the study.

The results of the San Francisco study were presented in 1967, and since that time my work has focussed on the growth of other large central districts (notably New York City, Boston, and London) as indicated in secondary sources, in an attempt to extend and modify the preliminary model of central-district growth developed in 1967.

This paper presents some of my preliminary findings. The first part is concerned with the process and timing of emergence of the Central District and its constituent nuclei within the fabric of the city. Threshold levels of emergence for certain districts will be presented, and suggestions made that the idea of the Central District and of specialized nuclei within it may have been diffused from London to the mercantile cities of the U.S. east coast, and replicated in the emerging central districts. The second part presents findings on the manner of growth of large nuclei within the Central District, and relates the three basic forms of Central District expansion to different types and patterns of internal growth.

II

LONDON: THE FIRST CENTRAL DISTRICT?

By the time Stow[19] wrote in 1598 London had a central business district (in the modern sense), but it had not had one for long. The London Stow describes is still predominantly medieval in that merchants, artisans, the rich and poor, storage and manufacturing were found scattered in all wards and parishes. Great parts of the city were primarily residential. Most people (although a declining majority) lived where they worked.

Yet specialized warehouses ("sheds") were remarked in the parishes at Thames-side, particularly in the old Steelyard area of the Hanseatic Merchants, in the old Vintry of the Bordeaux merchants, and the

---

[16] J. F. Hart, "Central Tendency in Areal Distributions," *Economic Geography* 30 (1954), pp. 48-59; Bowden, *op. cit.*, pp. 26-27; Rannells, *op. cit.*, pp. 102-103.

[17] Bowden, *op. cit.*, pp. 32-56.

[18] *Ibid.*, pp. 117-121, 523-591.

[19] J. Stow, *A Survey of London, Written in the Year 1598*, W. J. Thomas (editor) (London: Chatto & Windus, 1876).

old district of the Italian galleymen;[20] tenements and squatter settlements of aliens, primarily Flemish refugees, were concentrating in the suburbs, as well as within the city wall;[21] many formerly clustered activities that we think of as dispersed were seen by Stow as dispersing for the first time, e.g., grocers, vintners, and cooks;[22] and manufacturing—particularly that associated with the metal and leather trades—was gravitating to the North.[23] In sum, the city was in turmoil. From a population of 50,000 in the 1540s, the city's population had probably trebled by the turn of the century. Giovanni Botero was probably exaggerating a little in estimating London's population in 1606 as 160,000.[24]

For our purposes, however, the crucial change is the centripetal movement of the progenitors of the retailers of luxury shopping goods. "Men of trades and sellers of wares in this city have oftentimes . . . changed their places, as they have found their best advantages," wrote Stow,[25] and in the period of Stow's living memory (since 1535) most of the luxury traders and their great-merchant counterparts had moved toward the center of the city into the Cheapside area (often without moving their residences with them, particularly in the case of the great merchants).[26]

The impetus for the movement was almost certainly provided by the Exchange, which had grown rapidly in proportions in the 1530s. There had been proposals for a permanent covered bourse in the Cornhill area in 1534 and 1537, and another to convert part of the old Grain Market into an exchange in 1561. But the latter proposal was defeated partly because the old Leadenhall (Grain) Market was off center, which shows that the process of concentration had gone a long way by 1560. Gresham's massive Royal Exchange apparently met with widespread approval and was probably at the focus of the city's economic life when it was begun in 1564 and completed in 1568.[27] If a Central Business District did not exist in the early

---

[20] *Ibid.*, pp. 48-52, 87-89, 135.

[21] *Ibid.*, pp. 46-61, 74, 156-159; N. G. Brett-James, *The Growth of Stuart London* (London: George Allen & Unwin Ltd., 1935), pp. 47-49, 58-61, 475-481.

[22] Stow, *op. cit.*, pp. 31, 98-99.

[23] *Ibid.*, p. 31.

[24] Brett-James, *op. cit.*, pp. 495-499.

[25] Stow, *op. cit.*, p. 30.

[26] *Ibid.*, pp. 61, 98-101, 127-129.

[27] *Ibid.*, pp. 60, 73; N.S.B. Gras, *An Introduction to Economic History* (New York: Harper and Brothers, 1922), pp. 190-191, 197, 245-249; Brett-James, *op. cit.*, pp. 18, 43; R. J. Mitchell and M.D.R. Leys, *A History of London Life*, (Harmondsworth: Penguin Books, 1963), pp. 107-110; J. Strype, Addenda to Stow's *Survey of London, Written in the Year 1598*, J. Strype (editor), (London, 1720), Book 2, pp. 86, 135-317, 149-150.

1560s, it certainly did by 1570 in the form of the Royal Exchange, which had specialized storage of luxury goods and spices of the great merchants in the basement, exchange areas for both great wholesale merchants of luxury goods and for the money exchangers on the main floor, and shops for retailers above the main floor. There was in the building itself a fourfold breakdown by function.[28] Retailers not sufficiently fortunate to be in the Exchange clustered on the approaches to it. The population of London at the time of emergence of the Central District was probably 80,000-90,000.[29]

THE FORMATION OF DISTRICTS

In the Cheapside-Cornhill area developed perhaps the first modern Central District. But when did the constituent districts of the Inner City emerge?

In Stow's London, two internal clusters had begun to appear while the Central District as a whole crystallized. One was an exchange cluster to the east of Cheapside (Figure 2-1), a combination of the storehouses and residences of the great merchants in draperies, hosiery, fine leathers, and spices, together with the coffee houses and alleys of the money exchangers.[30] The Royal Exchange was in the western part of this cluster. On the western approaches to the Exchange was another well-formed cluster made up of overlapping concentrations of mercers, cordwainers, drapers, hosiers, haberdashers, and goldsmiths, as well as a cluster of inns.[31] This was a clearly defined cluster of shops, sheds, and storehouses.

Was this latter an embryonic wholesaling district of dry goods, leather goods, cloth, etc., or the beginning of a retail shopping district? The answer is that it was both in 1600. But what makes Stow's account so fascinating is that it reveals that some sorting of retailers and wholesalers within the district had already occurred, and that a complete spatial separation of the two groups was under way.

The large mercers (wholesalers?) and haberdashers had apparently moved into the eastern end of Cheapside recently[32] (Stow identifies three large storehouses for mercers in this area),[33] either replacing the shops and "solers" of the small mercers with large storehouses or becoming larger mercers in their place. Stow writes, "Now let us return to the south side of Cheape Ward. From the great conduit

[28] Gras, *op. cit.*, p. 191; Mitchell and Leys, *op. cit.*, pp. 109-110.
[29] Brett-James, *op. cit.*, pp. 496-497.
[30] Stow, *op. cit.*, pp. 71-78, 98-99.
[31] *Ibid.*, pp. 94-104, 111, 121, 129.
[32] *Ibid.*, p. 101.
[33] *Ibid.*, pp. 101, 103, 108.

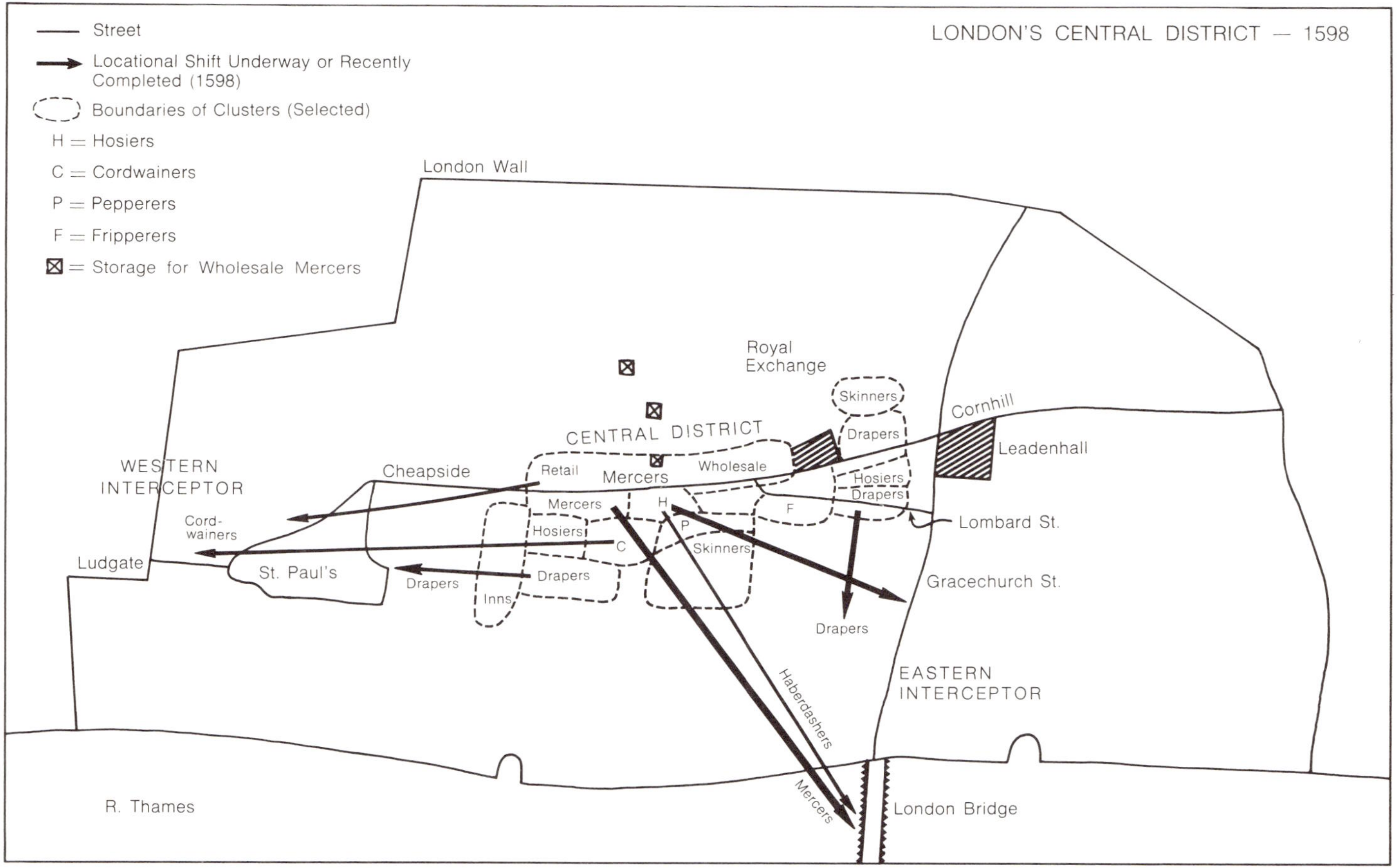

LONDON'S CENTRAL DISTRICT — 1598

— Street

↑ Locational Shift Underway or Recently Completed (1598)

⬭ Boundaries of Clusters (Selected)

H = Hosiers
C = Cordwainers
P = Pepperers
F = Fripperers
⊠ = Storage for Wholesale Mercers

London Wall

Cheapside

Ludgate

WESTERN INTERCEPTOR

St. Paul's

Cord-wainers

Drapers

CENTRAL DISTRICT

Retail   Mercers

Wholesale

Mercers

Hosiers

Drapers

Inns

Drapers

C

H

P

Skinners

F

Royal Exchange

Cornhill

Leadenhall

Skinners

Drapers

Hosiers
Drapers

Lombard St.

Gracechurch St.

Drapers

Haberdashers

Mercers

EASTERN INTERCEPTOR

London Bridge

R. Thames

Fig. 2-1

west be many fair and large houses, for the most part possessed of mercers . . . which houses in former times were but sheds or shops with solers over them . . . but those sheds or shops, by encroachments on the high street, are now largely built on both sides outward, and also upward, some three, four, or five stories high."[34] Elsewhere he points out that the small mercers and haberdashers—the "sellers of wares" as against the great merchants—"used to keep their shops on West Cheape [the same locale] . . . where partly they yet remain."[35] The retailers are on the west, the great merchants on the east, (Figure 2-1) although clearly overlapping.

The emerging pattern is made very clear by Stow, the small mercers were moving to two interceptors to the west and southeast of Cheapside: one to St. Paul's (and Lungate?); the other to London Bridge and Gracechurch Street (Figure 2-1).[36]

Similar changes had taken place among the drapers. Wealthy drapers were hard by the Royal Exchange (Birchin Lane and Cornhill) but retail drapers were concentrating at the two interceptors (to one of which some wealthy drapers had moved).[37] The wealthy hosiers had a location near the Royal Exchange but there was another off Cheap.[38] The haberdashers were still in the Cheap area, but were noticed by Stow in both interceptors; the cordwainers (sellers of shoes) were in Cheap but also clustering near Ludgate on the west.[39] The western interceptor was already surpassing the London Bridge cluster in 1600, for it had storage for mercery and a strong nucleus of drapers by that time.[40]

As the aristocracy and gentry poured into Westminster in the early 1600s the St. Paul's area became the first central retail shopping district. It probably warranted this title by 1620, when London's population was probably about 230,000.[41] The wholesale drapers and mercers were spreading into this area about this time, but, as John Graunt pointed out, both mercery and drapery were also leapfrogging westward to Ludgate Hill and Fleet Street (into Westminster) ahead of the great merchants, in the 1640's.[42]

---

[34] *Ibid.*, p. 101.

[35] *Ibid.*, pp. 30-31, 97.

[36] *Ibid.*, pp. 31, 79-80, 127.

[37] *Ibid.*, pp. 75, 82, 94, 129.

[38] *Ibid.*, pp. 31, 75.

[39] *Ibid.*, pp. 31, 80, 98-99.

[40] *Ibid.*, pp. 94, 97.

[41] Brett-James, *op. cit.*, pp. 495-500; Strype, *op. cit.*, 195-197, 206-207.

[42] Brett-James, *op. cit.*, pp. 391, 502; T. F., Reddaway, *The Rebuilding of London after the Great Fire* (London: Edward Arnold, 1951), pp. 301-302. (First printed 1940); Strype, *op. cit.*, pp. 206-207.

In sum, a Central district existed in 1570; it was essentially a retail district with a wholesaling and finance cluster concentrating on its eastern face. A central retail shopping cluster had emerged by 1600 as had a wholesaling dry-goods cluster. Taken together they constituted dry-goods and luxury-goods districts by 1620. The area was already markedly differentiated into mercers, drapers, and skinners by this time, and had been since 1600 (Figure 2-1). We have the apparent paradox of differentiation within the wholesaling district before the district itself had completely emerged, and of an internal differentiation within the retail shopping district rare even in the largest central retail shopping districts of the nineteenth century (where mixes of hosiery, lace, silk goods, shoe retailers were more common).

CENTRAL DISTRICTS IN THE NEW WORLD

In the colonial-type mercantile cities of the New World, the process of separation of the retailers and wholesalers was in some ways reversed. The retailer appeared to emerge as the landward adjunct to numerous yet unspecialized merchant wholesalers. A central retail district overlapping wholesalers had emerged in Boston by 1720 (and certainly by 1740—by which time the population had risen from 12,000 to 17,000),[43] and a similar district had developed around Hanover Square in New York City before the Revolution (population 25,000).[44] Separation of the retailing and wholesaling districts probably took place in New York City in the 1780s when the retailing district edged up William Street and the unspecialized wholesaling district remained to the east (population 25,000). The same sort of separation appears to have taken place in Boston 20 years later (population 25,000).[45] A full-fledged retail luxury goods district had emerged on Broadway, focussed on John Street, by 1805 (population 80,000), if not earlier

[43] Carl Bridenbaugh, *Cities in the Wilderness: Urban Life in America 1625-1742* (New York: Capricorn Books, 1964), pp. 143, 146, 171-172, 188, 192, 243-244, 338-341, 345, 403; Carl Bridenbaugh, *Cities in Revolt: Urban Life in America, 1743-1776* (New York: Capricorn Books, 1964), pp. 13-17, 77-78; W. M. Whitehill, *Boston: A Topographical History* (Cambridge, Mass.: Belknap Press, 1963), p. 24.

[44] Bridenbaugh, *Cities in Revolt*, pp. 5, 215, 275-276.

[45] S. I. Pomerantz, *New York: An American City 1783–1803* (Port Washington, New York: Ira J. Friedman, 1965), pp. 168-171, 199-201; Bridenbaugh, *Cities in Revolt*, pp. 77-83, 275-278; M. King, *King's Handbook of New York* (Boston: Moses King, 1893), p. 33; H. Kirker and J. Kirker, *Bulfinch's Boston, 1787–1817* (New York: Oxford University Press, 1964), pp. 135-140; Whitehill, *op. cit.*, pp. 47-72.

on William Street, and the same had occurred in Boston in the late 1830s (population 90,000).[46]

| In San Francisco all these thresholds were reached earlier. A central retail district had probably emerged by December 1849 when the population was a bare 8,000.[47] By June 1850 the last vestiges of overlap between the wholesaling and retailing districts had been removed (population 17,000),[48] and a fashionable retail shopping district was emerging and pushing other activities off Sacramento Street by 1853 (population 40,000–45,000) and was certainly large enough to be considered a fully fledged district by 1860 (population 60,000).[49] San Francisco's districting and specialization was old at birth.

As for wholesaling, specialization sufficiently marked to lead to spatial differentiation and the emergence of districts first occurred in New York City about 1795-1800. A cluster of dry-goods and textile wholesalers appeared on north Pearl Street in 1805 and a well-defined district had formed there by 1810.[50] (Population at the time of clear emergence in 1812 was 100,000.) This district had spread onto neighboring Liberty Street by the 1830s.[51] In Boston, David Ward recognizes a large wholesaling dry-goods district in the 1870s. If we take dry goods in the widest sense and including clothing and leather goods, it seems clear that there was a smaller wholesale dry-goods district in Boston by the 1850s (population 150,000).[52]

In San Francisco, once again, the threshold of emergence is very low. A wholesale dry-goods cluster had emerged by the late 1850s and had separated from the financial and retail shopping districts by the early 1860s when the city's population was less than 100,000.[53] By contrast, the emergence of a separate wholesale dry-goods and clothing district in Los Angeles in the mid-1900s occurred when

---

[46] King, op. cit., p. 33. Moses King, King's Handbook of Boston (Boston, Moses King, 1885), pp. 29, 329-353. I. N. Phelps Stokes, The Iconography of Manhattan Island, Vol. 1 (New York: R. H. Dodd, 1915), pp. 399-401, and Vol. 3, p. 521. J. H. Callender, Yesterdays in Little Old New York (New York: Dorland Press, 1929), pp. 91, 121.

[47] Bowden, op. cit., pp. 122-139.

[48] Ibid., pp. 90-96, 122-129.

[49] Ibid., pp. 174, 204-215.

[50] R. G. Albion, The Rise of New York Port 1815-1860 (New York: Charles Scribner's Sons, 1939), pp. 43, 60-61, 260, 276-282; Phelps Stokes, op. cit., Vol. 3, p. 521; various New York City directories.

[51] J. A. Kouwenhoven, The Columbia Historical Portrait of New York (Garden City: Doubleday, 1953), p. 149; Albion, op. cit., p. 266; Phelps Stokes, op. cit., p. 524.

[52] Ward, op. cit., pp. 160-164; various Boston Directories.

[53] Bowden, op. cit., pp. 229-239.

the central city had a population appreciably higher than this (230,000).[54]

A similar course of development is found for the financial district. London's financial district began, essentially, with the Royal Exchange in 1568. By 1600 this was surrounded by great merchants and some financiers and moneychangers. Yet the district did not crystallize as a separate entity even after the great merchant drapers and mercers shifted westward in the 1600s.[55] Even in the middle of the seventeenth century the goldsmiths—the prime financiers—were scattered and generally far from the Exchange.[56] And although London's first bank may have been founded before 1600 it was not until the 1680s that banks survived for long periods. The Bank of England was not founded until 1694.[57]

A banking cluster had developed by 1720, and clusters of insurance companies had also formed by this date. The stockbrokers had been ejected from the Royal Exchange in 1698 and had formed another cluster in Exchange Alley.[58] Taken together, these activities had begun to dominate the Cornhill-Lombard Street area and constituted the first full-fledged financial district. London's population at the time was about 600,000.[59]

Boston had a Royal Exchange in 1740, but no financial district had emerged by the time New York and Philadelphia challenged the Hub's supremacy. The first financial district to emerge was New York's on Wall Street between 1805 and 1810 (population 80,000).[60]

[54] R. M. Fogelson, *The Fragmented Metropolis; Los Angeles, 1850-1930* (Cambridge, Mass.: Harvard University Press, 1967), pp. 63-78, 138, 141-151; Los Angeles City directories published by W. Corran 1887-1893; Geo. Maxwell, 1887-1901; and the Los Angeles City Directory Company 1900-1916.

[55] Brett-James, *op. cit.*, p. 174; Reddaway, *op. cit.*, pp. 266-270.

[56] Brett-James, *op. cit.*, pp. 119, 390; Gras, *op. cit.*, p. 345; Stow, *op. cit.*, p. 129.

[57] Gras, *op. cit.*, pp. 245-246.

[58] *Ibid.*, pp. 247-253, 257-259. O.H.K. Spate, "The Growth of London, A.D. 1660-1800," in *An Historical Geography of England before A.D. 1800*, H. C. Darby (editor) (Cambridge: The University Press, 1935), pp. 534-535; Strype, *op. cit.*, pp. 149, 162-163.

[59] T. F. Reddaway, *The Rebuilding after the Great Fire* (London: Edward Arnold, Ltd., 1951), pp. 294, 304-305. M. D. George, *London Life in the Eighteenth Century* (Harmondsworth: Penguin Books, 1966), pp. 318-319 (First printed 1925); Strype, *op. cit.*, pp. 149, 162-164.

[60] Kouwenhoven, *op. cit.*, pp. 107, 135-139, 141; Pomerantz, *op. cit.*, pp. 178-194; Edgar M. Hoover and Raymond Vernon, *Anatomy of a Metropolis* (New York: Doubleday, 1962), p. 74. Albion, *op. cit.*, pp. 260, 265-266; Phelps Stokes, *op. cit.*, Vol. 1, pp. 383-391, pp. 419-421; 445-449; 453-458; Vol. 3, p. 517. Callender, *op. cit.*, pp. 120-121, 257-271.

Boston's emerged on State Street at practically the same threshold level in the 1830s.[61] In San Francisco, however, the financial district emerged a little earlier. A banking cluster existed almost from the start,[62] and formed a strong concentration on California Street, known as "the Wall Street of the West," by the early 1860s (population 70,000). All the elements of the financial district had moved to this axis by the mid-1860s, when San Francisco's population was about 90,000.[63]

In sum, as the new metropolises grew, the business innovations and improvements developed over a long period in London (and other European cities, notably Antwerp, Amsterdam, and Bruges) were quickly adopted and copied in the incipient metropolises of the eastern seaboard. Habits and patterns of business, and their spatial expression, were replicated in the expanding mercantile cities. To the Boston and New York merchants of the seventeenth century the advantages of competitive and complementary linkages were plain from the London example, which was familiar to the Boston merchants particularly, as Bernard Bailyn has shown so well.[64] The emergence of districts and separation, etc., was mainly a problem of attaining a critical mass of like specialized activities, and of overcoming inertia, and concentrating.

THRESHOLDS OF EMERGENCE FOR DISTRICTS

In London, like activities were frequently scattered over the face of much of the city and were only gradually drawn together. Even when the advantages of proximity were made clear, there was a great deal of inertia in the city's structure that had to be overcome before concentration could take place. Districts were very late in emerging. In San Francisco, by contrast, districts emerged perhaps as early as they have ever done in an American city, probably because of the lack of inertia. Whereas both Boston and New York were 150 years old when major districts began to form, San Francisco was five years old, and in a state of flux for the first twenty-five years of its existence. During this time its population rose from 500 to 200,000. It may also be that the theoretical threshold for emergence of districts has been lowered through time as suggested in Figure 2-2. In terms of

[61] Ward, op. cit., p. 158; H. P. Kidder and F. H. Peabody, "Finance in Boston," The Memorial History of Boston, Vol. 4, Justin Winsor (editor) (Boston: Ticknor & Co., 1881), pp. 151-178, see also 179-194. The thresholds for New York and Boston may be revised downward with further directory study.

[62] Bowden, op. cit., pp. 145-153.

[63] Ibid., pp. 118-195.

[64] Bernard Bailyn, The New England Merchants in the Seventeenth Century, (New York: Harper Torchbooks, 1964), pp. 16-40, 130.

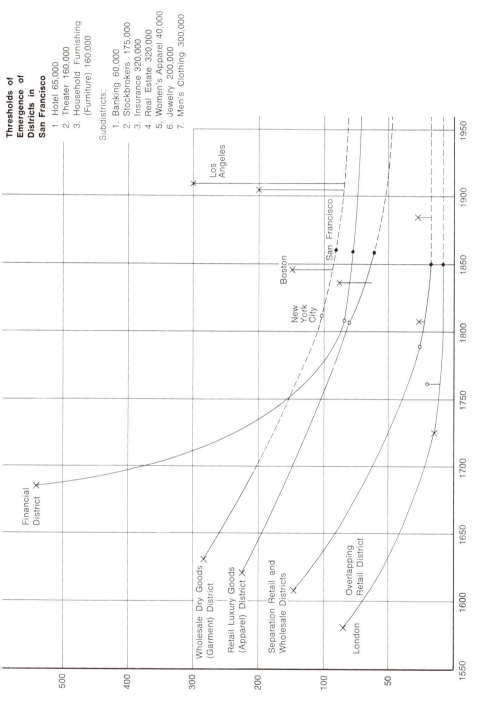

Thresholds of Emergence of Districts in San Francisco

1. Hotel 65,000
2. Theater 160,000
3. Household Furnishing (Furniture) 160,000

Subdistricts:

1. Banking 60,000
2. Stockbrokers 175,000
3. Insurance 320,000
4. Real Estate 320,000
5. Women's Apparel 40,000
6. Jewelry 200,000
7. Men's Clothing 300,000

Los Angeles

San Francisco

Boston

New York City

Financial District

Wholesale Dry Goods (Garment) District

Retail Luxury Goods (Apparel) District

Separation Retail and Wholesale Districts

Overlapping Retail District

London

1550 1600 1650 1700 1750 1800 1850 1900 1950

500 400 300 200 100 50

Fig. 2-2

development, rapidity of attainment of critical mass, and a minimum of inertia, San Francisco must be close to the optimal for the early emergence of districts. That is, the population level at the time of emergence in San Francisco (1850-1880) may be very close to the lowest thresholds of entry for districts.

In other words, in cities with a population of less than 70,000, a financial district will not emerge, but it is possible for such a district to emerge in a city with a population of between 70,000 and, say, 550,000 (conditional emergence), and a financial district will come into existence in a city whose population has reached 600,000 (unconditional emergence). This estimate is derived from the London experience (Figure 2-2), and roughly fits the experience of Los Angeles, where a financial nucleus struggled to district status in the mid 1900's[65] in the face of severe competition from the San Francisco financial district, which had a strong initial advantage as the financial capital of the west. The Los Angeles financial district may have emerged only when the population of Los Angeles *metropolitan area* approached the level of unconditional emergence.

A similar situation may have occurred in the rivalries between New York City and Boston concerning the emergence of districts. The wholesale dry-goods district emerged in New York by 1812 (population 100,000), and its hinterland must have extended deeply into New England, for it was not until Boston's population reached 140,000 in 1850 that a similar district emerged there. More telling examples of initial advantage are the emergence of the wholesale dry-goods (garment) district in San Francisco by 1860 and the delayed entry of a similar district in Los Angeles until after 1906 (Figure 2-2).

Because of extremely rapid and extensive growth in the first 30 years of the city's existence and the limited inertia in this period, San Francisco may provide the best example in the nineteenth century for establishing the lowest thresholds of entry of districts, and for illustrating the sequence of emergence of districts (see right of Figure 2-2). With its rapid but irregular growth in the early years, and its more stable, yet extensive, growth between 1880 and 1931, it also provides an excellent case for the study of the ways in which the large CBD and its constituent nuclei grow (i.e., expand areally—horizontally and vertically—and shift location, altering distance and direction).

[65] Fogelson, *op. cit.*, pp. 77-78, 138, 145-153; Los Angeles City Directories published by Maxwell and the Los Angeles City Directory Co. 1887-1907; Ira B. Cross, *Financing an Empire*, Vol. 2 (Chicago: S. J. Charles Publishing Co., 1923).

II

If we combine areal expansion and the locational component of growth (Table 2-1), we see 54 different ways in which nucleations in a central

TABLE 2-1   MANNERS OF GROWTH OF NUCLEATIONS

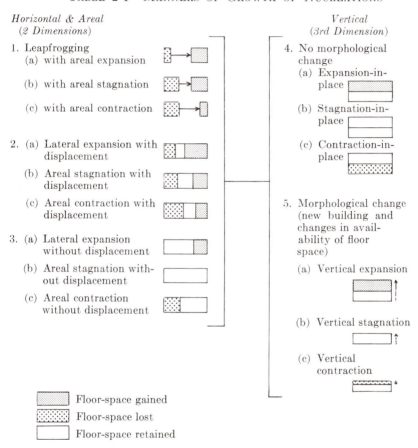

Horizontal & Areal
(2 Dimensions)

1. Leapfrogging
   (a) with areal expansion
   (b) with areal stagnation
   (c) with areal contraction

2. (a) Lateral expansion with displacement
   (b) Areal stagnation with displacement
   (c) Areal contraction with displacement

3. (a) Lateral expansion without displacement
   (b) Areal stagnation without displacement
   (c) Areal contraction without displacement

Vertical
(3rd Dimension)

4. No morphological change
   (a) Expansion-in-place
   (b) Stagnation-in-place
   (c) Contraction-in-place

5. Morphological change (new building and changes in availability of floor space)
   (a) Vertical expansion
   (b) Vertical stagnation
   (c) Vertical contraction

Floor-space gained
Floor-space lost
Floor-space retained

district might grow.[66] Several of these prevailed in San Francisco in the long periods between the phases of marked expansion of the Central District as a whole (Tables 2-2 and 2-3). But by far the greater part of the growth of nucleations was effected in short bursts

[66] Bowden, *op. cit.*, pp. 11-14, 266-269; 452-455; 708-711.

TABLE 2-2 LOCATIONAL CHANGES OF NUCLEI, 1850-75

Years in which Locational Changes Occurred and the Nature of the Change

Name of Nucleus	51	52	54	56	58	60	62	64	66	68	70	72	74	75
Theater		3a			3b						1a			
Central Hotel		1a		3b		1a		3b		2a				
Apparel-Shopping		3a												
Women's		2a			3b				1a	1a				2a
Men's Retail Jewelry		3a*		Development of Interceptors							2a			
Non-retail jewelry			2a?									1a	1a	
Household-Furnishing	stage one		Jackson Sq.		stage two					stage three				
East nucleus					arrested development—4 clusters				2a		3c			
West nucleus										2a				
District as a whole						1a					1a			
Financial nucleus	3a (+5a)								1a					
Banking	1a								1a					
Stockbroking				3b..........4a										
Real Estate		3b							1a	1a				
Insurance											2a			
Garment			2a			3b	4a				1a			
California economy	Prosperity		Depression		Recovery		Prosperity			Setbacks, Speculation & Depression				

* Mens' clothing zone separated into two sections. For manners of growth (1a, 5b, etc.) see Table 2-1. ⊢⊣ Years of major locational change. ☐ Climactic years of locational change.

TABLE 2-3 LOCATIONAL CHANGES OF NUCLEI, 1875–1906

Years in which Locational Changes Occurred and the Nature of the Change

Name of Nucleus	76	78	80	82	84	86	88	90	92	94	96	98	00	02	04	06
Theater		3b			1a					3b					3a?	
Central Hotel		3b			3b			3c				3b				
Apparel-Shopping	3a								2a			2c		2a		
Women's	2a								2a			3b		2a		
Men's		3a								2a				2a		
					middle Market phase									Union Sq. phase		
Retail jewelry	3b					3b		4a		2a				2a		
Non-retail jewelry	1a			3b					3b		3b					
Household-Furnishing																
East nucleus		2b				3b					1a		1a			
West nucleus		3b				3b		4a?			1a	3b				
Financial district																
Banking		2c		3b		4a	5a	3a				3b		4a	5a	
Stockbroking	2a				4a/2a	4a	5a	4a	2a			4a			5a	
Real Estate		2a						5a		2a	3b			3b		
Insurance					2a		4a	5a			4a		5a			
Garment	3a			3b							3b—4a/2a			3b		
California economy	Depression			Recovery			Prosperity			Depression				Return to Prosperity		

For manners of growth (1a, 5b, etc.) see Table 2-1.

——— Years of major locational change.

▢ Climactic years of locational change.

of activity by *lateral expansion* (2a and 3a); *vertical expansion* (5a), and *leapfrogging with areal expansion* (1a). See Figure 2-3.

LATERAL EXPANSION

Lateral expansion was the dominant form of growth in the nuclei of the central district, certainly after 1880. It was particularly characteristic of the core districts—the financial and apparel-shopping districts—and, to a lesser extent, of their contiguous nuclei. Lateral expansion was least common in districts farthest from the core. This form of growth has usually been accompanied by displacement—the nucleation advancing markedly on one front while contracting on the other. This is particularly true of the apparel-shopping district. In the financial district, by contrast, there has been little if any contraction: the district has experienced lateral expansion without displacement and vertical expansion simultaneously.

VERTICAL EXPANSION

Between 1850 and 1885, vertical expansion—the increase in the effective height of a nucleation following the construction of new, and additions to old, buildings[67]—was much less important than lateral expansion. Thereafter vertical expansion was important among the nuclei that could benefit the most from it, e.g., the financial, hotel, and medical-service districts, as distinguished from the apparel-shopping, household-furnishing, and theater districts, which could not. Increasing height presumably became common only when major morphological changes in central districts were made possible by technological advances in the construction industry. Such changes occurred in most American cities in the 1880s or 1890s, and, as a direct consequence, leapfrogging became less common among nuclei in the Central District.

LEAPFROGGING WITH AREAL EXPANSION

An unexpected revelation of my study has been the importance of leapfrogging,[68] in which a district jumps from one location to another, quite discrete one. Although this has occurred in San Francisco as a result of external pressures upon nuclei near the periphery of the Central District, more commonly it has been the consequence of both a heightened demand for space in, say, the main furniture nucleus by a large number of new furniture establishments (internal pressure

[67] *Ibid.*, pp. 465-468; 563-568; 710.
[68] *Ibid.*, pp. 266-269; 709-710.

within the activity-group), and by invading establishments—say, apparel shops—of a contiguous nucleus (external pressures). When internal pressures (within an activity-group) more than double within a decade, for example, the main nucleus of such a group has tended to leapfrog, especially if it has been subjected to external pressures, e.g., in the theater, garment, and furniture districts.[69]

Leapfrogging is rare in the financial district, more common in the apparel-shopping district. When it occurs in the core districts it does so as a result of internal pressures. In San Francisco the leapfrogging of both of the core districts occurred simultaneously on one occasion in the late 1860s. It prompted the leapfrogging of nucleations throughout the Central District, to such an extent that the Central District as a whole changed its locale, discarding most of the area that had been the Central District in 1850 (Figure 2-6).[70]

EXPANSION AND LOCATIONAL SHIFTS OF THE APPAREL
SHOPPING DISTRICT

In this case and most others, the most important element in initiating different types of Central-District expansion was the apparel-shopping district, which made four sizeable locational shifts between 1850 and 1931. Leapfrogging occurred once. On the other three occasions the manner of growth was lateral expansion with marked displacement (Figures 2-3 and 2-6 and Tables 2-2 and 2-3).[71]

The pattern of growth of the apparel-shopping district in San Francisco was essentially the same during all four locational shifts and probably similar in many other large Central Districts in the nineteenth century. A series of apparel-shopping nuclei (*potential interceptors*) began to emerge in a broken arc at a distance of between two and ten city blocks from the focus of the established apparel-shopping district. These nuclei were made up of establishments new to the Inner City, which were presumably able to pay the rents demanded or (more commonly) unable to find space in the main apparel-shopping district. In the *second phase* a few of these new establishments proved quite successful in one or two of the rival nuclei, and the nucleus generally thought to be the most successful was invaded by small and medium-sized establishments that came from nuclei that had been, or were soon to be, by-passed in the locational shift of the women's apparel-shopping district. The *third phase* saw the arrival of the medium-to-large establishments whose departure

[69] *Ibid.*, pp. 229-259.
[70] *Ibid.*, pp. 77-79, 196, 201, 206-208, 262-267.
[71] *Ibid.*, pp. 203-228, 359-403, 494-528, 595-607.

Fig. 2-3

from the former women's apparel-shopping district marked its eclipse and confirmed the dominance of the new district. The former district, in decline, served for a short while as an incubator (discard type)[72] for new retail establishments, some of which later moved to the new apparel-shopping district. Apparel nuclei by-passed in the migration generally became incubators (by-pass type),[73] although one occasionally retained its position as a potential interceptor in the new arc of apparel nuclei emerging to challenge the new apparel shopping district (Tables 2-4 and 2-7).

This was the pattern of development, 1865-1931. But in the early years, 1850-1865, there was a minor difference in that establishments were all relatively small, and growth was rapid and marked. Consequently, by the second phase of development a few of the new establishments had become medium-sized stores that directly challenged stores of a similar size in the established apparel-shopping district. The latter, in the third phase, did not confirm the dominance of the new apparel-shopping district by their arrival; rather they jumped to the new district for their own commercial survival. In

[72] *Ibid.*, pp. 363, 366. An "incubator" may be defined as an area or street that consistently "hatches" new establishments and presents them with a favorable environment for early development. A few of the establishments hatched in an incubator may move to a core district or to a potential interceptor location. Many are short-lived. Incubator areas, and particularly those in areas bypassed in the migration of the district, seem to have fulfilled a very important function in the growth of the Central District throughout the nineteenth century. Their importance may have been greatest at times of uncertainty as to the future line of migration, as in the early 1870s. The owner of a store that had been doing well in a retail cluster that struck him as having no potential for growth might gamble on a move to one of the potential interceptors emerging in the zone of assimilation. The moves of this type seem to have been largely accomplished before rents in the interceptor reached exorbitant levels. If a sufficient number of stores selected new locations in the same interceptor, they could go far toward establishing it as the new core of a district. Conversely, if a sufficient number of stores moved from the same retail cluster, it could lose its viability.

[73] Incubators of the discard type—former cores of the women's-apparel shopping district—tend to be short-lived compared to incubators of the bypass type. Their life-span is shorter simply because other activities with high-rent-paying abilities tend to move in quickly. Some of the more conservative elements in the women's-apparel shopping district, such as the furriers, tend to linger in the discard area for a decade or so after the large stores have moved out. While they are there, the incubator is viable. Also, if the old core is close to the new core, the former can rely on some overspill from the latter for a few years at least. For these reasons the attrition rate among new stores in the discard incubators is lower than in the bypass incubators. But rents are higher, and for this reason fewer establishments try themselves out there. For the retail incubator of a bypass type the prerequisites are (1) adequate facilities for vending, (2) low rents, and (3) a pedestrian count sufficiently high to allow establishments with new "lines" to try them out.

sum, in the early years new establishments[74] laid the foundations for a rival shopping nucleus and later some became dominant stores when the apparel-shopping district shifted to the nucleus. This was less true after 1865, when most of the founding establishments had disappeared or been displaced by the time the nucleus had become the focus of the main apparel-shopping district.

TABLE 2-4   WOMEN'S-APPAREL SHOPPING ESTABLISH-
MENTS IN SEVEN AREAS

Seven Areas	Number of Establishments				
	1858[a]	1860	1865	1869	1875
Sacramento St. Area[1]	19	44[b]	30	10	8
Lower Montgomery[2]	3	10	24	21	18
Second Street[3]	4	7	19	11	9
Stockton-Pacific Sts.[5]	24	33	20	24	29
Lower Kearny[4]	6	6	18	24	39
Third Street[6]	2	1	6	11	6
Middle Market St.[7]	0	0	3	4	18

[a] Milliners not included.

[b] Underlining indicates the largest total in a given year and the largest total for each area in the five selected years.

[1] Core to 1864; discard-type 1864-1875
[2] Interceptor to 1864; core 1865-1873; discard-type 1874-1875
[3] Interceptor to 1869; by-pass type 1870-1875
[4] Interceptor to 1873; core 1874-1875
[5] By-pass type 1858-1875
[6] Interceptor to 1872; by-pass type 1873-1875
[7] Interceptor 1865-1875

True leapfrogging with areal expansion occurred only once in the apparel-shopping district of San Francisco, during a period of extremely marked growth. It almost occurred in the early 1850s and in the early 1890s, and would perhaps have done so if rapid growth had not been curbed during protracted depressions that hit the city in the mid 1850s and mid 1890s. If leapfrogging had occurred on these two occasions, the type of expansion of the San Francisco Central District in the late 1850s and late 1890s would have been quite different, and the separation of the core districts might well

[74] *Ibid.*, pp. 204-209; for a discussion of the importance of new establishments as agents affecting the locational shifts of districts, see, *ibid.*, pp. 227-228, 239-240, 249, 259, 270-272, 711-713.

have become permanent, as had happened in New York City in the early nineteenth century.

CENTRAL DISTRICT EXPANSION AND RELATED INTERNAL GROWTH

What relation, if any, do the types and phases of growth in the constituent nuclei bear to the phases and patterns of peripheral expansion

TABLE 2-5 NUMBER OF "EMBRYONIC" DEPARTMENT STORES AND CLOAK & SUIT HOUSES IN SELECTED AREAS, 1860, 1865, 1869, AND 1875

	Number of Embryonic Department Stores			
Areas	*1860*	*1865*	*1869*	*1875*
Sacramento Street[1]	7	2	1	0
Lower Montgomery Street[2]	0	4	5	2
Second Street[3]	0	2	0	0
Lower Kearny Street[4]	0	0	0	3
Total	7	8	6	5

	Number of Cloak and Suit Houses			
Areas	*1860*	*1865*	*1869*	*1875*
Sacramento Street[1]	2	6	2	0
Lower Montgomery[2]	0	4	3	6
Lower Kearny[4]	0	0	1	4
Stockton-Pacific[5]	0	0	1	1
Mid-Kearny	0	1	1	1
Other	0	0	1	1
Total	2	11	9	13

[1,2,3,4,5] Explained in Table 4

of the Central District as a whole? A detailed analysis was made of the changing boundary of the San Francisco Central District delimited on the basis of a method described elsewhere. In addition, cursory surveys have been made of the changing outlines of the central districts of many large cities. These analyses make it clear that there are at least three basic types of peripheral expansion characteristic of the Central District as a whole, each roughly associated with different manners of growth among nuclei, and having a distinct morphologic expression.

TABLE 2-6 WOMEN'S-APPAREL SHOPPING STORES ON LOWER & MIDDLE
KEARNY STREET, 1879-80

Name of Store	Number on Kearny Street	Type of Store[a]	Date of Arrival	Approximate Age of Establishment Prior to Arrival (in yrs.)	Source Area[b]	Approximate Size on Arrival[c]
H. Friedlander	9	L.F.	70-75	5	B	3
E. Mansbach	26	D.G.	76-79	5	B	3
J. Samuels	28	D.G.	76-79	10	B	3
S. Hartman	36	D.G.	76-79	?	?	3
J. W. Davidson (White House)	101	C.S.	71	15	A	1
David Samuels (Lace House)	104	D.G.	75	5	B	2
Fratinger & Noll	105	C.S.	76	5	A	1
Keane Bros.	107-109	D.G.	71	5	B	2
S. Mosgrove & Co.	114	D.G.	70-75	5	B	2
Sullivan & Moorhead	120	C.S.	76	15	A	3
Mrs. H. Hahn	124	L.F.	76-79	—	B	1
Wurkheim Bros.	125	C.S.	76	15	A	2
Doane & Hinshelwood	132	D.G.	76	10	A	2
Julius Leszynski	113	D.G.	76-79	?	?	3
Lesser Leszynski	(212 Sutter)	C.S.	76-79	10	—	2
Samuel Leszynski	200	D.G.	70-75	?	?	3
Davis, Schonwasser	222	L.F.	72	15	C	2
Jacobs & Glass	226	L.F.	76-79	5	C	3
P. B. Kennedy	238	D.G.	65-69	5?	B?	3
S. Jacobs	403	L.F.	76-79	?	?	3
Solomon Jacobs	408	D.G.	65-69	?	?	3

[a] D.G.: Dry Goods; C.S.: Cloaks & Suits; L.F.: Ladies' Furnishings.

[b] A: Lower Montgomery St. (discard-type); B: Stockton-Pacific Sts. (bypass type; C Second & Third Sts. (bypass type).

[c] 1. Large; 2. Medium; 3. Small.

One has been a steady, if somewhat irregular, small-scale accretion following localized lateral expansion of a district or two within the Central District.[75] A limited chain reaction of locational shifts by nuclei may develop as a contiguous district is displaced by its expanding neighbor.[76] And a slight accretion takes place on a small section of the CBD boundary. Nuclei responsible for this type of accretion in San Francisco, 1850-1931, were the theater-entertainment, medical services, garment, hotel, furniture, and civic districts. During the greater part of San Francisco's history this was the only type of growth

[75] *Ibid.*, pp. 691-699.
[76] *Ibid.*, pp. 424-437, 457.

TABLE 2-7 WOMEN'S-APPAREL SHOPPING ESTABLISHMENTS IN
SIX AREAS IN SAN FRANCISCO 1875-1906

Types of Establishments	Lower Montgomery^a	Lower & Middle Kearny^b	Grant Avenue-Union Square^c	Middle Market^d	Upper Market^e	Other
Cloaks & Suits	6	6	0	1	0	0
Dry Goods	5	24	0	13	3	14
Ladies' F.G.	0	6	1	1	2	4
1875 Total	11	36¹	1	15	5	18
Cloaks & Suits	1	4	2	3	0	1
Dry Goods	2	13		8	6	6
Ladies' F.G.	0	5	5	5	2	2
1880 Total	3	22	9	16	8	9
Cloaks & Suits	0	7	4	2	1	0
Dry Goods	0	12	3	5	5	6
Ladies' F.G.	0	2	3	2	1	0
1885 Total	0	20	10	9	7	6
1896 Total	0	9	12	14	10	3
1906 Total	1	9	17	6	6	3

^a Discard-type to 1883.

^b Core 1875-1894; discard-type 1895-1906.

^c Interceptor 1875-1897; Core 1898-1906.

^d Interceptor 1875-1894; core 1894-1897; by-pass type 1898-1906.

^e Interceptor 1875-1897; by-pass type 1898-1906.

[1] Underlining indicates the two nuclei with the largest number of establishments at each cross-section.

going on, and when this was the case the Central District as a whole expanded little.[77] During the extended phases of lull in peripheral accretion a high proportion of the *transformation* (change-over of blocks from non-CBD to CBD) was concerned either with the *back-filling* of enclaves of formerly non-central business activities enveloped during previous phases of marked accretion, or with *infilling* of the interstices between the predominantly axial extensions that were the legacies of former phases of rapid growth.[78] Additions to the edges

[77] *Ibid.*, pp. 267, 451, 691-699, 705-707.
[78] *Ibid.*, pp. 627-646, 696-699.

TABLE 2-8 PHASES DURING WHICH GRID-BLOCKS ADDED TO
THE CENTRAL DISTRICT (1906-1931) WERE TRANSFORMED

Sector of the Periphery	Number of Grid-blocks Transformed, by Phase				
	1906-1915	1916-1920	1921-1926	1927-1931	Total
Embarcadero Extension	18	7	7	4(+2)	36(+2)
Northern Zones of Discard and By-pass	20	2	3(+1)ᵃ	6	31(+1)
Western Front	30	9	13(+2)	3	55(+2)
South-West	34	7	20(+1)	9	70(+1)
South	22	5	13(+2)	1	41(+2)
Total	124	30	56(+6)	23(+2)	233(+8)

ᵃ For explanation of brackets, see Table 2-9.

TABLE 2-9 PERIPHERAL ACCRETION TO THE CENTRAL DISTRICT
BY PHASE & SECTOR 1906-1931

Sector of the Periphery	Number of Grid-Blocks Added to the Central District				
	1906-1915	1916-1920	1921-1926	1927-1931	Total
Embarcardero Extension	7	18	7	4(+2)ᵃ	36(+2)
Nothern Zone of Discard	7	0	2(+1)	1	31(+1)
Northern Zone of By-Pass	13	2	1	5	
Western Front	26	6	20(+2)	3	55(+2)
South-West	20	2	39(+1)	9	70(+1)
South	19	3	18(+2)	1	41(+2)
Total	92	31*	87(+6)*	23(+2)*	233(+8)

ᵃ Number in brackets indicates the number grid-blocks of non-central-business-type in the central district in 1931 and the period in which they were enveloped by the advancing edge of the central district.

* Backfilling made up 10%, 2%, and 21% of the grid-blocks added to the Central District in 1916-1920, 1921-1926, and 1927-1931 respectively.

of the Central District were shallow, and took place on a broad front (Figure 2-4).

The second type of growth and accretion is the burst, in which the CBD expands rapidly in a very short time. There were five such periods in the history of San Francisco between 1850 and 1931, and most of the expansion of the Central District took place in these short spells, as it appears to have done in London and New York

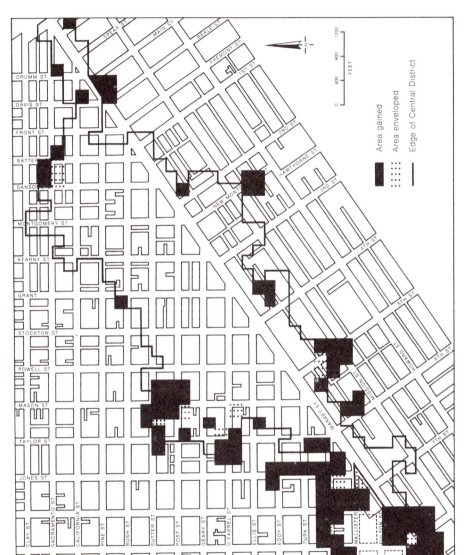

Fɪɢ. 2-4

City. In these phases of marked accretion, advances take place along the entire front of assimilation,[79] and there is frequently an axial component to growth—an extended linear advance of the Central District often to a former exclave of blocks of central business activities (Figure 2-5). In such a phase many blocks of non-central business activities are enveloped by the rapidly advancing edge of the Central District, and left inside the periphery as enclaves. These bursts on the edge of the CBD are the external expression of major morphological and functional changes taking place throughout the Central District, structural changes that take the form of a chain reaction of displacement and locational changes of most, if not all, of the constituent nuclei of the Central District. This *sequence of reaction,* as I have called it, gradually develops into a cumulative wave of displaced activities that surges to the advancing edge of the CBD some four to seven years after its inception in the core.

SEQUENCE OF REACTION AND A HIERARCHY AMONG NUCLEI

A full sequence of reaction occurs only when the financial district or the apparel-shopping district, or both, expands laterally at the expense of contiguous districts.[80] In San Francisco, the sequence generally began in the banking nucleus of the financial district or in the women's-apparel nucleus within the apparel-shopping district, whence the movement spread to the other nuclei of the *two core districts.* Expansion takes place into the contiguous districts, each of which is in the process of, or on the verge of, expansion, and the displacement becomes compound. In the contiguous districts external pressures to expand are frequently as great as the internal-growth pressures, and the contiguous districts expand laterally or sometimes leapfrog at the expanse of the peripheral districts. The latter are subject to so much external pressure during the sequence of reaction that they are frequently forced to leapfrog beyond the former boundary of the Central District, and to expand at the expense of occasional CBD nuclei and districts of non-CBD types of activities.

My study of the sequence of reaction has led me to a recognition of what Haig called an order of precedence among districts,[81] or what I have called the hierarchy among nuclei: the ranking of the nuclei in the central district based on each one's ability to displace any or all others. At the top of the hierarchy is the financial nucleus, which is displaced by no other nucleus, and only moves as a result

[79] *Ibid.,* pp. 592-646, 691-699.
[80] *Ibid.,* pp. 260-267, 456-457, 700-702.
[81] *Ibid.,* pp. 13-17; Haig, *op. cit.,* pp. 36-38; Hurd, *op. cit.,* pp. 81-85.

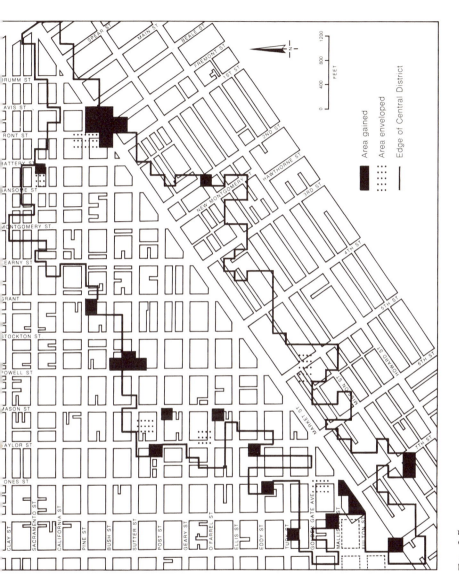

Area gained

Area enveloped

Edge of Central District

N

FEET

0   400   800   1200

SPEAR ST
MAIN ST
BEALE ST
TREMONT ST
1ST ST
2ND ST
HAWTHORNE ST
3RD ST
4TH ST
5TH ST
6TH ST
7TH ST
HOWARD ST
MISSION ST
MARKET ST
NEW MONTGOMERY

DRUMM ST
DAVIS ST
FRONT ST
BATTERY ST
SANSOME ST
MONTGOMERY ST
KEARNY ST
GRANT
STOCKTON ST
POWELL ST
MASON ST
TAYLOR ST
JONES ST

CLAY ST
SACRAMENTO ST
CALIFORNIA ST
PINE ST
BUSH ST
SUTTER ST
POST ST
GEARY ST
O'FARRELL ST
ELLIS ST
EDDY ST
TURK ST
GOLDEN GATE AVE.
MALLISON ST
FULTON ST

Fig. 2-5

of its own internal expansion. The other core district—the apparel-shopping district—has been broadly similar, although on occasion subject to external pressures from the financial district. It has tended to shift farther than the latter and in a different way. Third in the ranking, between the core and peripheral districts, has been the hotel district. Though subject to external pressures from the financial district and, to a lesser extent, from the apparel shopping district, it has undergone locational changes mainly as a result of internal pressures, and has tended to move farther than the two districts above it in the hierarchy.[82]

During bursts of expansion in the San Francisco Central District as a whole, all the other districts—those on the periphery—have been subjected to at least as much external as internal pressure to relocate. External pressures have been exerted by the three districts above them in the hierarchy, but in some cases a peripheral district has forced another from its local.[83]

In general, however, these districts have expanded at the expense of both the non-central-business activities that encircle much of the Central District, e.g., residential, wholesaling, manufacturing, construction, and transportation concerns, and of nuclei of activities of central business type that are sometimes inside the CBD and sometimes outside, e.g., club-church-organizational, automobile service, public administration, and entertainment nuclei.

SEPARATION AND THE POLYNUCLEAR CENTRAL AREA

The third type of growth—separation—is a special case of the "burst," in which the Central District breaks up into at least two discrete parts. It becomes in fact a polynuclear central area rather than a mononuclear CBD. In *laissez-faire* situations in the nineteenth century I have found this type of expansion only in large cities. It occurs when the set[84] is broken either (1) by catastrophe, fire, etc., or, more usually, (2) by the leapfrogging of one or more of the core districts during and following very rapid growth of the metropolis. Leapfrogging by the financial district is very rare, but it is more frequent in the apparel-shopping district, and when either or both jump to new and discrete locations, temporary separation is likely.

This happened for a few years in San Francisco in the early 1870s. The financial district, formerly contiguous with the apparel-shopping

[82] Bowden, *op. cit.*, pp. 700-702.
[83] *Ibid.*, pp. 458-459.
[84] The "set" is the position of nuclei relative to each other within the central district; once established it remains rigid and permanent in the main, increasingly so as the city grows. *Ibid.*, pp. 702-703.

district, leapfrogged two blocks to the southeast and the apparel shopping district jumped to a non-contiguous location five blocks south (Figure 2-6). These changes occurred between 1866 and 1869, and were followed by the leapfrogging of the theater, hotel, furniture, and garment nuclei to discrete locations between 1868 and 1873. For a short period four central nuclei, including the two core districts, were separated from each other by bands of non-CBD activities.[85] The leapfrogging was not extensive, and the interstices between the nuclei were quickly filled, so that by 1880 the Central District was once more intact. But the circumstances that lay behind this unusual growth epitomize the conditions necessary to this type of growth elsewhere. A tripling of the city's population between 1855 and 1865 and an increase of similar proportions in the number of apparel shopping establishments in the Inner City (particularly of medium-sized establishments) was sufficient to loosen the inertial burden and produce a polynuclear central area.

The extreme case of this type of Central District expansion is the semipermanent separation of the core districts in the central area, characteristic of metropolises that have undergone marked and rapid growth over a long period, e.g., London and New York City. The first polynuclear central area was probably London's, following the leapfrogging of the apparel-shopping district westward between 1610 and 1630.[86] During this period the population of London and the numbers of the gentry and aristocracy in the West End probably doubled.[87]

By the late nineteenth century, the apparel-shopping district had leapfrogged six times in moving almost three miles westwards from Cheapside; the financial district has remained in the region of its original crystallization.[88] Separation has been the rule for more than 300 years in London, where numerous districts have been isolated from other central nuclei by bands of non-CBD activities, although postwar development in these interstices may well reestablish a single and massive Central District in the next two decades.

In New York City, separation probably occurred between 1825 and 1835 as the apparel-shopping district leapfrogged northwards, soon

---

[85] *Ibid.*, pp. 178-274.

[86] Brett-James, *op. cit.*, pp. 67-104, 391, 502, 508; Reddaway, *op. cit.*, pp. 127-129; Strype, *op. cit.*, pp. 195-197, 206-207.

[87] Brett-James, *op. cit.*, pp. 498-499; George, *op. cit.*, pp. 318-319; Gras, *op. cit.*, p. 181; F. J. Fisher, "The Development of London as a Centre of Conspicuous Consumption in the Sixteenth and Seventeenth Centuries," *Transactions of the Royal Historical Society*, 4th Series, 30 (1948).

[88] Gras, *op. cit.*, pp. 243-260; Spate, *op. cit.*, pp. 530-537; Summerson, *op. cit.*, pp. 24-26, 262-267; Brett-James, *op. cit.*; Strype, *op. cit.*, pp. 149, 162-163.

105

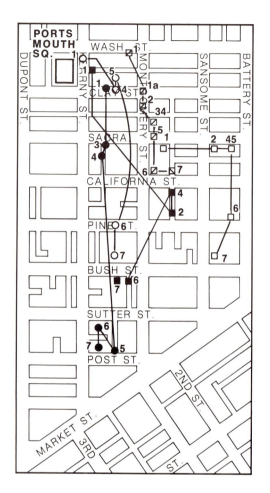

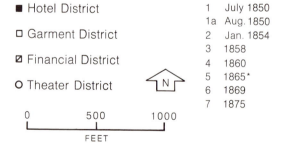

- ● Women's Apparel Shopping District
- ■ Hotel District
- □ Garment District
- ◩ Financial District
- ○ Theater District

1	July 1850
1a	Aug. 1850
2	Jan. 1854
3	1858
4	1860
5	1865*
6	1869
7	1875

0   500   1000
FEET

*No record of theaters in the 1865 Directory,
data for 1867 substituted

Fig. 2-6

to be followed by many other districts.[89] During this period the population of the city more than doubled. By the 1950s the apparel-shopping district had leapfrogged at least six times in moving four miles north of Wall Street.[90]

In sum, the type of growth prevalent in a central district at any given time under *laissez-faire* conditions would seem to depend in the main on the scale of demand for central-district space by certain types of linked establishments that form nucleations, and this demand, in turn, ultimately rests on the extent and rapidity of growth of the city and its hinterland. The lower and more steadier the rate of a city's growth, the slighter the probability that central district growth will be effected in the short bursts of what I have called "sequences of reaction," and the greater the probability that peripheral accretion will be of the shallow, piecemeal type. By contrast, the more rapid and marked the rate of a city's growth, the greater the chance that expansion of the central district will occur in bursts of peripheral accretion following sequences of reaction, particularly if the growth rate has been quite irregular, as in San Francisco.[91] And in those few metropolises where growth has been very extensive and whose growth rate has been continuously high, separation and the emergence of a polynuclear central area are probable.

III

CONCLUSION

The modern Central District is the morphological and functional expression of two major processes synchronous with the rise of the metropolis: (1) concentration in the area of high accessibility of estab-

---

[89] Hoover and Vernon, *op. cit.*, pp. 75-76, 110-113; Haig, *op. cit.*, pp. 97-104; King, *New York*, pp. 142-160, 843-912.

[90] Hoover and Vernon, *op. cit.*, pp. 110-113; Haig, *op. cit.*, pp. 102-104.

[91] In studying the rapidly shifting central districts of Japanese cities during recent decades of marked urbanization, Scholler feels that this "restlessness and unsteadiness demonstrates that *Western* forms of city structure and urban life have not yet come to a certain stability in Japan. . . . The technique is being mastered." (Italics mine.) He feels that four special facts concerning the Japanese—"psychological and sociological causes"—need to be taken into consideration to explain the "centre-shifting and centre-mobility" problem in Japan (P. Scholler, "Centre-Shifting and Centre-Mobility in Japanese Cities," in *Proceedings of the I.G.U. Symposium in Urban Geography, Lund 1960*, K. Norborg (ed.), Lund: C.W.K. Gleerup, 1962, pp. 576-593). No such special pleading is necessary, for historical studies show that the phenomena Scholler describes have been basic to central-district growth in the West (and particularly in the American west) during periods when cities were undergoing extremely rapid and relatively marked growth.

107

lishments linked by competition and complementarity, and (2) the separation of place of work from place of residence. I have implied that the Central District, in the Murphy-Vance sense, may have existed in what Gras called "the town economy," but that it was *not clearly defined* as an urban region until the beginning of "the metropolitan economy"—the late sixteenth century in London—and not perfected as an urban region until the late stages of what Gras describes as "the organizing of the market in the metropolitan economy"—the early eighteenth century in London.

Once the conception of the Central District was established and obvious, the idea was diffused to other cities, and the form and function of established central districts, like London's, was replicated in high-order central places. In the New World, Central Districts emerged in the dominant central places at threshold levels much lower than those characteristic in London, and at levels that continued to drop until the middle of the nineteenth century at least. And the same was true for the constituent nuclei of the Central District, as judged from the examples of the most rapidly growing metropolises of the New World. Threshold levels, measured in terms of the city population, were appreciably higher in central places of the middle order in the New World, threshold levels appear to have been higher largely because of the inertia in the long-established city structure. (Presumably this would be less true of such rapidly growing products of the Industrial Revolution as Liverpool, Manchester, and Birmingham.) I should stress that these statements are highly tentative.

A second and equally tentative conclusion is that a form of the Inner City different from the typical mononuclear CBD has been potentially present in the metropolis from the mid-seventeenth century onward—the polynuclear central area. I have suggested that this is not an Inner City form that is simply and exclusively an expression of size, but that it is rather a result of periods of very marked and rapid growth (possibly in small towns) in which the ever-present constraints of inertia were largely overcome by the growing Central District. The advantages of the polynuclear central area have been clear for 250 years in London, and obvious for more than 100 years in New York City, where the form was perfected. The fact that no internal pressures have been exerted to pull the separated nuclei together is some proof of the advantages of the polynuclear central area over the Central District. It is the form that Jean Gottmann sees as the future organizing framework in emerging megalopolises: his *novus ordo seclorum*.

The form came into existence before the telephone and the automobile, but these innovations make it possible for the form to be replicated in rapidly growing metropolises, both planned and unplanned. The Central District in large American cities is a form of the past, and the tragedy of downtown renewal programs in the postwar years is that, in spite of urban growth trends and processes, a nineteenth-century form has been rebuilt to carry out present-day functions.

3

Urban Deconcentration in the Nineteenth Century: A Statistical Inquiry*

KENNETH T. JACKSON

I

"Escape," suggest the advertisements. "Escape from cities too big, too polluted, too strident to call home." Find a new serenity in Druid Hills, or Scarborough Manor, or Houston Estates. Across the length and breadth of the land, the appeal is repeated every week, and with noticeable effectiveness. In 1970, the Census Bureau announced that suburbanites had become the largest single element in the American population, and predictions for the 1980s uniformly assert that the pattern will continue. Whether one regards low-density developments as "sloburbs" or as the hope of the future, there can be little doubt but that "spread city" is the dominant residential and commercial characteristic of twentieth-century urban growth.

The purpose of this inquiry is to examine the process of metropolitan sprawl in the United States before the widespread introduction of the electric streetcar in the 1890s and the private automobile in the 1920's. Specifically, I shall test the hypothesis that large American cities have always grown chiefly by peripheral accretion; or, as Robert Schmitt has suggested, that "there is nothing new about suburbanization."[1] The basic question is whether the spatial changes of the internal-combustion era represent a new urban pattern or are instead simply the logical extension of a long-established trend.

If it is a truism to say that the United States is now a suburban nation, it is a matter of considerable confusion as to how and when

* The author wishes to thank the National Endowment for the Humanities and the Columbia University Council for Research in the Social Sciences for financial support and Professors Herbert Gans of Columbia University, Leo Schnore of the University of Wisconsin, and John Modell of the University of Minnesota for their helpful advice. Mr. William Meyers generously granted permission to use data he compiled in my seminar.

[1] A research analyst with the Honolulu Redevelopment Agency, Schmitt included this suggestion in a lengthy letter to *Land Economics*. He offered no evidence to support his statement, which was challenged by Amos H. Hawley in the same issue. *Land Economics* 33 (February 1956), p. 86.

this came about.[2] Professor Carl Bridenbaugh's encyclopedic *Cities in the Wilderness: The First Century of Urban Life in America, 1625-1742* contains numerous references to "suburbs"; one was on the road to Kingsbridge near the Bowery and Astor Place in lower Manhattan; another was at Barton's Point on the periphery of built-up Boston where John Staniford advertised a new real estate development in 1719.[3] But these communities were isolated and small, and there was apparently little regular population movement between them and the larger cities.

As a pattern and a process, rather than as an occasional development, suburbanization was first noted more than three-fourths of a century ago in Adna Ferrin Weber's Columbia dissertation, *The Growth of Cities in the Nineteenth Century*.[4] More recently, Professors George Rogers Taylor, Sam Bass Warner, and Joel A. Tarr have found evidence of nascent urban deconcentration in the late nineteenth century.[5] But most urbanologists, social scientists, journalists, and historians obviously regard suburban growth as a twentieth-century phenomenon; some, like York Willbern, seem to find it only on this side of VJ Day.[6] The most charitable thing to assume is disagreement regarding definitions.

II DEFINITIONS AND METHODOLOGY

A suburb may be defined in terms of life style, jurisdiction, function, density, or some combination thereof. The study of the suburban "way of life" has been an important concern at least since the early 1950's, when William H. Whyte published his now classic study, *The Organization Man*. Subsequent research and debate have in fact been so extensive that Herbert J. Gans, Bennett M. Berger, and Scott Donaldson have begun to debunk the "suburban myth." Needless to say, the experts disagree among themselves.

The United States Bureau of the Census generally hews to a jurisdic-

---

[2] For a broad survey of American suburban history, see my recent essay, "The Crabgrass Frontier: 150 Years of Suburban Growth in America," in Raymond A. Mohl and James F. Richardson (editors), *The Urban Experience: Themes in American History* (Belmont, California: Wadsworth Publishing Co., 1973), pp. 196-221.

[3] (New York: Ronald Press, 1938), *passim*.

[4] Published by Columbia University Press in 1899 and recently reissued in paperback by Cornell University Press.

[5] Going beyond the well-known work of Taylor and Warner is Joel A. Tarr, *Transportation Innovation and Changing Spatial Patterns: Pittsburgh, 1850–1910* (Pittsburgh: Transportation Research Institute, Carnegie Mellon University, 1972).

[6] York Willbern, *The Withering Away of the City* (Tuscaloosa: University of Alabama Press, 1964), pp. 18-20.

tional definition and assigns metropolitan status to any county in which there is a city of 50,000 or more. Although "suburbs" are not mentioned, anyone living outside the central city but within the county is presumed to be a suburbanite. Thus, such densely settled, industrial, and aging towns as Hoboken, New Jersey, and Harvey, Illinois, are defined as suburbs, while fashionable neighborhoods like River Oaks, within the immense boundaries of Houston or similar areas in Oklahoma City, are regarded as part of the core. Such obvious disparities, which have to do with the annexation history of an area rather than with spatial patterns, should make anyone suspicious of official figures.[7] Urban geographers and economists, to their credit, assign suburban status on the basis of a functional relationship within the metropolitan area. Once again, however, there is little agreement about the proper indices or how to measure them.

Just as there is no satisfactory definition of "suburb," so also is there no consensus regarding the meaning of "suburbanization."[8] It is clear, however, that a suburb is a *place* and that suburbanization is a *process*. It is the *process* which is of concern here.[9] My methodology is to consider the five definitions of deconcentration which are most commonly used to dramatize and highlight the post-World War II move from the city, and to test those definitions in the context of nineteenth-century urban America.[10] My purpose is not to determine which of the definitions is most reasonable, but rather to demonstrate that all the so-called new suburban trends are at least a century old. Although traditional sources contain numerous references to the suburbs around every large city, the approach in this paper is frankly ecological and statistical—to analyze the changing composition and distribution of the urban population in space and time.[11] Obviously,

---

[7] If one uses jurisdiction as the measure, then suburbs come in all sizes and shapes. See Chauncy D. Harris, "Suburbs," *Amercian Journal of Sociology* 49 (July 1943), pp. 1-13; and Robin J. Pryor, "Defining the Rural-Urban Fringe," *Social Forces* 47 (December 1968), pp. 202-215.

[8] Henceforth, I shall use the terms "suburbanization" and "deconcentration" interchangeably.

[9] Other than Weber, the best books to consider deconcentration as a process are Graham R. Taylor, *Satellite Cities: A Study of Industrial Suburbs* (New York and London: D. Appleton and Co., 1915); Harlan Paul Douglass, *The Suburban Trend* (New York: Century Company, 1925); and Roderick D. Mc-Kenzie, *The Metropolitan Community* (New York: McGraw-Hill Book Company, 1933). Homer Hoyt's work on land values and residential neighborhoods is also extremely important.

[10] The five definitions I have chosen do not exhaust the list of possible suburbanization definitions, but they do represent the most commonly used.

[11] An excellent traditional study that is richly detailed is H. J. Dyos, *Victorian Suburb: A Study of the Growth of Camberwell* (Leicester: Leicester University Press, 1961).

this procedure does not explain everything about the suburban trend; it may in fact obscure more than it reveals. But because statistics are so often employed to define the urban condition in our own time, it seems appropriate to apply similar methods to an earlier period.

DEFINITION I

Urban deconcentration is a process of population redistribution that results in an increase in the proportion of people in a given area who live outside the core city. This definition, undoubtedly the most popular in use, lurks behind the official news that between 1940 and 1950 suburbs grew more than twice as fast as central cities, that between 1950 and 1960 they grew forty times as rapidly, and that between 1960 and 1970 virtually all metropolitan growth took place in the suburbs. This measurement calls for the establishment of geographical boundaries for the city and the fringe and the calculation of relative rates of growth over time. Suburbanization requires the existence of a higher growth rate on the periphery of a metropolis than at its center. Without an overall pattern of differential growth in favor of the outlying areas, suburbs could conceivably flourish but deconcentration would not be present. For example, if a peripheral region registered a 35 per cent rate of population increase over ten years while the core city was growing by 40 per cent, then the metropolitan area would be *concentrating*.

Using this growth-rate definition, Amos H. Hawley published a statistical volume in 1956 concluding that urban America moved toward concentration before 1920 and toward deconcentration after that date.[12] Several years later, a similar procedure convinced Professor Leo F. Schnore that Hawley's general conclusion was correct, but that ten American cities had begun to deconcentrate in the second half of the nineteenth century. According to Schnore's data, New York City began to experience suburbanization in the 1850's, followed by Cincinnati, San Francisco, and New Haven in the 1870's, Boston and Albany in the 1880s, and Baltimore, St. Louis, Scranton, and Duluth in the 1890s.[13] Conversely, Philadelphia, Chicago, Cleveland,

---

[12] Hawley, who studied 99 metropolitan areas, did not bother with the 19th century, which he regarded as a period of urban concentration. Amos H. Hawley, *The Changing Shape of Metropolitan America: Deconcentration Since 1920* (Glencoe: The Free Press, 1956). See also, Warren S. Thompson, *The Growth of Metropolitan Districts in the United States, 1900-1940* (Washington: U.S. Government Printing Office, 1947).

[13] Leo F. Schnore, "The Timing of Metropolitan Decentralization: A Contribution to the Debate," *Journal of the American Institute of Planners* 25 (November 1959), pp. 200-206. Professor Schnore generously shared his data with me.

Pittsburgh, and all other cities supposedly concentrated until the twentieth century.

The problem with this procedure is that it really measures political annexation much better than population movements. This occurs because Professors Hawley and Schnore, and in fact most demographers, essentially accept twentieth-century municipal boundaries and use them as a basis for making population comparisons over time.[14] In effect, this misleads us concerning the timing of deconcentration because it implies that a city is concentrating until it reaches its modern corporate limits and deconcentrating when its population moves beyond such arbitrary boundaries.[15] Thus, cities which have expanded their corporate limits enormously in recent decades, such as Memphis, Houston, Indianapolis, and Oklahoma City, exhibit a "concentrating" pattern when in fact their populations are quite spread out. Older cities with long-restricted boundaries, on the other hand, such as Buffalo, San Francisco, Boston, and St. Louis, appear to be "deconcentrating," when in fact their average population densities are comparatively high.[16]

Definition I, which essentially is the measurement of rates of growth within political areas, provides an excellent index of the ability of cities to expand their boundaries, but its usefulness as an index of deconcentration is entirely dependent upon one's definition of the center and the periphery. If this methodology were applied to large cities of the nineteenth century *according to the boundaries that existed in that century* then deconcentration would appear before 1830. New York's fringe would then have to be defined as Brooklyn or the Bronx rather than as Westchester, Nassau, or Suffolk Counties. Brooklyn, with tree-shaded streets, bluestone-paved walks, and excellent ferry connections to Fulton Street, actually maintained a higher rate of growth than that of neighboring Manhattan throughout the entire nineteenth century, beginning with the census of 1810.[17] (See

[14] Both men expressed concern over the problem of annexation, but except for Schnore's correction for the New York consolidation of 1898, their calculations were not affected.

[15] The only general overview of the American annexation experience is Kenneth T. Jackson, "Metropolitan Government Versus Suburban Autonomy: Politics on the Crabgrass Frontier," in Kenneth T. Jackson and Stanley K. Schultz (editors), *Cities in American History* (New York: Alfred A. Knopf, 1972), pp. 442-462.

[16] A suggestive study which compares cities without reference to political boundaries is David Harrison, Jr. and John F. Kain, "An Historical Model of Urban Form," Harvard University Program on Regional and Urban Economics Discussion Paper No. 63, September, 1970.

[17] This takes place even though Manhattan's northern suburbs, such as Harlem, are included in the city figures. By the terms of both the Dongan Charter and colonial legislation, the City of New York and Manhattan Island were

Table 3-1.) On the opposite shore, Newark, Jersey City, Hoboken, Hudson, and Elizabeth were, in percentage terms, outgrowing New York by the 1840s, and in 1861 a local booster claimed that "the Jersey suburb is the fairest, the most populous, and the most fruitful of any which surround the metropolis."[18]

TABLE 3-1 COMPARATIVE DECENNIAL RATES OF POPULATION INCREASE FOR FIVE CITIES AND THEIR SUBURBS, 1800-1860[a]

Metropolis	1790-1800	1800-1810	1810-1820	1820-1830	1830-1840	1840-1850	1850-1860
New York							
City	82.7%	59.3%	28.4%	63.8%	54.4%	64.9%	57.8%
Suburbs	48.3	85.1	63.0	114.6	135.4	167.3	88.5
Boston							
City	36.1	35.5	28.1	41.8	38.5	61.0	29.9
Suburbs	36.8	34.8	25.7	35.2	44.8	84.7	53.8
Philadelphia							
City	44.5	30.3	18.8	26.0	16.4	29.6	11.0
Suburbs	53.8	47.0	25.3	47.8	51.7	74.8	48.8
Cleveland							
City					393.7	50.4	10.8
Suburbs					128.0	89.2	72.4
St. Louis							
City			187.4	27.3	181.4	51.8	20.0
Suburbs			33.3	52.6	135.9	309.9	100.7

[a] The Boston periphery here includes Chelsea, Charlestown, Cambridge, Brighton, Brookline, Roxbury, and Dorchester. New York's suburbs here include Brooklyn, although the addition of New Jersey would not have altered the pattern. The Philadelphia periphery is defined as everything in Philadelphia County outside the city in 1850. The Cleveland periphery is defined as Cuyahoga County minus the city of 1830. The St. Louis suburbs are defined as those sections of St. Louis County that were outside the city in 1830.

SOURCE: Decennial United States Census Returns, 1790-1860.

Philadelphia affords an even better example of the importance of boundaries in dating the onset of suburbanization. If the core area is there defined as the municipal corporation after the 1854 consolidation, when the city grew from two to 127 square miles, then Philadelphia's rural areas absorbed the late-nineteenth-century population

---

legally coterminous as early as 1686. See also, Clay Lancaster, *Old Brooklyn Heights* (Rutland, Vermont: Charles E. Tuttle, 1961), pp. 13-16; and a half-dozen articles by Jacob Judd on Brooklyn published in the *Journal of Long Island History* in the 1960s.

[18] For example, Jersey City grew by more than 100 per cent every decade between 1840 and 1870. The quote is from J. Henry Clark, *The Medical Topography of Newark, N.J.* (New York: John A. Gray, 1861), p. 3.

increase and the city did not begin to deconcentrate until the twentieth century.[19] But if Philadelphia's fringe is defined as Spring Garden, Kensington, Germantown, and the other suburbs that were not annexed until mid-century, then it began to deconcentrate about 1800. If the peripheries of other cities are similarly redefined as they would have been in the mid-nineteenth century, and if relative rates of population growth are measured on that basis, then deconcentration in Boston, St. Louis, Baltimore, Cleveland, and New Orleans began before the Civil War (Table 3-1). The same pattern was also evident in England, where the inner suburbs of London were outstripping the core in the early nineteenth century. By the period 1861-1891 the outer ring of suburbs was growing by at least 50 per cent in each intercensal decade, and the fastest-growing cities in England were virtually all London suburbs.[20]

In contemporary America, reference is often made to the fact that high growth rates are constantly moving farther out on the exurban fringe. Yet certainly by the middle of the nineteenth century the same trend was evident in large cities. If we look closely at the population figures and distinguish not simply between city and suburb but among the suburbs themselves, then percentage growth rates in the higher ranges move steadily outward throughout the century. In Philadelphia County, for example, the highest population jumps between 1810 and 1830 were registered along the city's northern edges by the independent suburbs of Northern Liberties and Spring Garden.[21] In the next twenty-year period the areas of most spectacular growth had moved beyond the inner suburbs to Moyamensing, Penn District, Richmond, and Kensington.[22] By mid-century, numerous district and borough governments had been created to offer rudimentary urban service to the early suburbanites, and the Philadelphia Board of Trade was noting with pride that "the open grounds and commons in the

---

[19] For a description of the period when Philadelphia's various outer wards were settled, see Sam Bass Warner's stimulating, if not always convincing, *The Private City: Philadelphia in Three Periods of Its Growth* (Philadelphia: University of Pennsylvania Press, 1968), p. 181.

[20] Between 1881 and 1891, the four communities which claimed the most rapid population growth in England were Leyton, Willesden, Tottenham, and West Ham. Dyos, *Victorian Suburb*, pp. 19-20.

[21] In order to minimize the tendency for an area with a small population to show a higher growth rate than a densely settled area, the entire county rather than just the urbanized area was used as the statistical base. Significantly, the zones with the smallest population and lowest density, Byberry and Moreland, were never among the growth-rate leaders between 1810 and 1870.

[22] In 1850, Kensington, Northern Liberties, Southwark, and Spring Garden were all officially among the nation's largest cities, even though they would soon become Philadelphia neighborhoods.

116

suburbs are fast vanishing before the march of enterprise and construction."[23] In the late 1850s good commuter service began to be offered to Germantown, and the scion of an old Philadelphia family became so enthralled by the possibilities of that suburb that he predicted that "before long, town life, life in close streets and alleys, will be confined to a few occupations, and cities will be mere collections of shops, warehouses, factories, and places of business."[24]

As the map in Figure 3-1 indicates, Germantown became one of the areas of high-percentage growth between 1850 and 1870, by which time all the older suburbs were in relative decline. Throughout the century, the point at which growth rates in the Philadelphia area tended to level and then decrease moved centrifugally at the speed of about one half-mile per decade. Between 1900 and 1950, the wave of urban expansion moved outward at the rate of perhaps one mile per decade, and since 1950 the rate may have increased even further.[25] But the important fact is that it is the speed rather than the presence of deconcentration that most distinguishes the nineteenth- and twentieth-century suburban trends, according to the first definition of deconcentration examined.

DEFINITION II

Urban deconcentration is a process of population redistribution that results in a leveling of residential densities within an urbanized area. Perhaps there is no aspect of urban history less understood than intensity of land use, yet as Harrison and Kain have noted, net residential density is probably the best and most sensitive of the individual indices of urban form. The primary problem for the historian is that the component areas on which calculations must be based are not the smallest possible and they are not consistent over time.[26] With the establishment of census tracts in the twentieth century, more precise measures became feasible.

It is a generally accepted fact that in every large city, excepting

[23] Philadelphia Board of Trade, *Twenty-First Annual Report, February 6, 1854* (Philadelphia: Deacon and Peterson, 1854). The thirty suburbs and districts sometimes competed among themselves and with Philadelphia for basic urban amenities. Nelson Manfred Blake, *Water for the Cities: A History of the Urban Water Supply Problem in the United States* (Syracuse: Syracuse University Press, 1956), pp. 87-89.

[24] "The Diary of Sidney George Fisher, 1859-1860," *Pennsylvania Magazine of History and Biography* 87 (April 1963), p. 192.

[25] Hans Blumenfeld, "The Tidal Wave of Metropolitan Expansion," *Journal of the American Institute of Planners* 20 (Winter 1954), pp. 3-15.

[26] Harrison and Kain have developed a very sensible model demonstrating that the density of a metropolitan area is the cumulative or weighted sum

117

the business core, residential density tends to decline as one moves from the center to the edge. In fact, Colin Clark has demonstrated that this phenomenon follows a simple mathematical equation of *exponential* decline. If x represents the distance in miles from the business center and y represents the residential density then the equation may be expressed as

$$y = A e^{-bx}$$

This equation appears to be valid for all important cities at least since the year 1800, even though different areas show wide variation in the rate of decline of density, as measured by the coefficient b. A high value for b means a sharp drop in density as in a compact city, and a low value of b would mean that the city was more dispersed, as in contemporary Los Angeles.[27]

An equally important tendency, and one considered characteristic of the suburbanization process, is that over time cities tend to spread themselves out. In 1830, for example, urban populations tended to be very concentrated at the center and to drop off very sharply within a few miles. The distinction between city and country was clear and immediate. As late as 1860, fully three-fourths of Philadelphia's half-million inhabitants resided in an urban core of ten square miles.[28] The same number of citizens in 1970, in Philadelphia or any other automobile city, would require a land area many times greater in order to achieve the same facility of circulation that existed for pedestrian or horse-drawn traffic before the Civil War. Thus, the density curve representing the variation in density from one ward or census tract to the next is considerably higher for the nineteenth-century city than for the twentieth-century city. Prior to 1860, no American

---

of the density of its development over time to the present, as expressed by the following equation:

$$D_t = \frac{d_0 u_0 + d_1 u_1 + \cdots d_t u_t}{u_0 + u_1 + \cdots u_t} = \frac{\Sigma_{i=0}^t d_i u_i}{\Sigma_{i=0}^t u_i}$$

where D = average net residential density of the metropolitan area at time period t

d_i = net residential density of the dwelling units added to the area in time period i

u_i = number of dwelling units added to the area in time period i.

Harrison and Kain, "An Historical Model of Urban Form," p. 8.

[27] Colin Clark, "Urban Population Densities," *Journal of the Royal Statistical Society,* Series A, Part IV, 1951, pp. 490-496.

[28] Good descriptions of Philadelphia congestion are contained in William S. Hastings, "Philadelphia Microcosm," *Pennsylvania Magazine of History and Biography* 91 (April 1967), pp. 164-180; John Rannells, *The Core of the City* (New York: Columbia University Press, 1965), p. 68; and Warner, *Private City,* pp. 56-57.

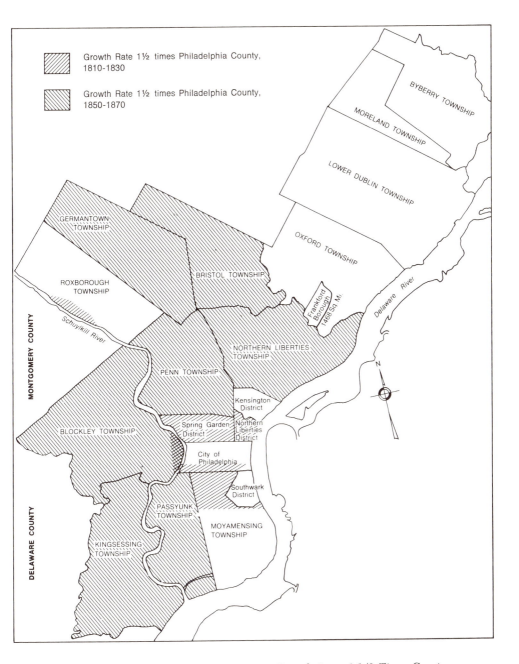

FIG. 3-1 Philadelphia Areas With Percentage Growth Rates 1 1/2 Times County as a Whole, 1810-1830 and 1850-1870.

community comprised a metropolitan built-up area of more than 40 square miles; in 1970, the urban agglomerations of New York, Chicago, and Los Angeles are calculated in thousands of square miles.

This disparity is indicative of the compactness and congestion of the large American city for perhaps a generation before and after the Civil War. In New York City, the "average" density in the built-up area in 1850 was 135 persons per acre, or 86,400 per square mile; in 1970, that degree of congestion can be achieved only through the use of dense tenements or high-rise apartments.[29] In 1870, the geographic center of New York's population was located roughly at Union Square (14th Street), and approximately 85 per cent of the population lived within two miles of the center.[30] In 1900, the tenth Ward on the Lower East Side reached levels of 900 persons per acre, or a half-million per square mile, the highest recorded density of population in world history,[31] even though large areas of undeveloped land remained available in upper Manhattan. At that degree of crowding, the city of New York could have accommodated the entire population of the United States as late as 1950. The density curve for New York County (Manhattan) is therefore more steep for 1900 than for 1970.

In Philadelphia, the leveling of densities had begun by at least 1850. At that time, it was a typically compact big city. Alleys proliferated in order to increase the intensity of land use. Typical row-house lots were less than 20 feet wide, and densities of 100 and more per acre were common. Meanwhile, large areas only a few miles

[29] The type of housing necessary to accommodate various levels of density per acre has been calculated as follows:

   3.2 to   12.8 Single Family Detached Housing
  12.8 to   32.1 Duplex and Single Family Detached
  32.1 to   83.6 Row Houses and Apartments
  83.6 to 238.0 Dense Apartments, High Rise Housing
  238.0 or more Very Dense Apartments

In contemporary urban America, densities exceeding 238 per acre are found almost exclusively in Manhattan and the Bronx. Joseph R. Passonneau and Richard Saul Wurman, *Urban Atlas: 20 American Cities* (Cambridge, Mass.: M.I.T. Press, 1968), p. 5.

[30] The percentage of people within two miles of the center has plummeted since 1870, but the center of population for the metropolitan area is probably somewhere in Manhattan even today.

[31] Bert F. Hoselitz reports a density of 840,000 per square mile in a section of Bombay, but the area is quite small. Hoselitz, "A Survey of the Literature on Urbanization in India," in Roy Turner (editor), *India's Urban Future* (Berkeley: University of California Press, 1962), p. 427; Weber, *Growth of Cities*, pp. 456-470; Peter Hall, *The World Cities* (New York: World University Library, 1966), p. 192; and Edward Ewing Pratt, *Industrial Causes of Congestion of Population in New York* (New York: Columbia U., Longmans, Green & Co., 1911).

distant from the waterfront were almost completely rural. Thus, as Table 3-2 and Figure 3-2 indicate, densities per square mile ranged from about 85,000 in Northern Liberties to about 100 in farming areas in the northernmost part of the county. If we take the city of 1854 as our unit of measurement, then the ratio between density extremes remains about 1000 to 1 from 1800 to 1850, when a marked decline begins. If we exclude rural areas which were not functionally a part of the Philadelphia urban network until about 1900, despite their legal status as neighborhoods, and if we confine our analysis to the built-up areas at the time of the Civil War, then the process of deconcentration according to Definition II began even before 1850. The ratio between the most densely settled areas (East and West Central City, Northern Liberties, Southwark) and the least densely settled suburbs in the built-up area (Penn District and West Spring Garden) narrowed from about 70 to 1 in 1820 to about 4 to 1 in 1860. Similarly, the density level at which the average citizen lived began to decline about 1850. In that year, less than 25 per cent of the population lived at densities of less than 50 per acre; by 1890, about 45 per cent of the citizenry lived at this level of dispersal. As Philadelphia spread itself out in the middle and late nineteenth century, its density curve over time and distance became less steep.

Nevertheless, the demurrer against Definitions I and II as indices of deconcentration is persuasive. It is, after all, only natural in a developing community for population to grow most rapidly on the edges, as the metropolis adds residential layers like rings on a tree. Thus, what we usually call the growth of Chicago or Los Angeles is actually the building up of new neighborhoods on the periphery. If large amounts of land suitable for development are not available within the municipal corporation, then many families seeking residences and businessmen seeking industrial sites will look to the suburbs. Not surprisingly, peripheral rates of growth will normally exceed those of the central city and residential densities will tend to level out in the metropolitan area.[32]

DEFINITION III

Urban deconcentration is a process of population redistribution in which the core area experiences an absolute loss of population and a reduction in residential density. As in the previous example, this definition assumes that residential land use is an important factor

[32] Among the few studies to consider the impact of annexation upon urban growth is Donald J. Bogue, *Components of Population Change, 1940-1950* (Chicago: Population Research and Training Center, University of Chicago, 1957).

TABLE 3-2 COMPARATIVE DENSITY PER SQUARE MILE OF SELECTED MINOR CIVIL DIVISIONS, PHILADELPHIA CITY AND COUNTY, 1800-1890

Civil Division	Area in Sq. Miles, 1853	Approximate Density Per Square Mile[a]						
		1800	1820	1830	1840	1850	1860	1890
East Central City	.683	50,000	60,000	65,000	56,000	65,000	59,000	42,000
West Central City	1.594	12,000	21,700	25,000	35,200	52,000	65,000	50,000
Northern Liberties	.556		35,400	50,000	62,000	85,000	75,000	65,000
Southwark	1.050	9,000	14,000	19,000	27,000	35,000	50,000	72,000
Kensington	1.899		3,700	1,800	12,000	25,000	25,000	65,000
East Spring Garden	.639		4,500	14,000	31,000	60,000	65,000	63,000
West Spring Garden	1.000		800	1,500	7,250	17,000	32,000	62,000
Penn District	1.984				1,000	4,500	16,000	60,000
Kingsessing	8.923	60	130	110	140	200	250	2,880
Moreland	4.779	75	90	85	98	102	110	800
Byberry	9.045	69	96	108	110	120	130	850
County Total	129.583	625	1,058	1,460	1,993	3,156	4,367	8,600

[a] These figures, which are averages for relatively large areas, have been rounded off in the case of heavily populated areas.

SOURCE: The square mile totals for different civil divisions are from William Bucke Campbell, "Old Towns and Districts of Philadelphia," *Philadelphia History* 5 (1942), p. 94. The calculations of density are based on the United States Census for the years indicated.

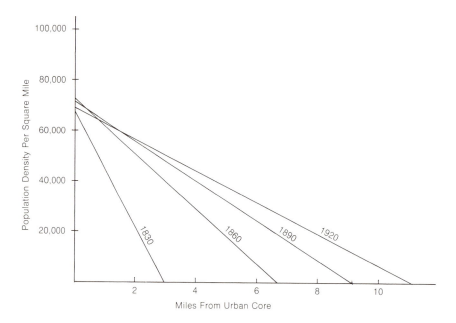

FIG. 3-2 The Relationship Between Population Density and Distance From the Urban Core in Philadelphia at Thirty-year Time Intervals, 1800-1920.

in metropolitan deconcentration and that the number of persons who ordinarily reside in a given area is a fairly objective index of settlement.

In the past four decades many cities have registered major population declines; in St. Louis the net reduction has been 270,000 or 30 per cent of the total. Between 1960 and 1970, Philadelphia fell from 2,003,000 to 1,927,000; Detroit from 1,670,000 to 1,493,000; Baltimore from 939,000 to 894,000; and San Francisco from 740,000 to 704,000. By 1950, most of the nation's big cities and all but one north of the Ohio River and east of the Mississippi River had attained their maximum densities; Manhattan actually reached its peak residential size in 1910 and Newark and Jersey City in 1930. This absolute decline is often cited as the most dramatic evidence that our cities are dying.[33]

Residential decline in the urban core is not, however, peculiar to the twentieth century.[34] In Philadelphia, the seven wards of the old city between Vine and South Streets that bordered the Delaware River (Wards five and six after the 1854 consolidation), taken as a group, reached their all-time population peak in 1830. Moreover, if allowance is made for the re-alignment of their western boundaries in 1825 from Fourth Street to Seventh Street, then the Chestnut and Walnut Wards apparently reached maximum residential densities about 1820 (Table 3-3), and the old High Street Ward actually recorded its peak population in 1800, the first census in which Philadelphia ward totals were reported. The process accelerated after the Civil War, and between 1860 and 1890 the two innermost wards were joined by nine additional wards in population decline.[35]

This phenomenon is not unique to Philadelphia. In New York City, the area south of Canal Street has been declining in residential density since 1850; the population of the second ward dropped particularly dramatically from 9,300 in 1825 to 3,300 in 1860.[36] In Boston, six out

[33] Cities outside the urbanized northeast and middle west, such as Savannah, Birmingham, Little Rock, and Chattanooga, have also recently suffered an absolute population loss.

[34] Many small towns (none of them suburbs, of course) in the northeast were losing population early in the nineteenth century. George Rogers Taylor, "American Urban Growth Preceding the Railway Age," *Journal of Economic History* 27 (September 1967), pp. 309-339.

[35] The process has continued in Philadelphia to the present. The city gained population until 1950 only because newer areas gained enough to offset the spreading section of decline at the core. Hans Blumenfeld errs in dating the initial period of downtown population loss between 1860 and 1890. Blumenfeld, "Tidal Wave," pp. 3-15.

[36] A vapid and superficial analysis of New York's experience is Frederick P. Clark, "Concentration and Decentralization in the New York Metropolitan Region," *Journal of the American Institute of Planners* 16 (Fall 1970), pp. 172-178.

123

TABLE 3-3 DECENNIAL POPULATION CHANGES OF PHILADELPHIA'S
INNER CITY WARDS, 1800-1860

	1800	1810	1820	1830	1840	1850	1860	1870	1880
Before Adjustment[a]									
Lower Delaware	3,377	3,526	3,237	6,863	5,996	6,425			
High Street	2,792	2,764	2,529	4,427	3,200	3,549			
Chestnut	2,693	2,732	2,930	4,115	2,639	2,443			
Walnut	2,169	2,306	2,817	3,428	2,405	2,544	(Wards 5 and 6)		
Dock	2,235	2,170	2,415	5,378	4,533	5,734			
Upper Delaware	3,067	3,644	3,396	5,763	5,783	7,224			
New Market	4,865	5,512	5,892	12,983	12,972	14,405			
Total	21,198	22,654	23,216	42,957	37,528	42,324	39,674	30,800	26,376
After Adjustment									
Lower Delaware	3,377	3,526	3,237	3,920	3,426	3,672			
High Street	2,792	2,764	2,529	2,528	1,828	2,028			
Chestnut	2,693	2,732	2,930	2,352	1,508	1,396			
Walnut	2,169	2,306	2,817	1,960	1,374	1,454	(Wards 5 and 6)		
Dock	2,235	2,170	2,415	3,074	2,590	3,276			
Upper Delaware	3,067	3,644	3,396	3,295	3,304	4,128			
New Market	4,865	5,512	5,892	7,418	7,412	8,232			
Total	21,198	22,654	23,216	24,548	21,444	24,185	22,672	17,600	15,072

[a] The ward totals are underlined for the census in which an all-time maximum population density is indicated. The totals given in the Before Adjustment column are those reported by the census. The figures in the After Adjustment column equal four-sevenths of the official total as listed from 1830 through 1850. This alteration, which was first applied by William Hastings for a smaller number of wards over a shorter period, takes account of the extension of ward boundaries from Fourth Street to Seventh Street in 1825.

SOURCE: Various U.S. Decennial Census Returns and John Daly and Allen Weinberg, *Genealogy of Philadelphia County Subdivisions* (Philadelphia: Department of Records, 1966), pp. 92-100.

of twelve wards showed a decrease in population between 1857 and 1867. In St. Louis and Baltimore, the central areas were also losing people while Abraham Lincoln was still a little-known Illinois politician.[37] Newer and smaller cities exhibited the same tendency at a slightly later date. Thus, the five innermost wards of Memphis all lost population between 1890 and 1910 while peripheral wards were registering gains of more than 400 per cent.[38]

To be sure, this pattern represents the expansion and differentiation of the Central Business District and the resulting encroachment of warehouses, factories, and offices upon formerly residential areas.

[37] In Chicago, the population within two miles of the business center reached its peak in 1890 and subsequently declined. Homer Hoyt, *The Structure and Growth of Residential Neighborhoods in the United States* (Washington: Housing and Home Finance Agency, 1939), p. 92. See also, Chicago Community Inventory, *Growth and Redistribution of the Resident Population in the Chicago Standard Metropolitan Area* (Chicago: Chicago Community Inventory, 1954), pp. 18-19.

[38] Inner areas of London and Dublin were losing residents by 1860, and in London eleven of thirty districts contained fewer persons in 1891 than in 1881. After 1891, the administrative County of London lost population.

Thus, population loss historically indicates not declining land use, but increasing congestion. One way to analyze this phenomenon would be to measure the changing intensity of land use as reflected by the amount of floor-space per acre or square mile. Such a floor-area calculation would give a more detailed picture of the kind of urban structure man has built for himself than would a residential index.[39]

Unfortunately, floor-area measurements are not readily available for most cities, and it is therefore difficult to determine whether housing demolition is to clear land for automobiles to maneuver and park (deconcentration) or to make available large plots for office buildings or institutions (concentration). This distinction is particularly important when land has important nonresidential uses. By a population measure, the island of Manhattan has been declining absolutely since 1910 and relative to its suburbs since 1800. A floor-area calculation, on the other hand, reveals that Manhattan remains the world's most intensively developed urban space and is becoming more concentrated every year. A single square mile in midtown New York contains 173 million square feet of floor space; only the Wall Street financial district and the Chicago Loop are as much as half as dense.[40]

In Manhattan as elsewhere, much of what passes for deconcentration actually represents the expansion and concentration of commercial and business organizations. Indeed, it is almost axiomatic that in any successful metropolis nonresidential uses of land will force population outward. In the absence of areal expansion even suburbs will often lose population.[41] This experience suggests that the centrifugal growth of American cities since 1820 represents not deconcentration, but rather, as Edgar Kant observes, a modified form of concentration.

DEFINITION IV

Urban deconcentration is a process of population redistribution that results in a positive and direct correlation between increasing

[39] On the importance of measuring the intensity of nonresidential land use, see Otis Dudley Duncan, "Human Ecology and Population Studies," in Philip M. Hauser and Otis Dudley Duncan (editors), *The Study of Population: An Inventory and Appraisal* (Chicago: University of Chicago Press, 1959), pp. 696-698.

[40] The entire 10 1/2-square-mile area of central London contains only 113 million square feet of office space. In New York, the Battery Park City complex will be a concentrating force because it will add 50,000 residents to the Wall Street area on a Hudson River landfill. The New York figures are from the 1969 City Plan; the London figures are from Hall, *World Cities*, pp. 32-33.

[41] Some London suburbs were losing population by 1911. American suburbs which have declined absolutely in population since 1950 include Hamtramck and Highland Park, enclaves within Detroit; Mount Vernon and Passaic near New York City; and Harvey and Cicero near Chicago.

socioeconomic status and increasing distance of residence from the central business district. This definition suggests that what is most significant about suburbanization is not the number of the out-migrants but their race and social class. Between 1950 and 1970 every central city in the nation's twelve largest metropolitan areas lost white residents and gained black citizens. Generally, the new city-dwellers were less affluent than the new suburbanites.[42] In *The Unheavenly City*, Professor Edward Banfield asserted a certain inevitability to this process: "The logic of growth does require that, in general, the lowest-income people live in the oldest, highest-density, most run-down housing."

The pattern, which in the United States is subsidized by the federal government, is a familiar one. First, businesses, industries, and individuals move out of the inner city—some because of taxes, others for need of more space, others for fear of minority groups. Low-income families move into the vacated apartments; they typically require services from the city government several times as costly as those provided the old residents. Thus the city government must increase expenditures. Additional taxes become necessary, and the cycle repeats itself. As a result, as Nathaniel Burt has said of Philadelphia, "the gentry, in a proportion of ten to one, live out of the city and prefer to stay there."[43]

Professor Banfield notwithstanding, there is nothing particularly inevitable or natural in this spatial structure. Contemporary cities all over the world, from Johannesburg and Durban to Vienna and Paris to Rio de Janeiro and Caracas, continue to offer a contrary pattern.[44] And prior to 1840 the most fashionable and respectable addresses in America's large cities tended to be located as close as possible to the center of town. In late-eighteenth-century Philadelphia, for example, the wealthy sought residences in the heart of the old city, not on the edges.[45] Meanwhile, the city's first suburb, Southwark,

---

[42] In New York City alone, the number of persons on some form of public assistance rose from about 4 per cent of the total population in 1960 to about 14 per cent in 1970.

[43] Nathaniel Burt, *The Perennial Philadelphians: The Anatomy of an American Aristocracy* (Boston: Little, Brown and Company, 1963), p. 11.

[44] There is some evidence to suggest that the American ecological pattern is beginning to appear elsewhere. Leo F. Schnore, "On the Spatial Structure of Cities in the Two Americas," in Philip M. Hauser and Leo F. Schnore (editors), *The Study of Urbanization* (New York: John Wiley and Sons, 1965), pp. 347-398. An exception to the normal nineteenth-century pattern was Manchester, where in the 1840's the middle and upper classes lived farther from the center than did the working class. Friedrich Engels, *The Condition of the Working Class in England* (New York: Macmillan, 1958), pp. 54-55.

[45] The residential location of church members of varying status is traced in Norman J. Johnston, "The Caste and Class of the Urban Form of Historic

TABLE 3-4 OCCUPATIONAL DISTRIBUTION, DISTRICT OF SOUTH-
WARK PHILADELPHIA COUNTY, PENNSYLVANIA 1790[a]

White-collar 26%		Blue-collar 74%			
Sea Captains	37	Laborers	128	Beekeepers	4
Merchants	26	Ship carpenters	56	Cabinetmakers	4
Innkeepers	22	Mariners	45	Plasterers	4
Grocers	20	Shoemakers	39	Painters	4
Shopkeepers	18	House carpenters	32	Porters	4
Schoolteachers	15	Tailors	30	Ship joiners	4
Pilots	14	Blacksmiths	29	Carters	3
Lodgehousekeepers	11	Coopers	26	Caulkers	3
Gentlemen	10	Weavers	17	Mantua makers	3
Gentlewomen	7	Bakers	15	Brewers	3
Clerks	5	Ropemakers	15	Wheelwrights	3
Doctors	4	Mates	12	Silversmiths	3
Justices of Peace	4	Joiner and cabinet		Sailmakers	3
Ministers	4	makers	11	Nailors	2
Tobacconists	3	Bricklayers	7	Potters	2
Attorneys	2	Ship caulkers	7	Tinmen	2
Constables	2	Butchers	6	Printers	2
Auctioneer	1	Mastmakers	5	Barbers	2
Broker	1	Seamstresses	5	Shallop men	2
Beerhouse keeper	1	Boatbuilders	4	Miscellaneous	25
Customs Officer	1			Total	571
Inspector	1				
Nurse	1	*Non-classifiable*			
Sheriff	1	Occupation not specified	207		
Supervisor	1	Spinsters and widows	34		
Surgeon barber	1	Free Blacks	221		
Total	213	Slaves	21		
		Total	483		

[a] The 1267 heads of families seems reasonable if compared to the total population of 5661 for the district in 1790. If anything, my percentages are weighted toward the white-collar side as all questionable occupations were listed under that category.

SOURCE: United States Bureau of the Census, *Heads of Families at the First Census of the United States Taken in the Year 1790. Pennsylvania* (Washington: Government Printing Office, 1908), pp. 208-214.

was populated mainly by artisans—carpenters, shoemakers, tailors—or persons whose life was in one way or another connected with the sea (Table 3-4).[46] Although not yet the slum it would later become, Southwark counted very few men of wealth or position among its

Philadelphia," *Journal of the American Institute of Planners* 32 (November 1966), pp. 334-349.

[46] Southwark, named for the London suburb guarding the "south work" of London Bridge, was settled by Swedes in 1638, forty-four years before Philadelphia was born. It was created a municipality in 1762 and incorporated in 1794. On the history of this community on Philadelphia's southern fringe, see M. Antonia Lynch, "The Old District of Southwark in the County of Philadelphia,"

residents. With fewer than four times as many citizens as Southwark in 1790, Philadelphia contained twelve times as many physicians, thirteen times as many merchants and dealers, and twelve times as many lawyers as the suburban community.[47]

Southwark, like other early suburbs, had little status, in part because mass transportation was in a primitive state and in part because of a long-established tradition in both England and America of forcing unwanted businesses such as slaughterhouses, leather dressers, and houses of prostitution out to the periphery.[48] As one observer noted as late as the mid-nineteenth century, "nine-tenths of those whose rascalities have made Philadelphia so unjustly notorious live in the dens and shanties of the suburbs."[49] Thus, decreasing desirability of location corresponded with increasing distance from the center. The primary exception to this pattern was the preference of the gentry for a country home, but this was a seasonal adjustment to escape the heat and threat of disease in the city in the summer months rather than an all-year residential abode. As might be expected, most urban blacks, whether in the south under slavery or in the north under a restricted freedom, tended to live toward the fringe.[50]

In the largest American cities, the shift in relative residential status between suburb and core began before 1860. In mid-century Philadelphia, the built-up area extended over about ten square miles, and the most important axis of growth was out Ridge Avenue toward

Philadelphia History 1 (1909), pp. 83-126; and *Southwark, Moyamensing, Weccacoe, Passyunk, Dock Ward for Two Hundred and Seventy Years* (Philadelphia: Quaker City Publishing Company, 1892).

[47] This author made a complete occupational breakdown of Southwark in 1790 because that was the year of the first census. The analysis was not continued into the nineteenth century because Philadelphia began to grow more toward the north and west and Southwark was no longer part of the developing fringe. The 1790 comparison with Philadelphia was made by John K. Alexander, "The City of Brotherly Fear: The Poor in Late Eighteenth-Century Philadelphia," in Kenneth T. Jackson and Stanley K. Schultz (editors), *Cities in American History* (New York: Alfred A. Knopf, 1972), p. 93.

[48] For example, see I. N. Phelps Stokes (editor), *Iconography of Manhattan Island* (New York: Robert H. Dodd, 1928), 1, pp. 162 and 197; and Justin Winsor (editor), *The Memorial History of Boston, 1630–1880* (Boston: Ticknor and Co., 1881), p. 595. The dance halls and brothels of early Wichita and Abilene were also on the outskirts; Robert R. Dykstra, *The Cattle Towns* (New York: Alfred A. Knopf, 1969), p. 233.

[49] George Rogers Taylor (editor), "Philadelphia in Slices: The Diary of George G. Foster," *Pennsylvania Magazine of History and Biography* 93 (January 1969), pp. 34, 39, and 41.

[50] In Philadelphia, the black population moved relatively, but not absolutely, closer to the center between 1811 and 1858. Johnston, "Caste and Class," *passim.* See also, Richard C. Wade, *Slavery in the Cities: The South, 1820-1860* (New York: Oxford University Press, 1965), pp. 69-70.

TABLE 3-5 OCCUPATIONAL DISTRIBUTION, DISTRICT OF PENN
(SOUTH PENN) PHILADELPHIA COUNTY, PENNSYLVANIA, 1850[a]

New Middle Class[a] 12.5%		Artisans 49.3%		Unskilled 38.2%	
Storekeepers	4	Carpenters	13	Laborers	33
Merchants	4	Bricklayers	8	Carters	13
Hotelkeepers	3	Shoemakers	8	Miscellaneous	12
Tobacconists	2	Brickmakers	4	Total	58
Clerks	2	Cabinetmakers	4		
Accountant	1	Tailors	4		
Horse-doctor	1	Machinists	3	Percentage	38.2
Manufacturer	1	Dyers	3		
Salesman	1	Blacksmiths	3		
Total	19	Jewelers	3		
		Hatters	2		
		Painters	2		
Percentage	12.5	Foremen	2		
		Farmers	2		
		Sashmakers	2		
		Weavers	2		
		Miscellaneous	10		
		Total	75		
		Percentage	49.3		

[a] By a systematic random-sampling procedure, 10 per cent of the total number
of households in the district were sampled. If the occupation of more than one
family member was given, that of the individual listed first was recorded.

[b] The classifications are those suggested by Sam Bass Warner in *The Private
City: Philadelphia in Three Periods of Its Growth* (Philadelphia: University of
Pennsylvania Press, 1968), pp. 64-65. Professor Herbert Gutman has advised me
regarding the skills of certain of these occupations.

SOURCE: U. S. Bureau of the Census, *Population Schedules of the Seventh Census
of the United States, 1850. Pennsylvania.*

the northwest. A systematic random sample of 10 per cent of the heads
of households listed on the manuscript census schedules of Penn District in 1850 and 1860, when that area was directly in the path of
advancing settlement (Tables 3-5 and 3-6), suggests the increasing
status of peripheral residence. Artisans and unskilled workers, most
of whom walked to jobs in the adjacent industrial suburbs of Spring
Garden and Kensington, were the dominant group in both 1850 and
1860.[51] But as the population soared in the decade, the proportion
of merchants, manufacturers, physicians, and grocers, the "new middle
class" in Sam Warner's phrase, approximately doubled.[52] After the

[51] Penn District was an exporter of workers in 1860, whereas Spring Garden
was an importer. Warner, *Private City*, pp. 60 and 135.

[52] Stuart Blumin has published a sophisticated and interesting analysis of occupational and residential mobility in Philadelphia between 1820 and 1860. He errs,
however, in suggesting that residential movement toward the periphery represented

TABLE 3-6   OCCUPATIONAL DISTRIBUTION, DISTRICT OF PENN
(WARD 20) CITY OF PHILADELPHIA, PENNSYLVANIA, 1860[a]

New Middle Class 26.9%		Artisans 48.4%		Unskilled 24.7%	
Clerks	31	Shoemakers	36	Laborers	69
Merchants	29	Carpenters	33	Car Drivers	7
Grocers	24	Tailors	19	Dressmakers	5
Manufacturers	14	Blacksmiths	15	Conductors	4
Physicians	5	Machinists	10	Paper Hangers	4
Contractors	4	Brickmakers	9	Carters	4
Realtors	4	Butchers	9	Coopers	3
Teachers	4	Moulders	7	Gasworks makers	3
Hotelkeepers	4	Stone masons	7	Tin workers	3
Attorneys	3	Cabinetmakers	7	Domestics	2
Druggists	3	Painters	7	Hatters	2
Clergymen	3	Coachmakers	6	Tanners	2
Chemists	2	Printers	6	Gardeners	2
Gentlemen	2	Jewelers	5	Morocco dressers	2
Tobacconists	2	Plasterers	5	Miscellaneous	16
Millers	2	Saddlers	5	Total	128
Traveling Agents	2	Bakers	4	Percentage	24.7
Miscellaneous	5	Ropemakers	4		
Total	141	Brewers	4		
Percentage	26.9	Stone cutters	4		
		Weavers	4		
		Wheelwrights	4		
		Three Each	12		
		Two Each	18		
		Miscellaneous	13		
		Total	255		
		Percentage	48.4		

[a] Both the methodology and the classification system are the same as those employed in Table 3-5.

SOURCE: U.S. Bureau of the Census, *Population Schedules of the Eighth Census of the United States, 1860. Pennsylvania.*

Civil War the number of commuters to the Central Business District continued to increase as more and more businessmen opted for "all the beauties of the country, within an easy and cheap communication with the city."[53]

If anything, residential analyses tend to understate the extent to

---

downward mobility, while movement toward the center certified increasing status. Certainly after 1850 and probably as early as 1840, the precise opposite was true. See his essay in Stephan Thernstrom and Richard Sennett (eds.), *Nineteenth Century Cities: Essays in the New Urban History* (New Haven: Yale University Press, 1969).

[53] Daniel Bowen, *A History of Philadelphia, with a notice of villages in the vicinity* (Philadelphia: Daniel Bowen, 1839), p. 183.

which suburban areas were becoming the preserve of the elite. In
the Boston area, the Chestnut Hill section of Newton was well on
its way toward attracting "the best class of residents" and becoming
"the most select of all Boston's First Family suburbs" in the 1850's.[54]
Throughout the latter part of the nineteenth century the town maintained an almost feudal image, and observers noted only the brilliant
sector of Chestnut Hill life.[55] But a careful analysis of Newton tax
lists and city directories for the period between 1850 and 1890 reveals
that a substantial portion of the heads of households (a maximum
of 39 per cent in 1875 and a minimum of 23 per cent in 1891) in
Chestnut Hill consisted of laborers, gardeners, and domestic servants.[56]
As it evolved into an upper-class community, it became a neighborhood
of economic extremes. Although the average taxable income and property were high and increasing, almost half the population paid no
tax or only a head tax. This disparity occurred because the extreme
economic segregation of the modern city had not yet fully taken
hold; the physical proximity of the poor was an advantage that was
not opposed by the barons of Chestnut Hill.

The movement of the affluent toward Germantown in Philadelphia
and Chestnut Hill near Boston was duplicated in other metropolitan
areas. In San Francisco, the city's bankers, merchants, and doctors
moved away from the downtown area between 1850 and 1860 and
put their new homes on the heights of Fern (Nob) and Russian
Hills. And after the establishment of steamboat and ferry service
on San Francisco Bay, Oakland and Alameda joined the competition
for citizens and quickly garnered a reputation as "steamboat
suburbs."[57] Because of competition from Brooklyn, newspaper editors
in New York were complaining as early as 1849 of "the desertion
of the city by its men of wealth." In Chicago, most of the high-grade
residential areas were still very near the center at the time of the
Civil War, but a tendency for the fashionable to move toward the

[54] Henry K. Rowe, *Tercentenary History of Boston, 1630–1930* (Newton, Massachusetts: City Clerk Department, 1931), pp. 168-169; and Cleveland Amory,
The Proper Bostonians (New York: E. P. Dutton, 1947), p. 106.

[55] The geographic area studied was constructed from the memoir of Mary
Lee, *A History of Chestnut Hill Chapel* (Newton, Mass.: Historical Committee
of the First Church in Chestnut Hill, 1937).

[56] Tax lists indicated not only the actual tax, but also the amount of taxable
property and income of each independent adult or head of household. The
value of land was also indicated. The compilations and tables are omitted;
they were put together by Julia Weinstein Tossell.

[57] Roger Lotchin, "San Francisco, 1846-1856: The Patterns and Chaos of
Growth," in Jackson and Schultz (editors), *Cities in American History*, pp.
151-160.

131

periphery was already apparent.[58] In almost every large city, the merchant princes and millionaires were searching for the hilltops and shore lands to build country estates; crowded cities offered fewer attractions with every passing year.[59]

The development of the typical urban pattern of peripheral affluence and central despair, which, as we have seen, began in the middle of the nineteenth century, can be traced to many causes. An important factor was the transformation of the nation's traditional rural ideal into a suburban ideal, a circumstance which owed much to the efforts of prominent landscape architects like Andrew Jackson Downing and Frederick Law Olmsted.[60] It also owed even more to the environmental deterioration of the city itself. The increasing size of factories and industrial operations, coupled with an influx of poor European immigrants and their settlement on the edges of the expanding business districts, served to create urban problems on an unprecedented scale. Who could forget the rancid odors of decaying garbage and animal waste that rose from the streets and pervaded the atmosphere, or the horrors of congestion and confusion that accompanied the head-on meetings of uncontrollable animals and unregulated pedestrians.

Then as now, many people preferred the lower taxes, the additional *lebensraum*, or the purer air of a less congested environment. As Sidney Low described the typical suburb-dweller of 1890: "If he does not live in the fields, he may have the fields at his door; he may be able to stretch his limbs by a walk over a breezy common, and get the smoke of the city out of his lungs by a ramble down a country lane."[61] But suburbanites wanted the best of both worlds; they sought to be "removed from the bustle of the city, and yet within a few minutes' ride of it." They wanted to separate work and residence, the

[58] Two sets of maps constructed by Homer Hoyt reveal an upper-class suburban trend by 1873 that had become widespread by 1899. Hoyt, *One Hundred Years of Land Values in Chicago* (Chicago: University of Chicago Press, 1933), Chapter 6.

[59] Zane L. Miller carefully describes the spatial patterns of residential growth in Cincinnati and interprets the city's turn-of-the-century political experience in terms of the interaction of these areas. The periphery was the high status or "hilltop" area. Miller, *Boss Cox's Cincinnati: Urban Politics in the Progressive Era* (New York: Oxford University Press, 1968), pp. 18-43.

[60] The popularization of the suburban ideal in the Progressive Era is treated in Peter J. Schmitt, *Back to Nature: The Arcadian Myth in Urban America* (New York: Oxford University Press, 1969). See also Jackson, "The Crabgrass Frontier," pp. 203-205.

[61] Sidney J. Low, "The Rise of the Suburbs," *The Contemporary Review* 60 (1891), p. 553.

city and the country. For this, they needed a mass transportation system, which brings us to our final definition.

DEFINITION V

Urban deconcentration is a process of population redistribution that results in increasing geographical distance between place of work and place of residence.
According to this interpretation, suburbanization requires that, over time, the average citizen commute increasing distances to work. Scholars generally agree that before 1800 the usual pattern was for urban residents to rest and to labor in close proximity—often in the same building. Because the easiest, cheapest, and most common method of getting about was by foot, there was a significant advantage, even for the affluent, in living within easy walking distance of the city's stores and businesses.

The lengthening journey to work of the average metropolitan resident over the past century and a half is obviously related to transportation technology. In a pioneering study of Boston's *Streetcar Suburbs* in the years between 1870 and 1900, Sam Bass Warner has documented the role of electrified transit in expanding the built-up radius of the old walking city.[62] The role of the private automobile and multi-lane expressway in the twentieth century in extending the urban boundaries even farther surely requires no special preachment; advances and innovations in mass transit in the three decades before the Civil War were just as important in encouraging suburbanization.

The achievement of the omnibus or horse-drawn bus, which was introduced in New York in the late 1820's, was that by lumbering along a fixed route according to a regular schedule and at an established price it made feasible the separation of place of work and place of residence.[63] Travel aboard such crude apparatus required a tolerance for cramped cars and bumpy rides, as well as a certain flexibility in working hours and an ability to pay perhaps ten cents per day in fares.[64] Placing the cars on rails in the late 1850s increased

[62] Warner, *Streetcar Suburbs: The Process of Urban Growth in Boston, 1870–1900* (Cambridge: Harvard University Press, 1962). See also, David Ward, "A Comparative Historical Geography of Streetcar Suburbs in Boston, Massachusetts and Leeds, England, 1850-1920," *Annals of the Association of American Geographers* 104 (1964), pp. 477-489.

[63] George Rogers Taylor, "The Beginnings of Mass Transportation in Urban America: Part I," *Smithsonian Journal of History* 1 (1966), pp. 35-52.

[64] The best study of passenger conditions on early forms of such vehicles is Glen E. Holt, "The Changing Perception of Urban Pathology: An Essay on the Development of Mass Transit in the United States," in *Cities in American History*, pp. 324-343.

133

the comfort, speed, and popularity of the vehicles; in New York City alone the number of streetcar passengers increased from less than seven million in 1853 to more than thirty-six million in 1860.[65]

Commuter traffic aboard steam railroads also grew at astonishing rates before the Civil War. Using such inducements as reduced fare for season tickets and family plans, the seven steam railroads serving Boston had managed to persuade perhaps 10 per cent of the area's work force to use the rails regularly by 1860, and had converted such quiet villages as Dorchester, Dedham, Quincy, Brighton, Newton, Medford, and Malden into "railroad suburbs."[66] The New York and Harlem and the Long Island Railroads provided similar service to lower Manhattan in the 1840s, and the Philadelphia, Germantown, and Norristown Railroad was the major commuter line into Philadelphia.[67]

My analysis of journey-to-work patterns is based upon an examination of the experience of Philadelphia merchants and bank presidents between 1829 and 1862, of New York attorneys between 1825 and 1915, and of Louisville businessmen and community leaders between 1865 and 1961. The methodology for examining Definition V is, therefore, the calculation of distance between work and residence for individuals. The emphasis in testing Definitions I through IV was upon "net" changes in population distribution. Unfortunately, a very small "net" change may conceal substantial residential mobility. An intensive analysis of population movement in Boston between 1830 and 1860 has shown that there were only very slight differences in the *total* numbers of people moving from the periphery to the center and vice versa, but that individual mobility was quite high. Peter R. Knights found that even though net demographic trends indicated deconcentration, most of the intra-Boston area moves were of a concentrating

[65] Harry J. Carman, *The Street Railway Franchises of New York* (New York: Columbia University Press, 1919), p. 145; Frederic W. Speirs, "The Street Railway System of Philadelphia: Its History and Present Conditions," *Johns Hopkins Studies in History and Political Science* 15 (1897), pp. 9-10; and Norman H. Keyser, "Early Transportation to Germantown," *Germantown History* (Philadelphia: Germantown Site and Relic Society, 1915), pp. 39-55.

[66] In 1855, however, one finds the contemporary problem of railroads losing money on commuter operations. Charles J. Kennedy, "Commuter Services in the Boston Area, 1835-1860," *Business History Review* 36 (Summer 1962), pp. 153-170.

[67] In Philadelphia and New York, local regulations required that horsepower rather than steam power be used to pull trains through thickly settled areas. Stations tended, therefore, to be some distance from the business core. Joseph Warren Greene, Jr., "New York City's First Railroad, The New York and Harlem, 1832 to 1867," *New York Historical Society Quarterly Bulletin* 9 (January 1926), pp. 107-123.

nature.[68] He concluded that for most five-year periods, however, suburbanizing moves slightly outnumbered those of a centralizing nature.[69]

In Philadelphia, as Figures 3-3 and 3-4 illustrate, the three decades before the Civil War, when mass transit systems were first developed, witnessed a significant movement of merchants and bankers toward the Schuylkill River in the western part of the city or toward Germantown northwest of Vine Street.[70] Between 1829 and 1862, the proportion of merchants living away from their stores and the average length of commutation approximately doubled. Similarly, the typical bank president, who had to live away from his office under any circumstances, also traveled about twice as far to work in 1862 as in 1829. Philadelphia's banks and large stores remained concentrated east of Seventh Street, but the fine residential districts moved progressively farther away.

In New York City, where the transit system was more extensive and population growth more rapid than in Philadelphia, the separation of work and residence proceeded even more swiftly, at least among the middle and upper classes.[71] An examination of the journey-to-work patterns of one hundred randomly selected Manhattan attorneys at ten-year intervals between 1825 and 1915 reveals that in terms of percentage increase of length of commutation, the most important decade was 1835-1845. Among the lawyers who lived in Manhattan or the Bronx (see Table 3-7), the average journey to work tripled

[68] This disparity was caused by the tendency of in-migrants to the metropolitan area to settle first on the periphery. Peter R. Knights, *The Plain People of Boston, 1830-1860: A Study in City Growth* (New York: Oxford University Press, 1971).

[69] Two other significant studies of residential mobility are Howard Chudacoff, *Mobile Americans: Residential Mobility in Omaha, 1880-1920* (New York: Oxford University Press, 1972); and Stephan A. Thernstrom and Peter R. Knights, "Men in Motion: Some Data and Speculations About Urban Population Mobility in Nineteenth-Century America," *Journal of Interdisciplinary History* 1 (Autumn 1970), pp. 7-35.

[70] The map of bankers' journey to work is not included because it is substantially similar to that of the merchants. Both groups were identified by lists at the back of the 1829 and 1862 city directories. The address of their place of business was then compared with their residence and a straight line drawn between the two. The two merchant samples are not precisely comparable because the 1862 directory was more exact about type of merchant than was the 1829 directory, which identified persons simply as "merchant." Lumber, china, glass, cotton, dry goods, and iron merchants were selected for the 1862 analysis.

[71] For roughly this same early nineteenth-century period, Allan R. Pred has found that Manhattan blue-collar workers who could best afford the time and money to commute tended to live farther from their place of employment than less skilled workers. Allan R. Pred, *The Spatial Dynamics of Urban Industrial Growth, 1800-1914* (Cambridge: M.I.T. Press, 1966), pp. 336-338.

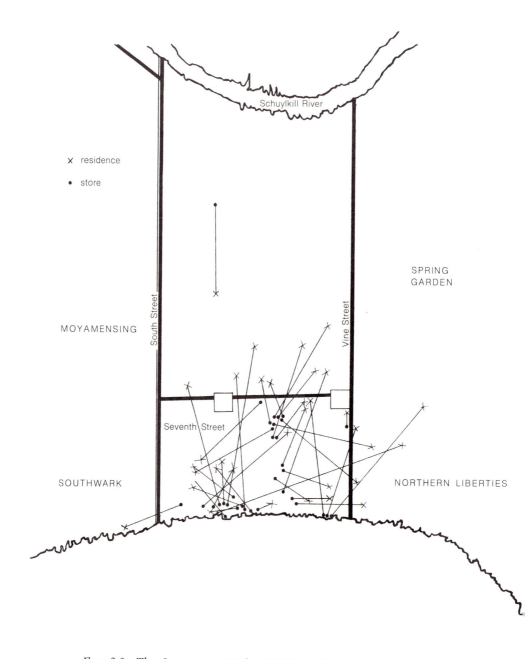

FIG. 3-3 The Journey to Work of Philadelphia Merchants, 1829. Forty-two persons of a sample size of eighty-six commuted and were plotted.
  SOURCE: *DeSilver's Philadelphia Directory and Stranger's Guide, 1829* (Philadelphia: Robert DeSilver, 1829).

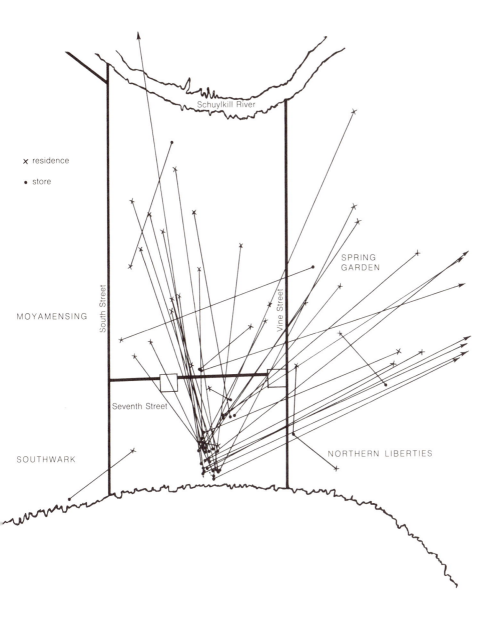

Schuylkill River

x residence

• store

MOYAMENSING

South Street

Vine Street

SPRING
GARDEN

Seventh Street

SOUTHWARK

NORTHERN LIBERTIES

FIG. 3-4 The Journey to Work of 56 Randomly Selected Philadelphia Lumber, China, Glass, Cotton, Dry Goods, and Iron Merchants. Seven men lived and worked at the same address and eight could not be plotted.

SOURCE: *McElroy's Philadelphia City Directory for 1862* (Philadelphia: E. C. and J. Biddle and Company, 1862).

TABLE 3-7   DISTANCE BETWEEN WORK AND RESIDENCE OF
MANHATTAN ATTORNEYS, BY DECADES[d]

Year	Number[a] Sample	Percentage Living in Brooklyn or N.J.	Increase in Brooklyn (%)[b]	Distance between Work and Residence of Attorneys Living Manhattan or Bronx[c]	Decennial Increase in Miles for Attorneys Living Manhattan or Bronx	Decennial Increase in % for Attorneys Living Manhattan or Bronx
1825	88	1.1%		.67 miles		
1835	84	2.3	110%	.81	.14 miles	20%
1845	84	14.2	510	1.39	.58	71
1855	97	21.6	52	1.80	.42	30
1865	99	35.3	63	2.43	.62	34
1875	100	45.2	28	2.91	.48	19
1885	100	47.0	3	2.97	.06	2
1895	96	34.4	−26	3.78	.81	27
1905	87	22.1	−35	5.57	1.79	47
1915	94	9.6	−56	7.48	1.91	34

[a] The sample size falls below one hundred on several occasions because the residences of some lawyers could not be located.

[b] The distance between work and residence of those living in Brooklyn and New Jersey was not plotted.

[c] The figures in this section are only for those attorneys living in either Manhattan or the Bronx.

[d] This table summarizes a portion of the data gathered by William Meyers in two seminars at Columbia.

SOURCE: Longworth's City Directories for the above dates.

between 1835 and 1865; it required another half-century for the figure to triple again.[72] The three decades between 1865 and 1895 were a time of relatively little increase, but the electrification of the streetcar lines in the 1890's and the rapid extension of the elevated and subway systems early in the century apparently encouraged a doubling of the distance between place of work and place of residence between 1895 and 1915.[73]

The New York data also indicate something of the changing popularity of Brooklyn as a place of residence for the city's professional

[72] The attorneys sampled were those listed on every fifth page of the relevant Manhattan directories. The calculations were made by William H. Meyers in my graduate seminar at Columbia University.

[73] Three of the better studies of the relationship between transit and residence are James W. Simmons, "Changing Residence in the City: A Review of Intra-Urban Mobility," *Geographical Review* 58 (October 1968), pp. 622-651; George M. Smerk, "The Streetcar: Shaper of American Cities," *Traffic Quarterly* 21 (1967), pp. 569-584; and Oliver Zunz, "Technology and Society in an Urban Environment: The Case of the Third Avenue Elevated Railway," *Journal of Interdisciplinary History* 3 (Summer 1972), pp. 89-102.

elite. As early as 1823, land developers were advertising the heights across the East River as a place with "all the advantages of the country with most of the conveniences of the city." With regular and dependable ferry service to Fulton Street, Brooklyn was particularly attractive to Manhattan attorneys who sought a degree of solitude for their families. As Table 3-7 indicates, the huge suburb was the home of 47 per cent of New York's lawyers in 1885. The opening of the Brooklyn Bridge in 1883, however, reduced the borough's appeal to the elite, who turned increasingly to upper Manhattan and the Bronx. By 1915, less than 10 per cent of New York's (Gotham's) attorneys called Brooklyn home.[74]

TABLE 3-8 AVERAGE DISTANCE BETWEEN DOWNTOWN LOUISVILLE AND RESIDENCES OF MEMBERS OF PENDENNIS CLUB, 1865-1961

Year	Membership	Average Distance in Miles	Increase in Miles Since Previous Reading	Percentage Increase Since Previous Reading
1865	43[a]	0.73[b]		
1890	299	1.16	0.43	58.9%
1923	550	2.57	1.41	121.6
1961	398	5.08	2.51	97.7

[a] Although the club was not established until 1881, 43 members in 1890 were found in the 1865 city directory.

[b] Distances were measured from Fourth and Broadway.

SOURCE: *Roster of the Pendennis Club, 1881-1947* (Louisville, 1947); and *The Louisville Blue Book, 1923; Edward's 1865 Directory of Louisville;* and *Caron's Directories for 1890 and 1961.*

The separation of work and residence that proceeded so dramatically in Philadelphia and New York in the early part of the nineteenth century took somewhat longer to develop in smaller cities. In Louisville, for example, an analysis of community and social leaders in 1865, 1890, 1923, and 1961 reveals some sharp differences from the Manhattan data. For Louisville, members of the prestigious Pendennis Club, founded in 1881, were selected as representative of trend-setters in the community. As in Philadelphia and New York, place of work was compared with place of residence and the resulting distance calculated in miles. As Table 3-8 illustrates, high-status Louisvillians lived only 1.16 miles from the center of the business district in 1890,

[74] New Jersey commuters are included in the Brooklyn total, but their numbers were never more than 10 per cent of the larger figure.

when the city's population was slightly over 161,000.[75] Even that distance, however, represents a 59 per cent increase in the journey to work over the 1865 measurement. Between 1890 and 1923 the suburban trend becomes clear. By the later date, many members of the Pendennis Club had moved to Cherokee Road in The Highlands, several miles from the urban core.[76] In those thirty-three years, the era of the electrified streetcar, the average distance between place of residence and the corner of Fourth and Broadway increased on a percentage basis more than it did in the thirty-eight years between 1923 and 1961, when mass transit was in precipitous decline.

III. CONCLUSIONS

DESPITE the wide publicity given to the post-World War II suburban trend and to the population decline of central cities, it is here suggested that the large-scale dispersal of urban residents into exurbia and suburbia is not a new phenomenon, but is rather the direct continuation of a spatial pattern characteristic of metropolitan America for 125 years. Five indications of deconcentration—higher peripheral rates of growth, leveling of densities, absolute loss of population at the center, movement of the upper and middle classes to the periphery, and lengthening of the average journey to work—were all present in the largest American cities before the introduction of the electric streetcar in the 1890s. These trends are not interesting anomalies or survivals from an earlier epoch, but rather are determining factors in our own urban crisis. Although suburbs now contain more people than central cities, although urban densities are now lower and more even, although metropolitan sprawl now infects thousands rather than dozens of square miles, although the poor and disadvantaged are now present in larger proportions toward the center, and although a journey to work is now more common and longer, these differences are largely quantitative rather than qualitative.[77] If nineteenth-century cities were not entirely modern in shape, they nevertheless exhibited a systematic pattern of population movement toward the periphery.

[75] In each of the primary years of comparison, 1890 and 1923, the older members tended to live closer to the center than their younger associates. The difference, however, was always less than one-third of a mile.

[76] Between 1890 and 1923, of the 108 members who had addresses in both years, 19 per cent moved *closer* to the center; between 1923 and 1961 that figure had fallen to less than 10 per cent.

[77] The statistical information on which the conclusions are based is admittedly fragmentary when compared with the broad scope of the subject. I feel confident, however, that additional refinement would not change the result. I have not treated the ideological factor of *why* people moved to the suburbs because it would have added inordinately to the length of the paper.

Almost every neighborhood in every large metropolis was at one time a suburb.

I would not argue, however, that "there is nothing new about sub-urbanization." Just because the demographic process of population deconcentration has long been operative does not mean that there are no new wrinkles in the suburban experience. At least five differ-ences suggest themselves. First, municipal annexation is no longer a workable procedure in most older cities; the result is a degree of governmental fragmentation that has made a crazy-quilt of metro-politan areas.[78] Second, the popularity of the private automobile has robbed cities of their focus as motorists move laterally toward shopping centers and fast-food outlets. In the mass-transit era, no matter how far an individual moved away from the center, his ties with the core remained because the system of streetcar tracks radiated from the Central Business District. Third, the innovation of the long-term, low-interest mortgage loan has made it possible, especially since World War II, for many more blue-collar and working-class families to enjoy the supposed benefits of suburban living. Fourth, the establishment of the home as a self-sufficient entertainment center has encouraged the development of a new way of life in the suburbs. Initially with the old crank-up phonographs and crystal sets, and more recently with the wide availability of stereophonic music, color television, and air-conditioning, the private dwelling has replaced the neighborhood and its institutions as the place of primary social contact.

Finally, I would suggest that fear and the economics of slum housing have created an entirely new form of deconcentration in contemporary America—abandonment. Throughout the nineteenth century, population was forced outward by pressures for more inten-sive use of land. What we witness now is not simply centrifugal growth, but the desertion of apartments, buildings, and even whole blocks. Abandoning neighborhoods to different ethnic or racial groups is not new, but some blighted areas are now left to the rodents, and some are devoid even of rats.[79] They are abandoned because their owners can no longer make enough money on them to cover

[78] Eric E. Lampard recently argued that the *decentralized* pattern of cities did not become predominant until the 1920s. Because he refers to growth rates, his real focus is political rather than demographic deconcentration. Lampard, "The Dimensions of Urban History: A Footnote to the Urban Crisis," *Pacific Historical Review* 39 (August 1970), p. 271. See also my article on annexation, "Metropolitan Government Versus Suburban Autonomy," *passim*.

[79] Using tax assessment figures, William S. Hastings has shown that some Philadelphia blocks were losing not only population but also land value before the Civil War. The period of his analysis was brief, however, and land values doubtless later recovered. Hastings, "Philadelphia Microcosm," pp. 164-180.

141

upkeep and taxes. In St. Louis, whole blocks of stores and row-houses lie empty; even Gaslight Square, renowned not long ago for chic restaurants and cabarets, is dark and quiet. The urban leprosy is infectious; in Wellston, a small community adjacent to St. Louis, 20 per cent of the houses are abandoned—and not even boarded up. As a federal official recently noted: "There are some parts of these cities so empty they look as though someone had dropped nerve gas." With minor exceptions, this is a new phenomenon in urban America.

But population deconcentration or suburbanization, as measured by the five ecological definitions tested in this paper, is not at all new. For more than a century and a half, the open spaces of the periphery have been looked upon as the salvation of the city. An anonymous English jingle of the 1870s caught the spirit of the suburban trend:

> The richest crop for any field
> Is a crop of bricks for it to yield.
> The richest crop that it can grow,
> Is a crop of houses in a row.

4

Patterns of Residence in Early Milwaukee

KATHLEEN NEILS CONZEN

I

Long before "ecology" became a popular catchword, and well before human ecologists began charting the social space of the American urban environment, Americans of all classes could hardly escape an awareness of the varying social characters of city neighborhoods. An early settler recalled that in Milwaukee, "while the upper and eastern part of the [first] ward, known as Yankee Hill, was the residence district of the better conditioned the lower part . . . was the home of the mechanic, the laborer, the shopkeeper, and the small manufacturer . . . in the main German-born. . . . That portion lying to the south of the hill and known as the Third Ward was almost wholly settled by the Irish as they landed here."[1] Most American cities possess their own equivalents of Milwaukee's Yankee Hill and *Klein Deutschland* and the Irish Bloody Third. During the nineteenth century, when the modern industrial city emerged, neighborhoods like those represented an important element in urban life, mediating for their inhabitants the "depersonalization" often noted as a pathological condition of urbanization. It was within the context of their neighborhoods that city dwellers made their adjustment to the urban environment; it was there that they found friends, went to school, attended church, shopped, voted, and in many cases worked. The city was no monolithic unit, but a congeries of such local communities, and an understanding of the conditions of urban life requires an understanding of the varying origin and character of city neighborhoods.

Although there is a plethora of urban ecological theory to explain the creation of these social areas, little of it contains an awareness of the historical dimension.[2] On the other hand, although some historians have begun to use residence as a means of charting social

[1] Taken from a paper read before the Milwaukee Old Settlers' Club by William G. Bruce, in *History of Milwaukee, City and County*, 1, William G. Bruce (editor) (Chicago: The S. J. Clarke Publishing Co., 1922).
[2] Leo F. Schnore, "Problems in the Quantitative Study of Urban History," in *The Study of Urban History*, H. J. Dyos (editor), (London: Edward Arnold, 1968), p. 189.

status and mobility, few have questioned the nature of residential areas or analyzed their role in the development of the city itself.[3] Urban social space in the nineteenth century thus remains almost virgin territory. Yet more thorough exploration of that *terra incognita* could yield dividends to both social scientists and historians. It could provide tests of models derived from the contemporary urban experience within the framework of a different time and technology, thereby isolating the culturally determined parameters of the models. At the same time, an adequate urban history requires a basic knowledge of the physical setting and the spatial distribution of subpopulations, and, in addition, analysis of changes in the city's constituent social areas provides an index of general social change.[4]

The present study will therefore use Milwaukee, Wisconsin, in the years 1836-1860 to assess the relevance of contemporary ecological models to a developing settlement during the formative period of the modern industrial city. In so doing it will evolve a descriptive model of those processes which divided the city into the neighborhoods that conditioned much of the social, political, and cultural life of Milwaukee's citizens.

II

NEIGHBORHOODS are created when people with similar social characteristics choose to live in the same general area. The physical features

[3] For the use of residence as an index of social status or mobility, witness the following studies in *Nineteenth-Century Cities: Essays in the New Urban History*, Stephan Thernstrom and Richard Sennett (editors) (New Haven: Yale University Press, 1969); Clyde Griffen, "Workers Divided: The Effect of Craft and Ethnic Differences in Poughkeepsie, New York, 1850–1880," pp. 49-97; and Stuart Blumin, "Mobility and Change in Ante-Bellum Philadelphia," pp. 165-208. See also Richard J. Hopkins, "Status, Mobility, and the Dimensions of Change in a Southern City: Atlanta, 1870-1910," in *Cities in American History*, Kenneth T. Jackson and Stanley K. Schultz (editors) (New York: Knopf, 1972), pp. 216-231; this article also contains a useful discussion of the spatial organization of the nineteenth-century city. Sam B. Warner, Jr., however, remains one of the few historians systematically to explore the spatial dimensions of urban social behavior; see, for example, his *Streetcar Suburbs: The Process of Growth in Boston 1870-1900* (New York: Atheneum, 1969); and *The Private City: Philadelphia in Three Periods of its Growth* (Philadelphia: University of Pennsylvania Press, 1968). See also Leo F. Schnore and Peter R. Knights, "Residence and Social Structure: Boston in the Antebellum Period," in Thernstrom and Sennett, *op. cit.*, pp. 247-257.

[4] This point is implied in Roy Lubove, "The Urbanization Process: An Approach to Historical Research," *Journal of the American Institute of Planners*, 33 (January 1967), pp. 33-39; and in Eric E. Lampard, "Urbanization and Social Change; On Broadening the Scope and Relevance of Urban History," in *The Historian and the City*, Oscar Handlin and John Burchard (editors), (Cambridge Mass.: The M.I.T. Press, 1963), pp. 248-250.

of the area, the operation of the housing market, and the area's location with reference to places of employment, recreation, and other facilities are all factors which influence the types of residents it will attract. A particular neighborhood thus results from the intersection of area with personal characteristics. Various models, describing the city in terms of concentric rings, sectors, or clusters, have been evolved to clarify the nature of the areal differentiation which results from this process. With continuing research, it has become increasingly evident that much of this work is complementary rather than contradictory, and what has been termed a "behavioral" synthesis of ecological and social-area-analysis theories has begun to emerge.[5] First, the socioeconomic status of individuals interacts with land values to create neighborhoods segregated on a class basis, which vary by sector. Second, individuals exhibit residential behavior influenced by their stage in the family cycle and therefore, within any given socioeconomic sector, will tend to form neighborhoods of young families toward the periphery while older couples and single persons will seek the convenience of central location. Finally, confusing the pattern of sector and ring is ethnicity: certain ethnic groups tend to cluster in particular locations regardless of their other characteristics.

To what extent can this composite model of urban structure be applied to a historical situation? It is generally recognized that the operative factors in the sorting of urban population by socioeconomic status have been land values and accessibility. The well-to-do can afford the cost, in time and transport, of spacious living on low-value land well away from the discomforts of the central city. The less flexible transportation requirements of the poor doom them to costly central locations, for which they pay with greater density.[6] However, such a pattern depends on the existence of modern means of transportation. Before the availability of streetcars or the automobile, as Leo F. Schnore has emphasized, the upper classes may well have rated

---

[5] Brian J. L. Berry, "Internal Structure of the City," *Law and Contemporary Problems,* 30 (Winter, 1965), pp. 111-119; for a review of literature and expanded discussion of the synthesis, see Philip H. Rees, "Concepts of Social Space: Toward an Urban Social Geography," in *Geographical Perspectives on Urban Systems,* Brian J. L. Berry and Frank E. Horton (editors) (Englewood Cliffs: Prentice-Hall, Inc., 1970), pp. 306-394.

[6] This represents a modification of the ecological model of concentric rings first presented by Ernest W. Burgess in "The Growth of the City: An Introduction to a Research Project," in *The City,* Robert E. Park, Ernest W. Burgess, and R. D. McKenzie (editors) (Chicago: University of Chicago Press, 1925), pp. 47-62; see the discussion in William Alonso, "The Historical and the Structural Theories of Urban Form: Their Implications for Urban Renewal," *Land Economics,* 40 (1964), pp. 227-231.

easy accessibility to the central business area higher than suburban amenities and consequently have used their superior economic power to occupy high-value land near the center.[7] Several studies of nineteenth-century cities provide evidence to support the view that suburbanization of the wealthier part of society has been a byproduct of technological revolution.[8] On this basis, one can hypothesize that frontier Milwaukee should also exhibit a reversal of the present-day pattern of socioeconomic residential areas.

Further questions arise, however. Although discussion of the historical city has emphasized concentricity, the sectoral influence of site characteristics, access routes, status affinities, and Central Business District expansion were as strong in the past as in the present.[9] Furthermore, the existence of any socioeconomic segregation whatsoever may be questioned. In preindustrial European cities, occupation rather than class influenced place of residence; for American cities with their shorter histories, the "rummage of class and occupations" which Sam B. Warner found in residence patterns in preindustrial Philadelphia may have been more characteristic.[10] As James E. Vance has stressed, only when the industrial revolution created diversified employment in different locations for several members of a family could a generalized housing market emerge in which socioeconomic status rather than occupation determined place of residence.[11] Thus, depending on the nature of the "employment linkage" in antebellum Milwaukee, a mixed residential pattern is a hypothetical alternative to the well-defined socioeconomic areas of either the modern or the inverse concentric-sectoral pattern. The social consequences of such an admixture would be of major significance.[12]

[7] Schnore, op. cit., pp. 199-204; Schnore, "Urban Structure and Suburban Selectivity," Demography, 1 (1964), pp. 164-176; smaller cities today continue to exhibit this pattern.

[8] Warner, Private City, p. 56; Streetcar Suburbs, pp. 15-34; Blumin, p. 188.

[9] Suggestions of such influence may be found in Walter Firey, "Sentiment and Symbolism as Ecological Variables," American Sociological Review, 10 (April, 1945), pp. 140-148; and David Ward, "The Emergence of Central Immigrant Ghettoes in American Cities: 1840-1920," Annals of the Association of American Geographers, 58 (June 1968), pp. 343-359.

[10] Warner, Private City, p. 11; James E. Vance, Jr., "Housing the Worker: Determinative and Contingent Ties in Nineteenth Century Birmingham," Economic Geography, 43 (April 1967), pp. 125-126.

[11] Vance, pp. 95-127; see also his "Housing the Worker: The Employment Linkage as a Force in Urban Structure," Economic Geography, 42 (October 1966), pp. 294-325. For examples of changes in work-residence patterns in early nineteenth-century New York, see Allan R. Pred, "Manufacturing in the American Mercantile City: 1800-1840," Annals of the Association of American Geographers, 56 (June 1966), pp. 307-338.

[12] Warner, Private City, pp. 16, 21, 56-57.

Underlying the preceding argument is the close relationship between the industrial revolution and the functional segregation of cities into discrete areas of work and residence. Only when production was transferred from the workshop to the factory could large-scale purely residential areas emerge.[13] The importance of the second residental-location factor (family structure) in this process is evident as well. Only after such functional separation occurred could family structure operate independently to influence residential location, and only then could the family-oriented neighborhood emerge. The extent of functional differentiation within a city at any given point in time thus appears crucial in predicting the importance of family structure as a locational influence.

Three general forces appear to interact in producing ethnicity as a third locational factor. A strong "congregational instinct" on the part of an ethnic group or, on the other hand, a strong tendency on the part of society at large to segregate the group can lead group members to select residence on the basis of ethnicity rather than socioeconomic or family status; then the economic status of the group as a whole would influence the general location of their cluster within the city's social pattern.[14] A so-called ghetto hypothesis has been developed to explain the historical operation of this factor.[15] Upon their arrival, ethnic groups were forced, by lack of money and skills and by the resulting dependence upon central casual-labor employment, to cluster in declining central areas abandoned by the wealthy. As they acquired skill and greater knowledge of American society, they or their children would then move out of the central ghetto and join the general sifting process of society as a whole, although some unusually cohesive groups might simply recluster farther out in higher-status areas. David Ward has clarified the forces influencing the sectoral location of such central ghettos, but has also emphasized that the concentration of an ethnic group in a central location is dependent on the extent of employment opportunities in the Central

[13] Eric E. Lampard, "The Social Impact of the Industrial Revolution," in *Technology in Western Civilization,* 1, Melvin Kranzberg and Carroll W. Pursell, Jr. (editors), (Madison: University of Wisconsin Press, 1967), p. 315; see also Hopkins, *op. cit.*

[14] See the discussion on this point in Stanley Lieberson, *Ethnic Patterns in American Cities* (Glencoe, Illinois: The Free Press, 1963), pp. 3-5.

[15] For statements of the process, see Oscar Handlin, *The Uprooted: The Epic Story of the Great Migrations That Made the American People* (New York: Grosset and Dunlap, 1951), pp. 144-169; Maurice R. Davie, *World Immigration* (New York: The MacMillan Co., 1956), pp. 250-252; Peter J. Rose, *They and We: Racial and Ethnic Relations in the United States* (New York: Random House, 1964), pp. 32-33. It is evident that the "ghetto hypothesis" represents a variant of the Burgess hypothesis.

149

Business District, and thus ultimately on the development of segregated work areas. Moreover, even if a central location is advantageous for a group, the city might be growing so quickly that there was not a sufficient stock of old central housing, and this problem would be particularly acute if the wealthy were still concentrating near the center.[16] The result would be growing shanty settlements on low-value peripheral land, a trend consonant with the inverted socioeconomic location pattern.

Rigorous application of the ghetto hypothesis has involved so many difficulties that Warner and Ward have questioned its utility for the period before transportation and industrial changes led to the reordering of the city's social space. They point out that only small proportions of most immigrant groups actually experienced ghetto concentration before the later nineteenth century, while slum areas often contained residents of many different ethnic groups.[17] The influence of ethnicity as a separate locational factor in a city such as Milwaukee would therefore depend both upon the nature of her ethnic groups and upon the rate of growth and the extent of functional differentiation within the city.

The foregoing discussion suggests major modifications in all three areas of the composite ecological model when applied to the mid-nineteenth-century city. But much of the research which has indicated the need for such modifications has dealt with major Eastern cities during the transitional period of the middle third of the nineteenth century, when they still functioned within frameworks inherited from the seventeenth and eighteenth centuries. Would the same conclusions result from a study of a smaller mercantile city created during the nineteenth century in the period of transition to an industrial economy? Milwaukee represents such a city; to assess its value in testing notions about mid-nineteenth century urban ecology, it is appropriate next to examine those characteristics of Milwaukee relevant to the formation of social areas.

[16] Ward, op. cit. See also his discussion of "The Internal Spatial Differentiation of Immigrant Residential Districts," in "Special Publication No. 3: Interaction Patterns and the Spatial Form of the Ghetto," Department of Geography, Northwestern University, Evanston, Illinois, February, 1970.

[17] Sam B. Warner, Jr. and Colin B. Burke, "The Ghetto Process of Cultural Change: A Limited Case in American Urban History," unpublished paper presented at the University of Wisconsin Political and Social History Conference, May 1968; Ward, "Internal Spatial Differentiation," op. cit., pp. 24-32. This point is also treated by Stephan Thernstrom and Peter R. Knights in "Men in Motion: Some Data and Speculations about Urban Population Mobility in Nineteenth-Century America," Journal of Interdisciplinary History, 1 (Autumn 1970), pp. 7-35.

III

THE HISTORICAL CONTEXT

In size, Milwaukee was perhaps more "typical" of its period than the more studied Eastern port cities; in its economy, it remained largely preindustrial through 1860. Founded amid high hopes by land speculators in 1836 on the site of a fur-trading post at the mouth of the Milwaukee River, the new settlement suffered severely in the depression of the late 1830s but grew rapidly after recovery in the early 1840s (see Table 4-1).[18] Milwaukee was the nation's thirtieth-largest city in 1850, and rose to twentieth place ten years later.[19]

TABLE 4-1   MILWAUKEE POPULATION

Year	Total	Per Cent Increase	Per Cent Native	Per Cent Foreign	Per Cent German	Per Cent Irish	Per Cent Other
1836	1,208						
1840	1,712	41.4					
1846	9,506	442.8					
1850	20,061	111.0	36.0	64.0	36.4	14.1	13.5
1855	30,448	51.8	35.6	64.4			
1860	45,246	48.9	49.5	50.5	35.3	6.9	8.3

Milwaukee's population was supported largely by the commercial functions of an entrepôt city for one of the nation's fastest-growing frontier regions.[20] Although it accounted for about a quarter of all Wisconsin manufacturing in this period, it ranked twenty-seventh among all American cities in manufacturing in 1860, and census-defined manufacturing activities occupied only 7.3 per cent of its population in 1850, and 7.6 per cent in 1860.[21] The average-sized

[18] Any discussion of Milwaukee's history owes much to Bayrd Still, *Milwaukee: The History of a City* (Madison: The State Historical Society of Wisconsin, 1965); sources for the population figures in Table 4-1 are: *Census of Wisconsin, 1836-80, U.S. Sixth Census, 1840, Compendium*, pp. 92-94; *Wisconsin Banner*, 25 July 1846; J.D.B. DeBow, *Compendium of the Seventh Census, 1850*, p. 399; *Annual Report* of the Secretary of State, State of Wisconsin, 1855, p. 71; *U.S. Eighth Census, 1860, Population*, p. xxxii.

[19] *Eighth Census, Mortality and Miscellaneous Statistics*, p. xviii.

[20] Still, pp. 168-199; Margaret Walsh, *The Manufacturing Frontier: Pioneer Industry in Antebellum Wisconsin* (unpublished Ph.D. dissertation, University of Wisconsin, Madison, 1969), chapter 3; William E. Derby, *A History of the Port of Milwaukee* (unpublished Ph.D. dissertation, University of Wisconsin, Madison, 1963), *passim*, especially pp. 168, 193-194, 212-216, 267-268.

[21] Walsh, *op. cit.*, pp. 74-75; *Eighth Census, Mortality and Miscellaneous Statistics*, p. xviii; the percentages were computed from manuscript census data summa-

manufacturing establishment employed only 6.5 workers in 1860, compared with Philadelphia's average of 15.6 for the same year.[22] Milwaukee in 1860 was still mainly a city of small workshops rather than large factories.

Nevertheless, a certain amount of areal differentiation according to function was already in evidence. A commentator in 1863 described the basic divisions evident at the time:

> A fine, high bluff, overlooking the lake and affording charming sites for private residences, follows the northern curve of the bay for nearly two miles when it subsides into the valley of the Milwaukee river. A similar, though not so lofty bluff, extends northerly from the south point of the bay for two or three miles. The intervening flat is occupied by the business and manufacturing portions of the city. The warehouses and lumber yards fringe the docks; the foundries and machine shops occupy the level ground a block or two back; while the heavy wholesale and retail houses line the main business streets, which run next to and parallel with the rivers. The bluffs, which retire from the Lake Shore, as they approach the mouth of the river, sweep round to the west, forming an amphitheatre, and on these high and inviting grounds the private residences of our citizens are thickly clustered.[23]

City directories provide further evidence of the city's emerging functional division.[24] The center of Milwaukee's retail trade in 1850 straddled the first and third ward boundaries on the east side of the Milwaukee River (see Figure 4-1). By 1860 it extended along the river for several blocks in both directions, and secondary centers emerged across the river to the south and the west, with an embryonic third area forming in the northwest. Most banks, business agencies, and professional offices located in the same central area in both years. Only doctors participated in the trend toward the secondary nuclea-

---

ries provided by Margaret Walsh. For comparison, see similar computations for 1860 in Eric E. Lampard, "The History of Cities in the Economically Advanced Areas," *Economic Development and Cultural Change,* 3 (January 1955), p. 120: Lynn, Mass., 45 per cent; Newark, 26.2 per cent; Philadelphia, 17.5 per cent; Cincinnati, 18.3 per cent; Chicago, 4.9 per cent.

[22] Walsh, *op. cit.,* p. 81; Warner, *Private City, op. cit.,* p. 77.

[23] A. Baylies, *An Exposition of the Business of Milwaukee* (Milwaukee: A. Baylies, Publisher, 1863), p. 13.

[24] Milwaukee City Directories for 1848-1849, 1851-1852, and 1859-1860. I am indebted to Sheila Kaplan Bradford, who analyzed the earlier directories in an unpublished seminar paper, "Milwaukee, 1850: A Study of the CBD and the Occupational and Ethnic Residence Locations Related to It," Department of Geography, University of Wisconsin, Madison, January, 1969.

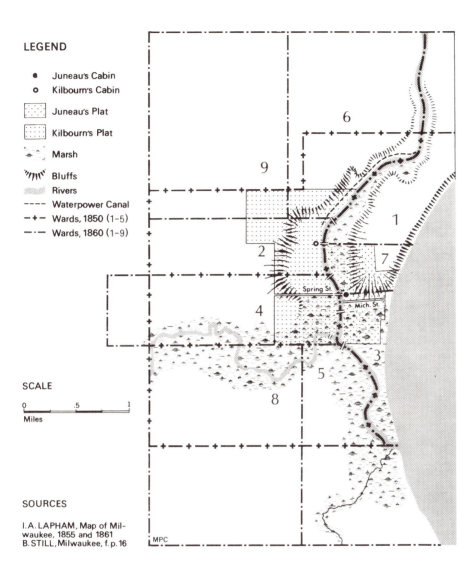

LEGEND

- ● Juneau's Cabin
- ○ Kilbourn's Cabin
- Juneau's Plat
- Kilbourn's Plat
- Marsh
- Bluffs
- Rivers
- ---- Waterpower Canal
- —+— Wards, 1850 (1-5)
- —·— Wards, 1860 (1-9)

SCALE

0   .5   1

Miles

SOURCES

I. A. LAPHAM, Map of Mil-
waukee, 1855 and 1861
B. STILL, Milwaukee, f. p. 16

FIG. 4-1

tions, as did businesses dealing in such daily necessities as groceries, bakeries, and saloons.

What major manufacturing and milling existed in 1850 was located along the length of both sides of the Milwaukee River, with clusters along the canal constructed in 1842, near the center of the central business area, and across the rivers in the south side. Locations had changed little by 1860. Processing industries followed a similar pattern, with the major exception of the breweries, which were scattered throughout the northern and western parts of the city. Woodworkers and the needle trades concentrated in or near the central area. Only shoemaking establishments appeared widely dispersed. It appears that, while much of Milwaukee's manufacturing was carried on in small shops, such workshops tended to concentrate along or near the river which formed the main axis of Milwaukee's commercial life. Although these areas also included the city's heaviest population concentration, large sections of the city apparently contained few workshops, as Table 4-2 suggests.[25]

TABLE 4-2 DISTRIBUTION OF MANUFACTURING EMPLOYMENT

Year	Ward	Per Cent of City Population Resident in Ward	Per Cent of Total Manufacturing Employment Located in Ward	Per Cent of All City Craftsmen Resident in Ward
1850	1	29.9	8.7	31.2
	2	24.3	22.3	29.8
	3	20.7	47.5	14.6
	4	12.2	12.3	12.4
	5	12.8	9.1	12.0
1860	1 & 7	25.5	6.5	22.3
	2	11.1	16.7	14.3
	3	11.2	32.1	7.2
	4	11.1	16.2	11.1
	5 & 8	17.4	22.6	15.2
	6	9.1	3.8	10.7
	9	14.6	2.2	19.2

A broadly defined central area in 1860 was thus the main source of employment. In effect, population growth expanded the residential area of the city, but most retail, manufacturing, wholesaling, and storage functions retained their old locations. Central areas of mixed

[25] Computed from manufacturing census manuscript data made available by Margaret Walsh, and from the 25 per cent samples of Milwaukee heads of households described below; for an approximate comparison for Philadelphia, see Warner, *Private City, op. cit.*, p. 60.

154

residence and workshops remained along the east side of the river and south and west of the canal, but for increasing numbers of Milwaukeans, the experience of life in undifferentiated mixed-function neighborhoods was passing, even if functional separation within the central area was not yet clear.[26]

Even for residents of peripheral neighborhoods, however, Milwaukee in 1860 remained a walking city. The farthest boundary was only three miles from the center of the retail area, and 92 per cent of the population lived within two miles of downtown, 58 per cent within one mile.[27] The first horsecar service was not introduced until May, 1860.[28] The forces distributing Milwaukee's population in this period, then, were essentially those of the preindustrial era, although they were doubtless affected by the beginnings of functional differentiation. Similarly, the conscious decisions of Milwaukee's city-builders, probably well aware of new urban forms appearing in the more industrialized eastern cities which they hoped to emulate, may have played a larger role in shaping the social space of Milwaukee than might be suggested by any model based on "the interplay of impersonal forces."

One final factor must be considered in assessing the nature of Milwaukee as a test case. The composition of Milwaukee's population differentiates it from eastern contemporaries. Although most major American cities experienced great increases in foreign-born population in the pre-Civil War era, the new city of Milwaukee differed from many in receiving its foreign-born at approximately the same time and in roughly equal numbers as the native-born (see Table 4-1). To a great extent, the natives lacked the advantage of prior occupancy. Milwaukee had no established neighborhoods and no existing stock of low-quality housing when immigrants began pouring in around 1840 and even earlier.[29] How would this situation affect ethnicity as a locational factor? If rapid city growth precluded the establishment of large ghettos in eastern cities, would it have the same result on the frontier with its presumably greater equality? However, the unstructured nature of the frontier community simply may have provided ethnic groups with even greater opportunities to cluster and recreate old-country society than was ever possible in eastern cities. The role of ethnicity in creating Milwaukee's social space therefore can be ex-

[26] Sample calculations indicated a clear trend toward absolute population decline in the central blocks along the river between 1850 and 1860.

[27] Calculated on the basis of the 25 per cent samples.

[28] Still, *op. cit.*, p. 249.

[29] For timing of arrival of Milwaukee's immigrants, see Rudolph A. Koss, *Milwaukee* (Milwaukee: Schnellpressen-Druck des "Herold," 1871), *passim*.

pected to differ from that in many other cities of the same time period.

IV

To test assumptions concerning the existence and development of social areas in a new commercial city in the mid-nineteenth century, the residential patterns of Milwaukee were reconstructed for 1850 and 1860 through the use of federal manuscript censuses, city directories, tax assessment rolls, and contemporary maps of the city. Poor census data and lack of city directories precluded a similar cross-section for 1840. An attempt will be made at the end of this chapter to indicate pre-1850 development through the use of more impressionistic historical sources.

A 25-per-cent sample of heads of household for the two census years provided the basic data. Only heads of household were selected, on the assumption that their ethnic status and occupational-residential decisions shaped the character of the entire household. Census information on personal and family status, ethnicity, occupation, property ownership, and other characteristics was coded for each household head, whose address was then located in the city directory.[30] For purposes of mapping the census data, a square grid of cells averaging four city blocks in size was laid over a map of the city, and households were assigned to cells according to their addresses. Some information was lost in this manner but aggregation became possible.[31] Household

---

[30] Increase A. Lapham, "Map of the City of Milwaukee," published by George Harrison, New York, 1855; for 1850, it was necessary to use both the 1848-1849 and 1851-1852 directories in conjunction. Of the names in the 1850 sample, 42 per cent could not be found in the directories, but it was generally possible to locate such households with a fair degree of accuracy by estimating the census-taker's route, using the addresses of neighbors and the location of structures on the Lapham map. Accuracy was greatest in the central wards and declined towards the periphery (35, 40, and 42 per cent unlocated in the three central wards as opposed to 49 per cent in each of the two outer wards); coverage was also more thorough for Americans (28 per cent unlocated) and British (30 per cent) than for Irish, German, and other immigrants (40, 52 and 52 per cent unlocated respectively). By 1860 coverage was vastly improved, with only 13 per cent of all names unlocated. In that year, inner wards had 7, 7, 10, and 10 per cent not in the directory, outer wards 22, 18, 16, 14, and 10 per cent; 7 per cent of the Americans, 8 per cent of the British, 12 per cent of the Irish, 15 per cent of the Germans, and 12 per cent of other immigrants were not covered.

[31] Pinpoint accuracy was impossible in any case, given the directories' vague way of noting addresses. Addresses such as "Martin corner Market," "Chestnut between 4th and 5th," "E. Water" were common.

characteristics aggregated by cell then formed a second set of data, providing a description of the social characteristics of *areas* rather than people. Finally, other cell data were added, such as distance from the city center, date of plat, a topographical index, and settlement density. The two sets of data, for households and for cells, form the basis of the following inquiry.

GRADIENT ANALYSIS

Analysis of Milwaukee's social areas begins with tests for the existence of locational gradients reflecting concentricity in the three hypothesized factors of socioeconomic status, family structure, and ethnicity. The first question is whether Milwaukee exhibited the suggested preindustrial pattern of high-status residential areas in the center and lower status towards the periphery. Selected indicators of the socioeconomic status of cell areas were grouped into quarter-mile tiers radiating outward from the Central Business District.[32] Definition of socioeconomic status in the mid-nineteenth century is difficult. Usual modern indicators include measures of income, occupation, and education, and the assumption will be made that in the nineteenth century they also provided a clue to that ill-defined something called "class."[33] Since no measure of income is available in the 1850 and 1860 censuses, real-property ownership and the number of servants employed are taken as proxies.[34] School attendance of children and literacy statistics are the only available indices of education. Since literacy statistics are notoriously inaccurate, only the school-attendance figures were used, on the assumption that higher-status families would value formal

[32] Cells were assigned to distance tiers according to the location of the cell midpoints. The result was tiers of equal distance-intervals rather than equal area. It should also be noted that due to the manner in which data were originally aggregated, tier-values represent mean cell percentages rather than the mean percentage of all households in the tier. The assumption is made that dominant household characteristics within any given cell determined the general character of that area as it would have been observed by contemporaries, and that present concern is with area rather than individuals.

[33] Occupation and wealth are often used as surrogates in nineteenth-century studies because of limitations of census data; ranking of occupations presents special difficulty. The occupational classification scheme used in this study was adapted with permission from that used by Peter R. Knights in *The Plain People of Boston, 1830-1860: A Study in City Growth* (New York: Oxford University Press, 1971).

[34] Personal property was not used because it was available only in the 1860 census. "Servant," especially in 1850, was often not listed as an occupation in the census; women of different surnames and different places of birth from the head of household and listed at the end of the household entry were so coded, as were men with similar characteristics listing no separate occupation. The category is therefore only approximate and subject to error.

157

education more and could better afford to have unemployed children. Finally, cell percentages of professional and major commercial occupations on the one hand, and laborers on the other, provide measures for the extremes of the occupational ladder.[35]

The resulting gradients (see Table 4-3), with a few exceptions, generally confirm the existence of the hypothesized high-status core and low-status periphery.[36] In 1850, with the exception of the fourth tier, real property declined steeply from center to periphery. High-

TABLE 4-3   GRADIENTS OF SOCIOECONOMIC STATUS, MILWAUKEE, 1850 AND 1860

Year	Tier	Mean Real Property per Household	Mean Per Cent Without Servants	Mean Per Cent At School	Mean Per Cent Professional and Business	Mean Per Cent Laborers
1850	1	191.25	59.19	71.00	13.94	11.90
	2	119.18	72.10	66.16	13.22	15.03
	3	113.80	82.45	46.56	10.10	24.09
	4	280.33	87.22	46.39	6.38	36.54
	5	40.36	89.95	36.81	3.66	35.56
	6	18.44	100.00	44.69	0.00	45.13
1860	1	487.11	61.17	64.81	19.57	6.59
	2	532.03	71.82	63.47	16.87	15.81
	3	655.12	72.73	71.01	16.34	25.53
	4	247.64	78.24	62.42	7.84	21.96
	5	85.33	93.49	60.77	3.85	26.42
	6	65.98	94.82	61.61	2.57	36.72
	7	43.85	96.99	46.15	2.49	47.36
	8	36.44	95.00	43.23	1.33	53.01
	9	34.08	97.43	24.49	2.56	66.41

status occupational dominance declined steadily, as did the percentage of households with servants, while the percentage of laborers increased. School attendance levelled off in the third and fourth tiers and actually increased in the last. The increase in owned property in the fourth tier was not reflected in any of the other indices. The exceptionally high standard deviation of real property for this tier suggests that the general downward slope of the gradient was prob-

[35] "Major commercial occupations" will also be termed "business," and distinguish propertied entrepreneurs and large-scale employers from small-scale shopkeepers and artisans.

[36] The last tier for 1850 and the last two tiers for 1860 were eliminated from consideration here and in the following sections because of greater possibility of sampling error given the sparse settlement on the fringes.

ably deflected by the property holdings of a few especially affluent men who had settled there.[37]

The gradients for 1860 indicate the same trend, with an important difference: three of the indicators reached their peaks only in the third tier, and the two which did not either levelled off in that tier or increased slightly in the next. This would suggest that in the ten years separating the two censuses, Milwaukee's central area began to acquire the character of a business district, with the wealthy moving to its periphery rather than residing in its midst. The 1860 gradients again exhibited a levelling off in the middle tiers before falling on the fringes. However, the slight rise illustrated by two of the indices in the last tiers may suggest the incipient suburbanization of the upper classes, the beginning of a wealthy "villa" settlement on the periphery beyond walking distance, whose members either commuted by horse or directed suburban enterprises which chance alone included within city boundaries.

These gradients generally present strong confirmation of the hypothesis that, in the pre-horsecar era on the nineteenth-century frontier, the upper classes sought residence near the Central Business District, while the propertyless, represented here by casual laborers, were forced to the periphery. But do these gradients present the entire picture? Although ecological theory has presented convincing evidence for the existence of socioeconomic gradients, equally forceful arguments have been advanced in favor of a *sectoral* pattern of socioeconomic groups. It could well be that the wealthy were sufficiently numerous near the city center to weigh the tier means in their direction, concealing the existence of sectoral variations; the higher standard deviations near the center would tend to confirm this.

In addition, Milwaukee's topography was sufficiently varied to offer differing grades of "desirability" of homesites within any given tier (refer to Figure 4-1 for elevations). This was important not only for scenic reasons, but more critically for health. The mid-nineteenth century homeseeker was pathologically sensitive to the dangers of fever and ague in low-lying swampy areas and undoubtedly placed a premium on high ground.[38] Finally, the same tier data could be

---

[37] The standard deviation for the fourth tier was 926.00 as compared with 285.18 in the first tier, 171.33 in the second, 250.99 in the third, 87.52 in the fourth, and 26.41 in the sixth.

[38] This concern is evident in "advice to immigrants" literature. See, for example, Fr. Pauer, *Die Vereinigten Staaten von Nord-America* (Bremen: F. C. Dubbers, 1847), pp. 104-105; in 1842, Milwaukee's bluffs were said to provide "airy and healthy residences," and an Episcopal rector who lived on one of those bluffs wrote to a friend in 1840 that "the country about here [is] much freer

interpreted in a third and not necessarily exclusive manner. The concentric tiers may conceal not only sectoral variations but also variations of the sort discussed earlier, where rich and poor shared the same general residential space but differed in their housing characteristics. This question will be considered in more detail at a later stage of the analysis; it is worth emphasizing, however, that the gradients clearly describe a pattern of socioeconomic sifting quite different from that of most larger present-day cities.

The attempt to analyze family-status patterns with similar tier-level aggregation proved somewhat inconclusive, despite the concentricity of such patterns in the modern city. Perhaps this was to be expected. The urban environment had not yet been identified with all the world's evils, and exclusively residential neighborhoods which could take on a "family" character were still embryonic in Milwaukee. Although young single persons may well have congregated in the rooming-houses of the central areas or boarded near their central places of employment, there is little reason to expect that family status alone would influence residence for other groups. Any evident patterns could equally well result from differential family characteristics of socioeconomic or ethnic groups.

However, since few gradients emerged from the analysis the problem does not arise. The lack of pattern may be real, or it may simply reflect the poor nature of the indicators.[39] There seems to be a slight trend towards increasing age of household head with increasing distance from the center, but the range of variation is small (see Table 4-4). Likewise, family size declines from the center; in conjunction with the first indicator, this could point to smaller families headed by older parents on the periphery, a finding difficult to interpret. Alternatively, the measure could be skewed by central boarding-houses, which would also account for the age gradient, or by the inclusion of servants in the family measures. Number of school-age children per household is equally inconclusive; the gradient dips in the center in 1850, where it peaks in 1860. Nor do households headed

---

from marshes and low ground than Michigan, and consequently much less subject to sickness. I never enjoyed such good health as here, nor was I ever so fleshy. . . ." Frank A. Flower, *History of Milwaukee, Wisconsin* (Chicago: Western Historical Co., 1881), p. 190; letter dated 14 December 1840 from Rev. Lemuel B. Hull to Samuel B. Read, Sharon, Michigan, reprinted in a Milwaukee newspaper, clipping dated 1904 in *Milwaukee* scrapbook, State Historical Society of Wisconsin, Madison.

[39] "Household size" includes boarders and servants as well as family members; children under school age were unfortunately not aggregated; "female heads of household" includes single women, widows, and women living apart from their husbands.

by females exhibit a pattern. Finally, the percentage of households living in single-family dwellings does decrease towards the center, again indicating the prevalence of boarding-houses but perhaps also of central high-density living. Aside from certain indications of centrality for younger and possibly unmarried persons, therefore, no concentric pattern emerges from these admittedly inadequate indicators of family structure.

TABLE 4-4 GRADIENTS OF FAMILY STATUS,
MILWAUKEE, 1850 AND 1860

Year	Tier	Age	Household Size	Per Cent Living in Single-family Dwelling	Number of Children Aged 5 to 17 per Household
1850	1	34.6	5.59	84.37	1.08
	2	36.5	5.23	82.99	1.10
	3	34.1	4.49	82.71	.85
	4	35.9	4.35	85.06	.84
	5	36.6	3.88	90.40	1.02
	6	39.1	4.17	93.28	1.80
1860	1	37.6	5.53	74.79	1.06
	2	38.8	5.24	84.53	1.24
	3	38.9	4.82	81.25	1.30
	4	37.7	5.51	83.92	1.48
	5	38.6	4.80	93.95	1.35
	6	39.9	4.77	94.92	1.37
	7	38.1	4.66	96.23	1.03
	8	42.2	4.36	100.00	1.19
	9	38.7	4.14	98.46	.88

Ethnicity is the third characteristic hypothesized as conditioning residential stratification. Cross-tabulation and chi-square tests indicate a strong correlation between ethnicity and economic status in Milwaukee, with the native-born on the upper rungs of the ladder and Germans and Irish on the lower.[40] As a result, these ethnic groups should exhibit the same spatial ordering as the economic classes of which they are a part, in the absence of ethnicity per se as a separate intervening factor. A test for concentric patterns can therefore be considered a negative test for the existence of an independent ethnic factor.

[40] These tests were carried out as part of the research for an unpublished dissertation, *"The German Athens": Milwaukee and the Accommodation of Its Immigrants, 1836-1860,* Department of History, University of Wisconsin (Madison), 1972.

161

TABLE 4-5 GRADIENTS OF ETHNIC DISTRIBUTION,
MILWAUKEE, 1850 AND 1860

Year	Tier	Mean Per Cent Native-born	Mean Per Cent Irish	Mean Per Cent German
1850	1	35.69	19.74	13.51
	2	32.14	25.70	24.10
	3	22.14	25.37	37.74
	4	19.48	22.18	42.99
	5	10.15	11.34	61.51
	6	14.35	9.26	63.42
1860	1	41.19	17.09	17.31
	2	26.09	30.16	24.26
	3	22.63	21.16	38.94
	4	20.74	20.31	40.69
	5	11.12	17.87	54.83
	6	8.09	4.75	75.09
	7	3.13	9.09	73.60
	8	8.91	17.22	68.85
	9	5.12	10.25	82.05

The expected pattern was indeed exhibited by the native-born and
the Germans (see Table 4-5), but the Irish, the lowest status group
in terms of occupation and property-ownership, followed a more confusing pattern, reaching peak percentages near the center. The anoma-
lous position of the Irish indicates that ethnicity cannot be dismissed
as an independent factor. It could also be consistent with either the
existence of a central low-status area hidden by the tier-level socioeconomic indicators, or with the mixed residential pattern of the preindustrial city suggested earlier. However, the inverse patterns of
the native-born and the Germans likewise indicate a certain relationship between ethnicity and economic status as residential factors.

V

FACTOR ANALYSIS

The preceding section has suggested both the utility and the limitations of examining gradients for a study of urban spatial ordering.
The next step, therefore, is to go beyond the simple concept of distance
tiers, in order to explore (1) whether the concentric socioeconomic
status pattern remains a better descriptive concept than one based
on sectors or intermingled settlement; (2) whether in fact any non-
zonal family-stage sifting can be discovered; and (3) whether ethnicity has an independent role in the spatial sorting of Milwaukee's

population. To test the relative importance and sufficiency of these three concepts in explaining the spatial variations in the characteristics of Milwaukee's neighborhoods, and to provide a means of mapping similar locational patterns, twenty-three cell-level variables were subjected to principal-components factor analysis.[41] Factor analysis so used is a way of reducing the complex interrelationships of these variables to a more meaningful descriptive scheme of the city's residential space. The choice of variables (see Table 4-6) was dictated by available data and the limitations of the collecting procedure, but the variables nevertheless all possess a logical relationship with residential location. The analysis yielded nine factors (see Table 4-6) with eigenvalues greater than 1.0 for both years, accounting for 69.3 per cent of the total variance for 1850, and 70.5 per cent for 1860.[42] Standardized factor scores were then mapped to yield the locational dimensions of each factor.

The first factor in 1850 may be termed a family-structure factor. High scores on this factor identify cells with a greater than average number of school-age children per family, with larger households often headed by older men. Such cells also exhibit a good school attendance record. By 1860, family structure drops to fourth place in explanatory strength among the factors, but continues to identify areas of well-established family life, with high loadings on numbers of school-age children per family, school attendance, and size of household. The "solid middle class" character of this factor is underlined in 1860 by the strong positive loading on skilled labor and the tendency to exclude unskilled labor; families larger than average tend to be found where skilled craftsmen rather than casual laborers reside.

Mapping of the family-structure factor scores (see Figure 4-2) reveals little spatial bias in 1850. High positive and negative scores are found side by side and in all areas of the city, although there is some tendency towards lack of negative scores in the central area. For 1860, clearer patterns emerge. Family residence as indexed by this factor is found neither at the center nor at the fringes, but begins

[41] For a discussion of the advantages and pitfalls of factor analysis for ecological research, see Carl-Gunnar Janson, "Some Problems of Ecological Factor Analysis," in *Quantitative Ecological Analysis in the Social Sciences*, Mattei Dogan and Stein Rokkan (editors) (Cambridge, Mass.: The M.I.T. Press, 1969), pp. 301-341; see also Rees, pp. 316-323. Factor analysis is discussed in Leslie King, *Statistical Analysis in Geography* (Englewood Cliffs: Prentice-Hall, 1969), pp. 165–193; a statement on the mapping of factor scores may be found in J. P. Cole and C.A.M. King, *Quantitative Geography: Techniques and Theories in Geography* (New York: John Wiley and Sons, 1968), pp. 297-302.

[42] Loadings of less than .400 were removed from the table for the sake of clarity.

TABLE 4-6 ROTATED FACTOR MATRIX, 1850
(Normal Varimax)

Variable	F I	F II	F III	F IV	F V	F VI	F VII	F VIII	F IX
School-Age Children	.867								
Household Size	.737								
Per Cent at School	.637								
Age	.530								
Per Cent Professional		.770							
Per Cent Native		.676			.464				
Per Cent Without Servants		-.511							
Per Cent Shopkeepers		.424							
Per Cent Irish			-.804						
Per Cent German		-.417	.777						
Topography Index			.578						
Per Cent Unskilled				.764					
Per Cent Skilled		-.409		-.635					
Date of Plat				.575					
Per Cent British				-.503					
Real Property					.751				
Per Cent Business					.726				
Per Cent Female Heads						.797			
Per Cent Illiterate						.601			
Density							.791		
Per Cent Clerical							.686		
Per Cent Semiskilled								.915	
Per Cent Dutch									.716
Per Cent Single Family									.688

TABLE 4-6 ROTATED FACTOR MATRIX, 1860 (Continued)

(Normal Varimax)

Variable	F I	F II	F III	F IV	F V	F VI	F VII	F VIII	F IX
Real Property	.815								
Per Cent Professional	.785								
Per Cent Without Servants	-.752								
Per Cent Native	.703							.409	
Density		-.776							
Date		.721							
Per Cent Single Family		.637							
Per Cent German	-.414		-.588					-.412	
Per Cent Irish			.833						
Per Cent Illiterate			.686						
Topography Index		.490	-.544						
Per Cent Skilled				.747					
School-age Children			.434	.632					
Per Cent at School				.548	.401				
Per Cent Unskilled		.415		-.470			.412		
Per Cent British					.778				
Per Cent Business	.513				.619	.807			
Per Cent Shopkeepers				.415		.556			
Household Size	.493						-.784		
Per Cent Semiskilled							.602		
Age								.799	
Per Cent Clerical									
Per Cent Dutch						-.372			.849
Per Cent Female Heads							.381		

to form a roughly defined band around the older "workshop" area of the city. The family-structure factor therefore tends to confirm the lack of concentricity noted in the 1850 gradient analysis, but by 1860 a tendency to decentralize becomes evident, although the outer edges of the city remain an area of less family-oriented settlement.

Factors II and V combined in 1850 to delineate the high-status areas of Milwaukee. Cells scoring high on Factor II tended to be the homes of professionals (principally doctors and lawyers) or small

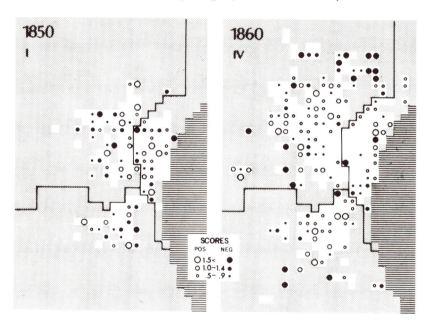

Fig. 4-2   Family structure factor

businessmen, often native-born, who employed servants more frequently than did the average. Negative scores indicate cells tending toward German population, and skilled rather than nonmanual occupations. The fifth factor distinguishes the high-status residences of the city's leading businessmen. Cells scoring high on this factor exhibit the same dominance of native-born population as do high-status professional cells, but they also indicate extensive property ownership. The latter combines with the employment of domestic servants to demonstrate the high-status character of the factor. These two factors therefore distinguish within the high-status group the more propertied businessmen from the professionals. Factor II also indicates the relationship between socioeconomic status and ethnicity: it was the native-born who reaped the greatest profits from Milwaukee's economy.

Ten years later, socioeconomic status emerged as the most important factor in describing Milwaukee's residential patterns, combining both 1850 socioeconomic-status factors. Factor I in 1860 indexes property-ownership and native dominance, and separates areas whose residents were mainly professional men and entrepreneurs living in large households staffed by domestic servants from areas occupied by Germans lower on the economic ladder. Both businessmen and professionals now shared the same prosperous neighborhoods. Note that the Irish, though of low economic status, did not emerge on this factor. Given the ambiguous trends noted in Irish residential behavior earlier, it may be assumed that the socioeconomic-status factors in both census years segregate those two groups which were most distinct from one another both residentially and economically. The corollary is that ethnicity and socioeconomic status did not vary directly with regard to residential location.

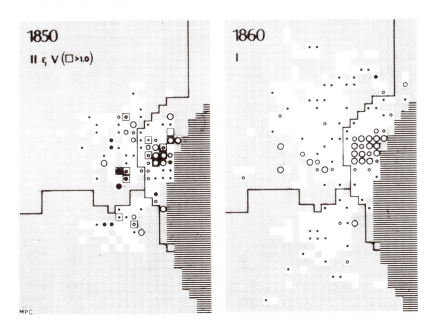

FIG. 4-3   Socioeconomic status factor

Scores for Factor II in 1850 (see Figure 4-3) show a concentration of high-status cells near the lake shore north and east of the central business area, with scattered concentration elsewhere, while the low-status German cells predominate on the south and northwest sides. The business factor in 1850 was not mapped separately; areas with scores greater than +1.0 are outlined on Figure 4-3, indicating the proximity of those cells to the high-status area of Factor II. By 1860 the lake-shore high-status area had concentrated and expanded, and a lone 1850 high-status cell on the west side proved to be the nucleus of a second Yankee area ten years later. Incipient Yankee areas in the northwest and south disappeared by 1860, and German settlement expanded in these directions.

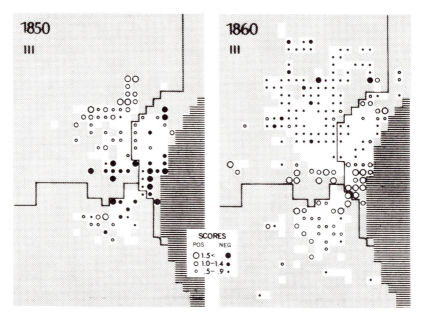

Fig. 4-4   Ethnicity factor

High loadings on Factor II in both 1850 and 1860 denote its character as an ethnicity factor distinguishing German and Irish settlement. This factor in 1850 loads high positive on per cent German, negative on per cent Irish; patterns remain the same in 1860, with the signs reversed. German areas tended to be located on higher ground, and Irish areas exhibited greater illiteracy and larger families by 1860. When scores are mapped (see Figure 4-4), the dichotomous nature of the settlement of these two ethnic groups stands out. Each of the four Irish nuclei of 1850 had expanded by 1860. The northern and south-side areas were generally scattered, but strong Irish cores existed south and east of the central business area and to the west across the river. Both areas bordered directly on high-status Yankee areas. (See Figure 4-3 for comparison.) German communities appeared on both sides of the river north of the center, with greatest expansion occurring to the northwest by 1860. The south-side German community, which appeared in the socioeconomic-status factors, does not score highly on ethnicity, especially in 1860. There could be greater Irish-German residential admixture in this area, or general economic similarity of its German and Irish residents. One final point to note is the internal differentiation within the German areas implied by differences in distribution of scores on the socioeconomic and ethnicity factors.

The last factor of major significance for the overall spatial ordering of Milwaukee's neighborhoods is a "centrality" index which appears as Factor VII in 1850 but rises to second in explanatory power by 1860. The centrality factor in 1850 isolates central areas of high density, with a large population employed in shops and offices. High positive loadings in 1860 describe an inverse situation: the factor picks out low-density recently settled areas on high ground. In such areas much of the population lives in single-family housing, and many are unskilled laborers.

The centrality factor in both years appears to distinguish those central cells in which residence is closely associated with economic activity from the outer, more purely residential areas of the day laborers. With its increasing strength from 1850 to 1860, it charts the growing functional division of the city noted earlier. Mapping of factor scores (see Figure 4-5) clarifies this interpretation, as high scores accentuate the central areas of mixed retail, workshop, and business employment combined with residence, where no one occupational or socioeconomic group dominated. While the core east of the river remained relatively stable, the clear expansion of this area northward and westward is evident, as is the retreat of the fringes. The centrality factor has therefore added a fourth element to the areal divisions on the basis of family status, socioeconomic status, and ethnicity.

To be sure, socioeconomic divisions are implied, as the fringe areas scoring low on centrality are low-status areas. But high-scoring areas are not necessarily high in status. They seem to be rather those areas in the new mercantile city in which an older form of urban life prevailed, one involving high-density living in a central area of mixed employment and residence, where all groups, rich and poor, master and apprentice, lived close to, or indeed at, their places of work. But by 1860 the expansion of the mixed central area had not kept

169

pace with population expansion, and more occupationally uniform peripheral residential areas were developing, whose residents must have walked to workplaces located elsewhere unless the expansion of the city itself provided local jobs.

The remaining factors in both census years are of lesser importance to the overall spatial differentiation of the city and will therefore be discussed only briefly without reproducing factor-score maps. British concentration appeared as Factor IV in 1850 and V in 1860. In 1850, it combined with skilled-labor concentration to contrast with peripheral settlement of the unskilled. Areas of such British skilled-

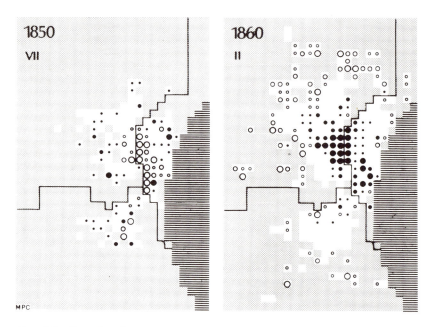

Fig. 4-5   Centrality factor

labor residence were found mainly on the fringes of the high-status Yankee area and near the center of the northwestern German area. By 1860, the loading of British on the factor was stronger and was clearly associated with high socioeconomic-status indicators, differentiating it from German areas. Mapping of scores confirmed the tendency of the British to settle in high-status Yankee areas, with some scattered south-side residence as well.

If the British by 1860 tended to share upper-class native-born residential areas, the Dutch found room at the periphery of the German area. Dutch concentration was indexed by Factor IX in both census

170

years; high scores appeared in six cells on the fringes of the German northwest in 1850, and in these and six others farther out by 1860. The Dutch settlement pattern was more cohesive than that of the British; the relationship of both, in residence and socioeconomic status, to similar-speaking groups is clear.

It may be noted that the distinction between residence of skilled labor on the edges of the central district and unskilled on the city fringes indicated by Factor IV in 1850 documents an earlier phase of the same trend made evident by Factor IV in 1860, previously identified as a family-structure factor. Further clarification of the occupational pattern is provided by Factor VIII in 1850 and VII in 1860. Both exhibit heavy loadings for percentage of semi-skilled, and both delimit concentration of such occupations on the south side, although by 1860 the semi-skilled are also scattered throughout most of the northwestern German area. Since the south side was not uniquely described by any of the major factors, the semi-skilled factors substantiate an occupational unity for an otherwise mixed area.

The two remaining 1860 factors are likewise occupational. Factor VIII stresses concentrations of clerical occupations, associated with native birth to the exclusion of Germans. Clerical occupations loaded highest on the centrality factor in 1850; mapping of the 1860 clerical-factor distribution indicated fairly central locations, with some tendency to disperse to the northern edges of the eastern Yankee area and to the new south-side business area. Factor VI indicates residential areas of small businessmen, often areas of larger households as well. These small businessmen were associated with high-status Yankees in 1850; factor scores for 1860 placed them in central German areas on both sides of the river, to some extent in the eastern Irish core, and in the southern business area.

The remaining 1850 factor, Factor VI, isolates cells with high proportions of households headed by females, unmarried, widowed, or otherwise bereft. Factor scores exhibited little spatial pattern, and the variable produced no high loadings in 1860.

How has this analysis clarified the process of neighborhood formation in antebellum Milwaukee? A comparative summary of the factor structures is provided in Table 4-7. Most notable is the declining importance of family status factors by 1860, at the same time as the differentiation in character between central core and periphery became more marked. The three hypothesized social-area variables of socioeconomic status, family structure, and ethnicity were identified in the factor analysis. Residence on the basis of family was found to exhibit few initial spatial patterns, but by 1860 "well-established"

TABLE 4-7 SUMMARY OF FACTORS, 1850 AND 1860

Factor	Identification	Factor Variance	Per Cent of Total Factor Variance	Per Cent of Total Variance Explained by Factor
1850				
Factor I	Family Structure	2.440	14.7	10.2
Factor II	Socioeconomic Status (Professional)	2.295	13.8	9.6
Factor III	Ethnicity	2.114	12.7	8.8
Factor IV	British-Skilled	1.945	11.7	8.1
Factor V	Socioeconomic Status (Businessmen)	1.807	10.9	7.5
Factor VI	Female Household Heads	1.684	10.1	7.0
Factor VII	Centrality	1.618	9.7	6.7
Factor VIII	South Side Semiskilled	1.409	8.5	5.9
Factor IX	Dutch Concentration	1.322	7.9	5.5
	Total	16.635	100.0	69.3
	Total Variance	24.000		
1860				
Factor I	Socioeconomic Status	3.253	19.2	13.6
Factor II	Centrality	2.315	13.7	9.6
Factor III	Ethnicity	2.313	13.7	9.6
Factor IV	Family Structure	1.776	10.5	7.4
Factor V	British Concentration	1.744	10.3	7.3
Factor VI	Shopkeepers	1.508	8.9	6.3
Factor VII	South Side Semiskilled	1.494	8.8	6.2
Factor VIII	Clerical	1.423	8.4	5.9
Factor IX	Dutch Concentration	1.105	6.5	4.6
	Total	16.931	100.0	70.5
	Total Variance	24.000		

families tended to avoid both the core areas and the outer fringes. The economic-status factor revealed definite sectoral bias, with the main high-status area located north of the central area and a second to the west by 1860. The concentric pattern found in the gradient analysis was therefore only a partial explanation. Although the upper class exhibited a definite central tendency, they did not occupy the entire central area.

The socioeconomic-status factor was related to ethnicity, but the two were not direct proxies for one another. Therefore a separate ethnicity factor emerged to differentiate the two major lower-status foreign-born groups, one occupying generally central locations and balancing the high-status Yankees, the other dominating a quadrant of the city extending to the northwest from the center. Separate factors identified British concentration within Yankee areas and a Dutch community at the outer fringes of German area. Some indication of internal status segregation especially within the German areas appeared; the eastern German area was best described in terms of skilled labor, shopkeepers, and centrality, the main northwestern area in terms of skilled labor, and the fringes in terms of unskilled.

Joining the three main types of locational behavior was a *fourth* factor which appeared to distinguish city areas on the basis of density of settlement and occupational characteristics. Termed a "centrality" factor, it segregated the mixed work-residential heart of the city from both high-status inner city residential areas and low-status fringe residential areas. We have suggested that this factor isolated an older form of central-city urban life; its areal strength corresponds to the cells of mixed function noted in the city directory analysis, and its area overlaps that of both central German and Irish clusters.

These four factors were ambiguous in characterizing one area of the city, the south side, which (perhaps because of ethnic intermixture) was best mapped by scores on occupational factors describing concentrations of semi-skilled labor. Finally, although the two socioeconomic indicators of 1850 merged by 1860, the separate appearance of two middle-class occupational factors in the latter year suggests increasing economic and ethnic divergence within what had been a more cohesive non-manual laboring group when the city was younger. By 1860 the relatively fluid social structure of early Milwaukee appeared to be yielding to more marked cleavages along occupational and ethnic lines, as the internal differentiation of the city's space itself became more evident. One can only speculate on the relative importance of increasing city size, greater maturity, and changing economy in stimulating these trends; only transportation innovation was clearly absent.

VI

ETHNIC AREA ANALYSIS

Both the tier gradients and the factor analysis have clarified the extent and nature of Milwaukee's structural patterns. Although some economically "integrated" areas existed, sizable proportions of the lower classes must have lived well away from the well-to-do. Factor analysis also suggested that ethnic groups may have been more strongly separated from one another in Milwaukee than evidence from other cities would have implied. If the frontier city was able to sort its residents efficiently by wealth, it appears to have done even better in segregating ethnic groups. The final stage of this analysis, then, will attempt to probe more deeply into the nature and extent of the ethnic clustering.

By any standards, Milwaukee was an ethnically segregated city from a very early date. If one applies the commonly used "index of dissimilarity" as a summary measure of residential separation of major ethnic groups at the ward level, relatively high levels of dissimilarity appear (see Table 4-8).[43] The Irish pattern is most dissimilar

TABLE 4-8 RESIDENTIAL DISSIMILARITY,
WARD LEVEL, MILWAUKEE 1850 AND 1860
(1850 above the diagonal, 1860 below)

	Total Population	Native	Irish	German
Total population	—	14.2	35.3	16.4
Native-born	34.6	—	33.1	30.8
Irish	44.5	26.0	—	51.2
German	19.8	44.4	53.2	—

to that of the total population of the city in 1850, and in 1860 they were joined by the native-born. The Germans, as the largest group, inevitably influenced the distribution of the city population more than the other two and thus do not appear highly segregated. A better picture of the city's ethnic division is provided by the indices measuring the extent of dissimilarity in residential patterns between individual groups. Both Irish and German residential patterns are quite dissimilar to the natives in 1850, but by 1860, though German dissimilarity increased, Irish residential patterns more closely approximated those of the native-born.

To clarify Milwaukee's ethnic divisions further, ethnic neighborhoods were mapped by assigning to an ethnic area any cell in which more than 60 per cent of the heads of household belonged to that ethnic group. It was assumed that if a group occupied more than 60 per cent of the residences in a four-block area, the character of the area would be easily recognized by residents and nonresidents

[43] Values of this index tend to increase as the size of units decreases, and therefore computation at the ward level may conceal segregation within wards. The index indicates the percentage of any one group which would have to move in order that its distribution resemble that of the group with which it is being compared; lack of segregation would yield a minimum index of 0, complete segregation a theoretical maximum of 100. For discussion of the index of dissimilarity, see Karl E. and Alma F. Taeuber, *Negroes in Cities* (Chicago: Aldine Press, 1965), pp. 203-204, 223-238; and Lieberson, *op. cit.*, pp. 30-39.

174

alike.[44] The resulting neighborhoods, based on the single variable of ethnic dominance, appear in Figure 4-6. They confirm the broad ethnic divisions isolated by factor analysis and substantiate increasing separation between 1850 and 1860.[45]

In 1850, 73 per cent of the sample German households lived in the German neighborhoods thus defined, increasing to 83 per cent in 1860.[46] Fifty per cent of the Irish lived in Irish areas in 1850, while a slight decline to 47 per cent occurred by 1860. The 41 per cent of the native-born living in Yankee neighborhoods in 1850 increased to 53 per cent in 1860. Conversely, the percentage of natives and Germans living in neighborhoods of other ethnic groups declined, while the percentage of Irish doing so rose. The proportion living in neighborhoods dominated by no one ethnic group declined for all three groups. The social consequences of these patterns are easily visualized. The vast majority of Milwaukee's Germans lived surrounded by fellow-countrymen, with little neighborhood contact with English-speaking groups. Likewise the upper-class Yankees attempted to isolate themselves residentially from the foreign-born. The Irish were the only ones to begin breaking the pattern, but more than a quarter still remained resident in 1860 in the central east-side Irish cluster alone, in which fully three-fourths of the residents were Irish. It is worth noting that many more Irish than Germans had lived elsewhere in America before migrating to Milwaukee, an experience which could have given them a head start toward assimilation.[47] More importantly, many of the "integrating" Irish were laborers and probably reflected "back-to-back" residence rather than true integration.

There can be little doubt that economic factors influenced the ethnic clustering, but they do not provide a fully satisfying explanation. Table 4-9 charts the general occupational structure of the three major

[44] The construction of areas for statistical purposes is discussed in Jack P. Gibbs (editor), *Urban Research Methods* (Princeton: D. Van Nostrand Co., Inc., 1961), pp. 145-146.

[45] None of the other ethnic groups was sufficiently large to create its own areas given the criteria established. A large percentage of the total Dutch population concentrated in the northwest area noted earlier, while the British duplicated the settlement patterns of the native-born, as did the smaller group of Canadians. A small Scandinavian colony congregated on the south side. Negro settlement patterns were not analyzed; they are the subject of a study by William J. Vollmar, "The Negro in a Midwest Frontier City: Milwaukee 1835-1870" (unpublished M.A. thesis, Marquette University, 1968).

[46] These and following statistics were computed from the 25 per cent samples.

[47] Based on inspection of the birthplaces of children born in the United States to foreign-born parents as recorded in the census for the 25 per cent samples. See also Humphrey J. Desmond, "Early Irish Settlers in Milwaukee," *Wisconsin Magazine of History*, 13 (June 1930), pp. 366-367.

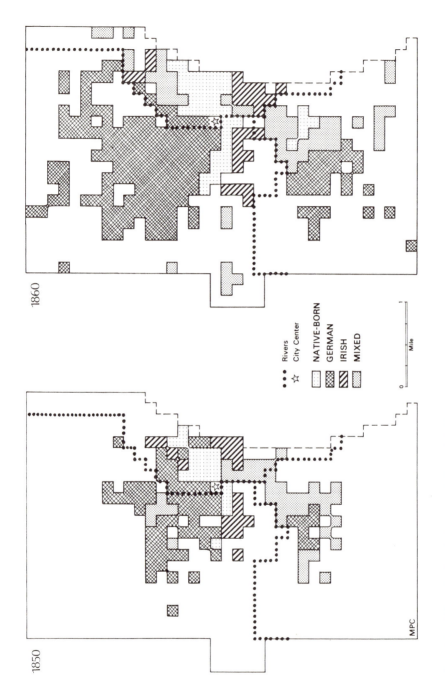

1860

Rivers

City Center ☆

NATIVE-BORN

GERMAN

IRISH

MIXED

0   Mile

1850

MPC

Fig. 4-6   Milwaukee's ethnic areas, 1850 and 1860

TABLE 4-9 OCCUPATIONAL DISTRIBUTION OF MILWAUKEE ETHNIC GROUPS

Occupation	Native		British		Irish		German		Total Population
	Per Cent	Index	Per Cent	Index	Per Cent	Index	Per Cent	Index	Per Cent
1850									
Professional	12.4	2.58	1.0	.20	1.6	.32	3.4	.70	4.8
Managerial	11.1	2.52	5.9	1.33	2.6	.59	1.7	.38	4.4
Clerical	6.2	2.05	1.0	.30	1.0	.35	2.7	.87	3.0
Shopkeepers	15.9	1.38	11.8	1.02	7.3	.63	9.9	.85	11.6
Artisans	32.3	.91	53.9	1.52	16.7	.47	40.6	1.14	35.5
Semiskilled	9.3	.89	11.8	1.12	9.9	.95	9.9	.94	10.5
Unskilled	2.7	.12	2.0	.09	54.7	2.40	26.1	1.14	22.8
Other	11.5	2.09	4.0	1.54	1.0	.41	1.6	.66	2.6
Unoccupied	4.9	1.01	8.8	1.84	5.2	1.09	4.1	.85	4.8
Total	100.0		100.0		100.0		100.0		100.0
1860									
Professional	11.1	3.24	1.4	.40	.8	.24	2.0	.59	3.4
Managerial	20.6	4.11	3.4	.68	1.9	.38	2.0	.41	5.0
Clerical	10.0	2.56	8.8	2.25	1.9	.50	2.3	.58	4.0
Shopkeepers	16.2	1.44	14.3	1.28	6.6	.59	9.8	.87	11.2
Artisans	26.2	.78	45.6	1.34	19.1	.57	38.0	1.12	33.8
Semiskilled	7.2	.61	10.2	.85	15.2	1.28	12.5	1.04	12.0
Unskilled	3.6	.15	8.8	.37	43.5	1.81	27.9	1.16	24.1
Other	1.1	1.10	3.4	3.34	0.9	.82	.8	.78	1.0
Unoccupied	3.9	.71	4.1	.74	10.0	1.81	4.6	.83	5.5
Total	100.0		100.0		100.0		100.0		100.0

groups.[48] The native-born tended to specialize in white-collar occupations and skilled craftsmanship, and dominated the former in both census years. Irish concentrated heavily on the lower end of the occupational spectrum, and skilled labor predominated among the Germans.

The ethnic neighborhoods therefore reflect the fact that, given native-born dominance of upper occupational categories, any upper-class neighborhood would almost inevitably take on a Yankee tone. But the same economic distinctions are insufficient to explain German-Irish segregation. The main Irish cluster on the east side produced heavy concentrations of unskilled laborers, and transport and service workers. But those few Germans who settled in this area included smaller percentages of such workers than the German population as a whole. Similarly, the Irish in the heavily commercial and manufacturing German east-side area were mainly unskilled. Only on the south side was there evidence of relatively mixed settlement, primarily on the basis of occupation rather than ethnicity. German areas in effect presented a microcosm of the economic differentiation of the city as a whole, with internal economic differentiation, in a way that the Irish neighborhoods did not. Indicative of this is the fact that three-quarters of the Germans in the top two occupational categories resided in German areas in 1850, and two-thirds in 1860, whereas all but one of the ten Irishmen in those categories in 1860 lived outside Irish areas.

VII

THE DEVELOPMENT OF MILWAUKEE'S RESIDENTIAL PATTERN

The broad outlines of social differentiation of Milwaukee's urban space have been sketched. A final question remains, the answer to which can best be suggested by more traditional historical data: given the differing locational tendencies of the economic and ethnic groups,

---

[48] There is a strong significant relationship between occupation and property ownership for the city area as a whole and for major ethnic groups in both census years, so occupation can be considered a general measure of economic standing. The "index" figures on Table 4-9 represent a measure of over-concentration or under-concentration of an ethnic group in an occupational category; an index of 1.00 indicates normal distribution. For example, the index of 2.58 for native-born professionals in 1850 means that the percentage of professionals who are native-born is slightly over two and a half times the percentage of native-born heads of households in the city as a whole, and the Irish index of .32 in the same entry signifies that there are only a third as many professionals among the Irish as their share of the total population would imply.

what influenced the specific location of the various social areas? The theoretical importance of the Central Business District as a source of employment and as a consumer of land in influencing residence was discussed earlier. It has been the contention of this chapter that Milwaukee's development was such that, despite residential expansion, most employment remained relatively central. Therefore central locations would have been important for most occupational groups in Milwaukee, except for those casual laborers and skilled builders whose labor furthered the expansion of the city itself. Can the location of Milwaukee's social areas be clarified with reference to the developing central area?

Milwaukee's Central Business District grew up around the site of Solomon Juneau's trading post on the east bank of the Milwaukee River (refer to Figure 4-1). Juneau's rival in city promotion, Byron Kilbourn, attempted to establish a second business center a few blocks north on his side of the river, but it remained a secondary node.[49] The first stores were erected close to the docks and warehouses along the river near Juneau's cabin, and at the foot of the bluff stretching eastward to the lake, where piers were constructed after 1843. East Water Street and Michigan Street ran along these lines and formed the city's first business axis.[50] The third line of expansion was created when the hill along the river north of the first site was graded, providing access to a freshwater spring where a marketplace was established, and an easier route to the wooded bluffs whose summits offered more appealing homesites than the swamps along the river and south of Michigan Street.[51] Those who could afford it moved up to this attractive area, creating the nucleus of "Yankee Hill," convenient to the business district yet with a pleasant view and well above the miasmas of the swamp. The secondary center of Yankee culture developed in the 1850s on the west side after the Spring Street hill was graded to give easy access to the west-side heights from the central business area.[52]

Meanwhile, in the early 1840s, a dense Irish settlement developed along Michigan and farther south on poorly drained land. Here formed a "somewhat disreputable" neighborhood of "modest and unpretending frame buildings," many little more than shanties, often "erected

[49] Flower, op. cit., p. 143; Koss, op. cit., p. 74.
[50] A. C. Wheeler, The Chronicles of Milwaukee: Being a Narrative History of the Town from its Earliest Period to the Present (Milwaukee: Jermain and Brightman, 1861), pp. 74-76; Koss, p. 74.
[51] Wheeler, op. cit., pp. 15, 121; Milwaukee Sentinel, 16 October, 1895.
[52] Ibid., p. 112.

179

on posts above the marsh water."[53] The poor site undoubtedly reduced the cost of central location, as did high density living.[54] The area's Irish residents could find day-labor in draining swamps, cutting trees, and grading roads for town promoters, in house construction, in work at the nearby docks and warehouses, and in the growing business district. There is evidence that Juneau actively encouraged this settlement. A similar Irish nucleus grew up on swampland across the river, south of Spring Street on Kilbourn's plat, and undoubtedly fulfilled similar functions. Later Irish arrivals, stepping off the boat in either area, would have found a community ready to receive them and provide them with jobs.[55]

The initial German settlement was located on swampy land immediately north of the central business crossroad. The land here would have been as undesirable as that to the south and was not as close to major sources of casual labor, but most of the early German settlers were craftsmen who could benefit sufficiently from a central business location to bear with the poor site. Fortuitous factors were undoubtedly also important. One of Milwaukee's first German settlers, a gunsmith who enjoyed the good hunting the site offered, located his shop on the hillside near the spring; another German pioneer, after being cheated of his earnings by his Yankee patron, moved his boarding-house to the same area and established the first German tavern; a German baker and an amiable shoemaker settled not far away near Juneau's cabin. Around this nucleus of conviviality and mutual aid, German settlement converged. The area filled with small workshops and became the first focus of Milwaukee's German culture.[56]

This first mention of German settlement on the west side occurs in 1839, when a large colony of German Pietists arrived in Milwaukee.

[53] Robert Sutherland, "Reminiscences of a Twenty Months' Residence in Milwaukee in 1851-2-3," *Evening Wisconsin*, Milwaukee, 16 July, 1904; Robert Davies, "Early Buildings of Milwaukee," *Milwaukee Sentinel*, 16 October, 1895. Sutherland indicates that many of the settlers, especially those along the lake shore, may well have been squatters on land to which they had no title.

[54] The average value of ownership-parcels of land per cell was considerably lower in this area than in the central business block or the Yankee Hill area; similar low values were found in the German areas and on the south side. Based on calculations from data in the City of Milwaukee's "Assessment Roll, and State, County and School Tax List for the Year 1861," manuscript in the Milwaukee County Historical Society.

[55] E. E. Barton, publisher, *Industrial History of Milwaukee, The Commercial, Manufacturing and Railway Metropolis of the Northwest* (Milwaukee, 1886), p. 14; Wheeler, *op. cit.*, pp. 56, 112; concerning employment opportunities in urban construction, see Still, *op. cit.*, pp. 22-24. In 1843 harbor improvement provided another source of labor in the ward; Still, *op. cit.*, p. 46; *Milwaukee Courier*, 31 May 1843.

[56] Koss, *op. cit.*, pp. 50, 90-92; Wheeler, *op. cit.*, p. 56.

180

It was in the depths of a depression and, with poor land sales, Kilbourn and Juneau were engaged in bitter competition for settlers. Kilbourn therefore gave one of the Germans a piece of land near the center of his plat, on which the colonist built a half-timbered house. Such promotion evidently encouraged further German settlement in the area, and Kilbourn's embryo town center filled quickly with numerous small German boarding-houses.[57] The attractiveness of the area for Germans undoubtedly increased after 1842, when the construction of the water-power canal brought factories and mills to the area and bridges connected it to the older German nucleus.[58] There is little doubt that the higher land on the west side made living more pleasant, and for those Germans whose work did not require immediately central locations, or who could not afford even unhealthful and crowded central quarters, the west side offered an alternative. Soon the area's "almost purely American settlement" of the 1840s "dissolved like a mist" before the newcomers.[59] Here was good land available for the fine homes of "the aristocracy of the older German families," and numerous small combined workshops and residences located near Kilbourn's center and along the main outward arteries; laborers swelled the population farther outward, many perhaps living in shanties.[60] The German community could expand freely in a northwestern direction, and for the time being expansion of the east-side German area was blocked by topography and the high-status Yankee area.

By the 1850s, when new German arrivals were the main factor in swelling the city's population, most of the new subdivision took place in the northwestern sector. The new lots were smaller than the city average, and many of the small-scale developers were themselves German.[61] As the German population increased, it became almost inevitable that segregation—or perhaps congregation is a better term—would also increase. The newcomer welcomed the chance to live close to fellow-countrymen; he found little in the way of cheap vacant downtown housing, so he went to the fringes, where the city had prepared a place for him. Heavy German clustering therefore was a result not so much of exclusion, or even of impersonal economic

[57] *Ibid.*, pp. 103, 126, 158.

[58] Wheeler, *op. cit.*, pp. 128, 142-144; Koss, *op. cit.*, p. 129; canal construction also was a source of employment; *Milwaukee Advertiser,* 13 October, 1840.

[59] *Milwaukee Sentinel*, 16 October, 1895.

[60] *Milwaukee Free Press*, 21 May, 1911; Wheeler, *op. cit.*, p. 279; for reference to shanty living, see *Wisconsin Banner*, Milwaukee, 25 July 1846.

[61] Koss, *op. cit.*, p. 60; city maps provide evidence of lot-sizes and names of subdividers.

segregation, but simply of the great numbers of the Germans and the ability of the frontier city to satisfy spatially their congregational instincts.

The major alternative area of available housing was the south side. This area grew more slowly than the east and west sides had, partly because of the poor nature of the land, partly because of a contested title which was not cleared until the early 1840s. The construction of plank roads and the coming of the railroad opened the area and provided employment; several brickyards, a tannery, and engine works gradually attracted more laborers, and the industrial future of the area was becoming evident by 1860.[62] Though German and Irish laborers settled here, strong ethnic communities did not develop as they did elsewhere in the city, and this may well have been a mixed area of growing class, rather than ethnic, attachment.[63]

VIII

A MIXTURE of chance, site characteristics, economic status, and the locational requirements imposed on ethnic groups by their occupational characteristics can be used to clarify the initial location of Milwaukee's ethnic-economic social areas. Such areas then expanded along sectoral lines unless stopped by entrenched groups or physical obstacles, and set the spatial framework within which the city has evolved. Given the interaction of such complex forces, a discussion of Milwaukee's social areas in purely concentric terms is necessarily inadequate. However, gradient analysis has confirmed for Milwaukee the hypothesized pattern of central high-status settlement and low-status periphery. Factor analysis, while permitting a broad multi-variable delineation of Milwaukee's neighborhoods, also indicated that family status as well as socioeconomic status had different locational dimensions at the earlier period, and it suggested the existence of a central mixed residential area oriented toward the needs of the mercantile city. Finally, Milwaukee exhibited a high degree of ethnic clustering, which may well have differentiated it from older cities of the same period, cities where no one immigrant group so completely dominated, cities with inherited physical and social structures and with more diverse employment patterns. If Milwaukee is in any way representative of other midwestern cities of the same generation, the

[62] Wheeler, op. cit., p. 95; Harry H. Anderson, "Early Scandinavian Settlement in Milwaukee County," Historical Messenger of the Milwaukee County Historical Society, 25 (March 1969), pp. 7-8.

[63] The area did see the growth of a small but concentrated Scandinavian community after 1847; Anderson, op. cit., pp. 2-19. The south side was to be the site of major Polish settlement in following decades.

eastern city came much closer than the frontier city to being the crucible of Americanization hypothesized by the Turnerians.[64] Class and ethnic divisions appeared rapidly on the frontier and quickly were given spatial expression.

This study as it stands, however, remains incomplete. The precise nature of the "employment linkage," the relationship between residence and place of work, requires further investigation before more conclusive statements are made concerning the basis of neighborhoods. Similarly, the internal differentiation of ethnic neighborhoods deserves more detailed consideration. The nature of the sampling and aggregation techniques in this study have also presented certain problems, and an extra dimension could be added by tracing the residential behavior of sample individuals over time, in order to compensate for the weaknesses of the census "snapshots." The larger question of the representativeness of a Milwaukee study for the mid-nineteenth-century city in general has received only implicit treatment here. Nevertheless, the case of antebellum Milwaukee has provided both a caution against facile generalizations about urban social-spatial structure drawn from other times or other places, and an illustration of the advantages to be derived from testing such theories in different historical and geographical contexts.

[64] Frederick Jackson Turner, *Frontier and Section: Selected Essays* (Englewood Cliffs: Prentice-Hall, Inc., 1961), p. 51.

5

Urban Blacks in the South, 1865–1920:
The Richmond, Savannah, New Orleans,
Louisville and Birmingham Experience

ZANE L. MILLER

I

FOR at least a century after 1820 a series of influential observers of Negro life in America contended that cities did not provide an environment congenial to blacks. Negroes who left the countryside, it was felt, would either stagnate, regress, or develop into a permanent and chronically tumultuous, undifferentiated, and criminally inclined mass. This attitude was explicit in the writings of Charles C. Jones and Daniel Drake, both of whom were close students of southern cities in the ante-bellum years, and the same idea forms a central theme in Professor Richard C. Wade's study of urban slavery in the south.[1]

The rush of blacks to cities after Appomattox reinforced the notion. As one Savannah resident put it to the local Freedmen's Bureau agent:

> Nothing is more demoralizing to the negro than a town and city life. . . . They cannot obtain regular employment . . . and they will be tempted to pillage and steal . . . or starve. . . . [And] it is ruinous to their health as well as morals. They crowd together in small and often filthy apartments, and disease and death follows. It is best for them . . . that so far as possible they be kept in the country.[2]

---

[1] See Charles C. Jones, *The Religious Instruction of Negroes in the United States* (Westport, Connecticut: Negro Universities Press, 1969; first published in Savannah, 1842); Henry D. Shapiro and Zane L. Miller (editors), *Physician to the West: Selected Writings of Daniel Drake on Science and Society* (Lexington: University of Kentucky Press, 1970); Richard C. Wade, *Slavery in the Cities* (New York: Oxford University Press, 1964).

[2] E. H. Bacon to Capt. N. C. Dennett, October 11, 1865, in the National Archives, Washington, D.C., Record Group 105, Bureau of Freedmen, Refugees and Abandoned Lands, Box 32.

From the Reconstruction era until 1920, journalists, physicians, socio-logists, and such different Negro leaders as Kelly Miller and Booker T. Washington reached substantially the same conclusion.

Yet by 1900 important dissenters from this view had appeared. "There is a notion among Southern people," George Washington Cable complained just after the turn of the century, "that it is highly impor-tant that the Negro should be kept on the plantation. . . . That is false. What is civilization? The cityfying of a people. . . . True the city has many temptations. . . . But it only means a more energetic process of selection, and as much as some go down, others go up." W.E.B. DuBois was both more emphatic and more optimistic in his assessment of the influence of the urban environment on blacks in the latter half of the nineteenth century. The "country was peculiarly the seat of slavery," he argued in 1908, "and its blight still rests . . . heavily on the land, . . ." but "in the cities . . . the Negro has had his chance."[3] This chapter is an attempt to evaluate the views of the "anti-urban" and "pro-urban" spokesmen by examining some aspects of the black experience between 1864 and 1920 in Rich-mond, Savannah, New Orleans, Louisville, and Birmingham. The evi-dence from these places supports the thesis that the cities produced diversified and lively, rather than demoralized and inert, black communities.

II

It ought to be made clear at the outset that Negroes seeking a place in southern cities faced incredible obstacles. An analysis of differential public expenditures by race provides one way to gauge the odds. Broadly speaking, local officials adopted a budget policy which, gen-erously interpreted, might appropriately be characterized as one of "benign neglect."

The situation in Richmond at the turn of the century illustrates the point. In 1900 city contributions to charitable organizations aiding blacks totaled $550 and 9,787 bushels of coke, while contributions to organizations identified as white totaled $7,722 plus 12,500 bushels of coke and $500 worth of coal. Though the blacks made up a dispro-portionately large segment of Richmond's poor, only 611 black families and 886 single persons received meal from the city compared to white figures of 537 and 857 respectively. Negroes fared much worse at getting wood. Only 572 black families and 943 individuals were pro-

---

[3] For both quotes see W.E.B. DuBois (editor), *The Negro American Family,* Atlanta University Publications, Number 13 (Atlanta, 1908), pp. 64-65.

vided for, while the white totals came to 945 families and 1,605 individuals.

The city's record on health care was only slightly better. At the City Free Dispensary, Negroes received the bulk of the services rendered, but only 468 blacks were admitted to the hospital for treatment as opposed to 565 whites. Home visits by the Physicians to the Poor were similarly skewed. The records show 9,415 visits to white patients and 8,427 to blacks. And since Negroes constituted almost 39 per cent of the total population, and a much larger percentage of the poor, the 44 per cent of the visits made to them scarcely comes to a fair share.

The balance in the field of education was not much better. The city had no public library, but the city council appropriated $500 toward the support of a quasi-public institution which served whites only. Still, in 1898-1899, 50.9 per cent of the black school-age population was enrolled in public schools while whites registered 49.2 per cent; and 10 per cent of the black pupils received free textbooks (a total of 444) compared to only 3 per cent (a total of 317) among the whites. Black teachers, however, were not as well paid as their white colleagues. The salary gap for men, on the average, was $315.50 per year; for women $34.87; and all principals were white. Nor did expenditures per pupil on school property even out. Blacks cost the city $24.41 per student, and whites $46.09 per student.

Other indicators of educational opportunity fall into the same unequal pattern. In 1920 the city had four white junior high schools manned by 112 teachers and accommodating 2,969 students. There was no black junior high. At all-white Marshall High School the student-teacher ratio was 21.1, while at all-black Armstrong it mounted to 29.9 students per teacher. Marshall's library owned 14,000 volumes, Armstrong's but 1,000; Marshall had $39,000 of laboratory equipment to Armstrong's $1,300. The general per capita cost of instruction at Marshall was $68.58, while at Armstrong it was $34.83 per student.

The grim litany could be extended. Analyses covering recreation facilities, police and fire protection, and rapid transit all produce similar results, and the returns from the other four cities indicate that conditions there were just as bad. Indeed, in only one respect did the Negroes of Richmond receive the lion's share of the public goods. In 1900 the city provided blacks with 172 free coffins and 115 free burials; whites got only 29 and 44, respectively. The black advantage in this respect stemmed in large part from the fact that Negroes did not survive as well as whites the institutional care available to indigents. Of the 155 inmates of the almshouses who died that year, 112 were black and 43 white. The discrepancy had little effect on the budget. Out of $1,000 allotted for construction, $804.25 went to the white almshouse.[4]

Given these grossly discriminatory conditions, one can understand why contemporaries might conclude that blacks could only stagnate in the cities. A review of the federal census reports makes such a conclusion even more inescapable. In virtually every category covered by the population statistics, the blacks consistently turn up at the "wrong" place in the tables. Their illiteracy rates stood higher than those of either the native or the foreign-born whites; their death rates ran well above those of all whites; their school-attendance records came out generally weaker; and among them the indices of family instability seemed most ominous. They scored no better in the volumes on occupations. Throughout the period disproportionately large numbers of blacks tended to hold jobs offering the lowest pay, the most irregular employment, the longest hours, the worst working conditions, and the least status and authority.

Yet this interpretation, evoking the familiar image of an undifferentiated and retrograde black urban mass, is distorted. Despite the failure of city governments to adhere to a strict construction of the separate-but-equal doctrine, and regardless of the inability of the blacks to catch up with the whites in the decennial statistics, a closer look at the federal censuses, supplemented with data from other sources, indicates that the black communities in these cities contained lively and dynamic elements as well as large numbers of poor, oppressed, and dispirited individuals.

III

THE census figures on the differential growth rate for the black and white populations for each city provides a convenient point of departure.[5] (See Table 5-1). In general, 1900 marked an important change in growth rates for each race. To that date the black population increased in most of the cities at a faster rate than that of the total white population, but thereafter the black growth rate fell below that for native whites. With the exception of Louisville, the size of the Negro communities did not decline in absolute terms, but they did decline relative to the proportion of whites.

There are at least two explanations which might account for the

[4] This account is based on Richard Mendales, "Differential Public Expenditures by Race: Richmond," and "Sic Transit Richmond," Research Memoranda, Typescript, The Urban Negro Project, Center for Urban Studies, University of Chicago.

[5] I am indebted to Allen Emrich, my research assistant on the Urban Negro Project, who compiled the tables on population and occupations and made the preliminary analyses on which this and following discussions of the census data are based.

187

	1880	1890	1900	1910	1920
BIRMINGHAM					
Growth Rate					
Total	—	748%	47%	254%	35%
Negro	—	—	47	216	34
White	—	—	46	268	35
Population Composition					
Total	3,086 (100%)	26,193 (100%)	38,415 (100%)	132,685 (100%)	178,806 (100%)
Negro	—	11,254 (42)	16,575 (43)	52,305 (39)	70,236 (39)
White	—	14,909 (58)	21,840 (57)	80,380 (61)	108,550 (61)
RICHMOND					
Growth Rate					
Total	25%	28%	5%	50%	35%
Negro	20	16	0	45	16
White	28	37	8	53	45
Population Composition					
Total	63,597 (100%)	81,364 (100%)	85,050 (100%)	127,628 (100%)	171,667 (100%)
Negro	27,832 (44)	32,330 (40)	32,230 (38)	46,733 (37)	54,093 (32)
White	35,765 (56)	49,034 (60)	52,820 (62)	80,895 (63)	117,574 (68)
LOUISVILLE					
Growth Rate					
Total	23%	30%	27%	9%	5%
Negro	39	37	37	4	−1
White	20	29	25	11	6
Population Composition					
Total	123,752 (100%)	161,108 (100%)	204,731 (100%)	223,928 (100%)	234,891 (100%)
Negro	20,905 (17)	28,651 (18)	39,141 (19)	40,538 (18)	40,122 (17)
White	102,847 (83)	132,457 (82)	165,590 (81)	183,390 (82)	194,769 (83)

SAVANNAH

Growth Rate

Total	9%	41%	26%	20%	28%
Negro	20	46	23	18	18
White	0	35	29	22	38

Population Composition

Total	30,695 (100%)	43,174 (100%)	54,244 (100%)	65,064 (100%)	83,252 (100%)
Negro	15,654 (51)	22,963 (53)	28,090 (52)	33,246 (51)	39,179 (47)
White	15,041 (49)	20,211 (47)	26,154 (48)	31,818 (49)	44,073 (53)

NEW ORLEANS

Growth Rate

Total	13%	12%	19%	18%	14%
Negro	14	12	21	15	13
White	12	12	18	19	14

Population Composition

Total	215,954 (100%)	241,867 (100%)	287,104 (100%)	339,262 (100%)	387,219 (100%)
Negro	57,617 (27)	64,491 (27)	77,714 (27)	89,262 (26)	100,930 (26)
White	158,367 (73)	177,376 (73)	209,390 (73)	249,813 (74)	286,289 (74)

failure of Negroes to match the pace of the white population growth after 1900. Based on what we know of the south-to-north pattern of black migration for this period, one might assume that it was due to the increasing numbers of (presumably) more able southern rural blacks who moved to northern cities after 1890. There is, however, an alternative explanation. A two-step process could have been under way. Southern rural Negroes may well have continued to migrate to southern cities at nearly the same rate after the turn of the century as before, but as they arrived they merely filled a void left by young black urban adults who were moving from southern centers to homes in cities beyond the cotton curtain.

This latter explanation is based primarily on the fact that the number of young Negroes between fifteen and twenty-five in every city except Savannah increased at a slower rate than adult Negroes over twenty-five (and often at a slower rate than Negroes under fifteen). (See Table 5-2.) To be sure, the fifteen-to-twenty-five group is precisely the group most likely to be underenumerated in the census returns. But granting this precaution, the fact remains that the growth rate for young black adults was nearly identical to that for adults

TABLE 5-2 GROWTH RATES, BY AGE GROUPS, FOR
NEGRO MALES, FIVE SOUTHERN CITIES, 1890-1920

	1890–1900	1900–1910	1910–1920
BIRMINGHAM			
15-24 Years	30%	187%	25%
25 Years and Over	50	259	35
0-14 Years	35	278	35
RICHMOND			
15-25 Years	9%	43%	0%
25 Years and Over	3	57	22
0-14 Years	−8	42	13
LOUISVILLE			
15-24 Years	42%	−4%	−23%
25 Years and Over	55	13	6
0-14 Years	16	−11	−8
SAVANNAH[a]			
15-24 Years	18%	15%	30%
25 Years and Over	31	28	26
0-14 Years	9	7	6
NEW ORLEANS			
15-24 Years	26%	18%	10%
25 Years and Over	28	34	13
0-14 Years	11	−11	21

[a] Savannah is noted as an exception.

over twenty-five from 1890 to 1900, yet fell behind that pace between 1900 and 1910, and 1910 and 1920. Moreover, the higher growth rates for black adults after 1900 also support the view that rural Negroes were continuing to migrate to southern cities after the turn of the century. Rural-to-urban migration has usually been concentrated among adults between twenty-five and forty-five years of age, and that age category made up the bulk of the adult Negroes in these five cities.[6]

The data on illiteracy do not entirely substantiate this line of argument. If rural blacks were migrating to southern cities at a high rate after 1900 one would expect the Negro illiteracy levels to remain very high in those cities. And they were high in 1910 and 1920 when compared to the rate among whites, especially the native whites. But at the same time the proportion of illiterate Negroes over ten years of age dropped by more than 50 per cent in every city but one between 1890 and 1910, with the largest reduction in illiteracy taking place between 1900 and 1910. The exception was Savannah, where the decline was less than 50 per cent. (See Table 5-3.) This seems difficult to explain if rural migration continued at near pre-1900 levels (assuming a direct relationship between rural residence and illiteracy and an ineffective urban educational system for blacks).

Yet this evidence is not conclusive. Data on the illiteracy rate among blacks in Chicago from 1890 to 1920 tend to support the notion that large numbers of Negroes who were moving north had lived in southern cities at least long enough to benefit from the informal and formal educational facilities available in these places. Only 11 per cent of the nearly 15,000 blacks in Chicago in 1890 were illiterate, and this already low rate dropped to less than 8 per cent in 1890, while the city's black population doubled. In addition, the rate dropped to just under 4 per cent in 1920, although by then the black population had jumped to nearly 100,000. This rate was considerably below that in any of the five southern cities (see Table 5-3), and one that reflected the probability that southern blacks with at least some urban experience in the south constituted a significant proportion of those Negroes who participated in the Great Migration, and that their places in southern cities were filled by black newcomers from the countryside, large numbers of whom either were literate or managed somehow to become literate after their arrival.

There is additional census evidence which buttresses the two-step migration interpretation. In every city the black population had a

[6] See Donald J. Bogue, *Principles of Demography* (New York: John Wiley and Sons, 1969), p. 472.

TABLE 5-3 ILLITERACY RATES FOR PERSONS
10 YEARS OF AGE AND OVER, FIVE SOUTHERN
CITIES, 1890-1920

	1890	1900	1910	1920
BIRMINGHAM				
Negro				
Total	52%	40%	22%	18%
Male	47	37	—	19
Female	57	43	—	18
White	2	1	1	0
Foreign White	7	14	15	16
RICHMOND				
Negro				
Total	46%	32%	20%	15%
Male	44	30	—	14
Female	47	34	—	16
White	2	2	1	1
Foreign White	10	9	7	8
LOUISVILLE				
Negro				
Total	42%	31%	19%	14%
Male	39	29	—	14
Female	45	33	—	15
White	2	2	1	1
Foreign White	10	11	10	8
SAVANNAH				
Negro				
Total	51%	34%	27%	21%
Male	45	29	—	19
Female	57	39	—	23
White	2	1	1	1
Foreign White	9	8	7	6
NEW ORLEANS				
Negro				
Total	45%	36%	18%	16%
Male	38	32	—	13
Female	48	40	—	18
White	3	2	1	1
Foreign White	16	18	13	14

higher proportion of adults than did the white, a surprising statistic given the steeper death rates for black adults between twenty and forty. The black bulge in this age category might be explained, as noted above, by the high proportion of black adults who migrated to southern cities, and stayed there, as compared to those under twenty-five. Yet this raises a question: why did not the larger proportion of black adult residents, over the years, produce enough children to offset the mobility of black urban youths, and thus even up the growth rate of the total black and white populations and balance the proportion of black and white children?

Although the federal census does not bear directly on birth rates, it seems possible that the relative scarcity of children in the black communities might have stemmed from a declining birth rate. The evidence is strongest for Savannah. There the increase in children between 1890 and 1920 did not begin to match the increase of Negro adults. The returns for the other cities are more mixed, but the fact remains that they also have proportionately fewer black children than white. And Reynolds Farley's work in this field provides support for the hypothesis concerning a declining black urban birth rate. He has argued that the birth rate for Negroes throughout the United States generally began to fall in the last quarter of the nineteenth century, a trend which persisted until World War II.[7] If Farley is correct, and if it is true that birth rates have usually been lower in the city than in the country, it seems likely that the birth rate for blacks in these five cities did indeed decline at a faster rate than for whites.

A consideration of the great imbalance between males and females in their teens and early twenties also helps clarify migration patterns. The ratios ran as low as seventy males to every hundred females between fifteen and twenty-five, and it is unlikely that such a wide gap can be entirely discounted as the product of the greater propensity for underenumeration among young black males. (See Table 5-4). Another possible explanation is that black women tended to migrate to the city at a younger age than black men.[8] That this was probably the case in these five cities is partially substantiated by the higher rates of illiteracy among women than among men in the black communities, indicating that a heavier proportion of rural in-migrants were women. And, of course, the relative lack of young black men may be an indication that more of them were moving north than were young black women. In summary, then, both black men and women were moving into the southen cities, but the women came in larger numbers and a larger proportion of them were apt to stay.

IV

THE idea that the city somehow had a demoralizing effect on blacks is not supported by the census statistics. A comparison of the proportions of married, widowed, and divorced males by race reveals few

[7] See Reynolds Farley, *Negro Cohort Fertility* (University of Chicago, unpublished Ph.D. dissertation, 1964).

[8] Bogue, *op. cit.*, p. 167.

193

significant differences. Black men tended more often to be married, the percentage of widowers was several points higher among blacks than among whites, and a higher proportion of white men remained single. In short, on the basis of these figures alone, it seems that black men were not significantly more susceptible to family instability than were whites.

TABLE 5-4   NUMBERS OF MALES AND FEMALES, NEGRO POPULATION AGED 15-24, FIVE SOUTHERN CITIES, 1890-1920

	1890	1900	1910	1920
BIRMINGHAM				
Male	1,471	1,913	5,482	6,870
Female	1,626	2,518	6,485	8,890
RICHMOND				
Male	3,096	3,379	4,842	4,843
Female	3,466	4,706	6,379	6,945
LOUISVILLE				
Male	2,893	4,105	3,939	3,042
Female	3,418	4,890	4,493	3,701
SAVANNAH				
Male	2,190	2,576	2,951	3,846
Female	2,986	4,168	4,490	5,327
NEW ORLEANS				
Male	5,365	6,763	7,947	8,776
Female	7,793	9,468	11,002	11,636

The marital statistics for black women, on the other hand, show striking contrasts. Often one-fifth and sometimes one-fourth of all Negro women over fifteen were widows. These figures ran 50 to 100 per cent higher than the proportion among native white women, though often less than the proportion among foreign-born women. (See Table 5-5.) The high death rate among Negroes, especially for those under forty, was undoubtedly the major factor behind these differences.

The marital-status data by age group for Louisville and New Orleans, for example, show that by far the largest number of widows among native and foreign-born whites and blacks were over thirty-five. Since a much higher proportion of foreign-born white women were over thirty-five than Negroes or native whites, the percentage of widows for all foreign-born white women was raised substantially, and this accounts for the difference between them and Negro women.

194

	1890	1900	1910	1920
BIRMINGHAM				
Negro Male				
Married	—	50%	57%	63%
Widowed	—	6	9	7
Divorced	—	1	1	1
White Male				
Married	—	44%	56%	61%
Widowed	—	5	4	4
Divorced	—	0	0	1
Widowed Female				
Negro	—	25%	22%	21%
White	—	14	12	12
Foreign White	—	18	14	15
RICHMOND				
Negro Male				
Married	—	48%	52%	60%
Widowed	—	6	6	6
Divorced	—	0	0	1
White Male				
Married	—	48%	51%	59%
Widowed	—	4	4	4
Divorced	—	0	0	0
Widowed Female				
Negro	—	21%	20%	18%
White	—	14	14	13
Foreign White	—	27	24	19
LOUISVILLE				
Negro Male				
Married	50%	45%	49%	57%
Widowed	6	7	8	8
Divorced	1	1	1	2
White Male				
Married	43%	47%	51%	57%
Widowed	3	3	4	4
Divorced	1	1	1	1
Widowed Female				
Negro	22%	23%	22%	22%
White	10	12	11	12
Foreign White	28	32	33	35
SAVANNAH				
Negro Male				
Married	—	—	61%	63%
Widowed	—	—	6	6
Divorced	—	—	1	1
White Male				
Married	—	—	52%	59%
Widowed	—	—	4	4
Divorced	—	—	0	0

TABLE 5-5 *(Continued)*

	1890	1900	1910	1920
Widowed Female				
Negro	—	—	19%	17%
White	—	—	14	12
Foreign White	—	—	27	22
NEW ORLEANS				
Negro Male				
Married	59%	56%	58%	61%
Widowed	5	6	6	5
Divorced	0	0	0	0
White Male				
Married	40%	44%	49%	56%
Widowed	3	4	4	5
Divorced	0	0	0	1
Widowed Female				
Negro	24%	24%	21%	20%
White	12	13	14	18
Foreign White	40	42	35	30

In the twenty-five-to-thirty-five age category, however, the incidence of widowhood among Negro women was two to three times that among native white or foreign-born white women. This can be attributed, at least in part, to the mortality differentials by color, which show that the probability of death before forty was much higher for Negroes than whites. And just as the death rate among blacks dropped after 1918 in every city, so too did the percentage of widows.

Yet not all the census evidence leads to the conclusion that death was everywhere the major cause of broken homes in the black neighborhoods. The comparative percentages of male and female widows among Negroes in Louisville and New Orleans show three to four times as many females widowed between twenty-five and thirty-five as males; and the same difference extended to those over thirty-five. It is possible but unlikely that the incidence of death was that much higher among men than women.

Other explanations are feasible. Black and white clergymen, social workers, public health officials, and other close observers and students of life among the black urban poor often asserted that common-law alliances were frequent, and they repeatedly condemned the practice before black audiences. It is possible that black women, confronted by a curious stranger who identified himself as a government official (the census-taker), preferred to conceal their "peculiar" domestic arrangement behind the veil of widowhood. Beyond that, all women

196

seemed inclined to hide the fact that they had been deserted, for native and foreign-born white as well as black women were three or four times more likely to list themselves as widowed than were men. In addition, the greater attraction of cities generally for widowed and divorced women has to be taken into account. And, finally, the black-white widow differential may also be another reflection of the high mobility of young adult blacks, both rural and urban.

Two other sets of figures from the population volumes ought to be considered. Both the school-attendance and illiteracy records contradict the notion that black southern city-dwellers constituted an inert and backward group. Whatever the quality of the schools, the differences between the proportions of black and white children recorded as attending school diminished steadily until, by 1920, 90 per cent of the children of grade-school age of both races attended school. But blacks still found it difficult to secure access to high schools. (See Table 5-6.)

Illiteracy rates reflect the increase in elementary-school enrollment among blacks. (See Table 5-3). Over the years, illiteracy among Negroes above ten years of age decreased. Most of the improvement occurred between 1900 and 1910, and there was some progress during the next decade when the Great Migration was reaching its peak. Despite these gains, however, the differences between native whites

TABLE 5-6 SCHOOL ATTENDANCE, BY COLOR AND AGE GROUP, FIVE SOUTHERN CITIES, 1890-1920

		1890			1900			1910		1920	
Age	5-9	10-14	15-19	5-9	10-14	15-19	5-14	7-13	14-15	16-17
BIRMINGHAM											
Negro	20%	48%	10%	28%	59%	11%	73%	90%	72%	32%
White	33	74	20	41	85	30	75	91	88	51
RICHMOND											
Negro	34%	66%	19%	27%	71%	18%	65%	90%	67%	27%
White	45	85	24	45	82	26	79	95	78	39
LOUISVILLE											
Negro	44%	75%	21%	48%	80%	24%	87%	95%	83%	31%
White	55	82	17	53	83	21	89	96	78	30
SAVANNAH											
Negro	33%	61%	14%	28%	68%	21%	66%	91%	66%	26%
White	51	86	23	44	86	27	83	96	82	44
NEW ORLEANS											
Negro	37%	66%	13%	22%	68%	15%	68%	89%	69%	31%
White	48	79	16	34	79	19	80	93	80	30

and blacks remained great. The percentages of illiterate blacks ranged from 15 in Louisville and Richmond to 21 in Savannah, while among native whites it spread from a low of 0.7 to a high of 1.2 per cent.

Like the population figures, the federal occupational statistics can be (and were) used both to support and to dispute DuBois' optimistic assessment of the effect of city life on Negroes. Though space limitations forbid a thorough discussion here, a survey of the census data (Table 5-7), the Atlanta University Publications on urban blacks, the *Negro Year Book*, the proceedings of the National Negro Business League, biographical dictionaries, local directories, and study of residential patterns all suggest that after 1880 a new and larger black middle class took shape in these cities. Clergymen, as before, topped the list, but a substantial segment of them, unlike their predecessors in the immediate post-bellum years, had attended seminaries. By 1900 each of the five towns also contained growing cadres of black teachers, many of them in secondary-school or college and in administrative posts, and smaller and more gradually expanding groups of lawyers, doctors, dentists, and pharmacists. And each of the black communities supported sizable numbers of black entrepreneurs.

This assortment of people constituted the "talented tenth" of the black urban south. Along with the energetic, restless, and highly mobile youths and younger adults concealed in the population reports, they brought a new vitality to the black communities. At a sharply accelerating rate after 1890 they added a new layer of organizations to the post-bellum structure of churches, secret societies, political clubs, and benevolent and military organizations. Though strategies and goals varied, between 1880 and 1920 the black bourgeoisie organized an imposing array of clubs, societies, and associations which (whatever their particular programs) above all stressed racial pride, unity, and achievement.

V

But the race-uplift movement had another dimension. In the early 1920's, the *Negro Year Book* announced that the new black groups were pushing for greater participation in politics. They sought not to elect black officials but rather "to secure . . . paved streets, well-lighted streets, clean streets and alleys, water and sewer facilities and, most important of all, protection under the law."[9] That remark implies that the emergence of the new Negro in the urban south was not exclusively due to rural-urban and interurban migration pat-

[9] *Negro Year Book,* 1921-1922, p. 53.

TABLE 5-7 OCCUPATIONS OF THE BLACK MIDDLE CLASS, FIVE SOUTHERN CITIES, 1900 AND 1920[a]

RICHMOND	1900	1920
Professional		
Clergy	51	105
Dentists	N.A.	N.A.
Doctors	8	28
Engineers	N.A.	—
Gov. Officials	—	2
Journalists	N.A.	N.A.
Lawyers	9	12
Teachers	205	266
Business		
Bankers	8	5
Bldg. Contractors	N.A.	N.A.
Com. Travel	2	4
Insurance	N.A.	52
Mfg. & Co. Officials	6	12
Real Estate	N.A.	12
Total	289	498

NEW ORLEANS	1900	1920
Professional		
Clergy	126	183
Dentists	N.A.	22
Doctors	22	30
Engineers	3	1
Gov. Officials	21	4
Journalists	N.A.	N.A.
Lawyers	7	5
Teachers	206	338
Business		
Bankers	5	—
Bldg. Contractors	N.A.	21
Com. Travel	10	2
Insurance	N.A.	36
Mfg. & Co. Officials	26	12
Real Estate	N.A.	5
Total	429	659

LOUISVILLE	1900	1920
Professional		
Clergy	88	135
Dentists	N.A.	9
Doctors	19	47
Engineers	N.A.	2
Gov. Officials	4	6
Journalists	5	N.A.
Lawyers	7	10
Teachers	205	232
Business		
Bankers	3	—
Bldg. Contractors	N.A.	5
Com. Travel	2	1
Insurance	N.A.	19
Mfg. & Co. Officials	15	7
Real Estate	N.A.	3
Total	348	476

SAVANNAH	1900
Professional	
Clergy	71
Dentists	N.A.
Doctors	13
Engineers	N.A.
Gov. Officials	9
Journalists	N.A.
Lawyers	5
Teachers	104
Business	
Bankers	6
Bldg. Contractors	N.A.
Com. Travel	1
Insurance	N.A.
Mfg. & Co. Officials	3
Real Estate	N.A.
Total	212

BIRMINGHAM	1920
Professional	
Clergy	222
Dentists	N.A.
Doctors	13
Engineers	N.A.
Gov. Officials	9
Journalists	N.A.
Lawyers	5
Teachers	104
Business	
Bankers	—
Bldg. Contractors	22
Com. Travel	2
Insurance	43
Mfg. & Co. Officials	2
Real Estate	11
Total	665

[a] These data underestimate the size of the black middle class. Other sources, including W.E.B. DuBois, (ed.), *The Negro in Business*, Atlanta University Publications, No. 4 (Atlanta 1899), indicate that a substantial number of barbers and merchants ought to be considered "middle-class," and the census provided no figures for druggists and undertakers.

terns, improved educational opportunities, higher levels of literacy, or the development of a larger and better-educated middle class. For the *Negro Year Book*'s list of goals are those associated with neighborhood politics, and it was the appearance after 1880 of a new kind of Negro neighborhood—the central-city ghetto—which combined with these other forces to open the modern era in the history of American urban blacks, both above and below the Mason-Dixon line.

An analysis of the federal census ward figures, available only for New Orleans, Richmond, and Louisville, barely hints at this development (in part because of shifting ward boundaries). In New Orleans the index of segregation by ward declined after 1870 and did not return to the level of that date until 1920. Moreover, the New Orleans index never approached the heights reached in Chicago which, in 1920, stood just above 75 on a scale of 100. Clearly, residential segregation did not conform to ward boundaries in New Orleans, though the tables do reveal a tendency for certain wards to become Negro wards. (See Table 5-8).

In Louisville, however, there was a progressive increase in the segregation index. Although it did not match Chicago's record, it was, nonetheless, more than twice the rate in New Orleans. And as in New Orleans, the Louisville index alone fails to reflect the existence of a black neighborhood in wards nine through eleven. Finally, the index for Richmond shows the continuing occupation of Jackson Ward by blacks between 1880 and 1900, but the juggling of boundaries thereafter reduced the figure to about the level of New Orleans in 1920.

VI

REFERENCE to the occupation statistics, maps, and literary sources not only sharpens the picture but also bares the outline of the process. Before 1860, as Wade has pointed out, southern cities had a dual residential system for blacks. Some were scattered across the cityscape, but others accumulated on the periphery in small and geographically distinct but heavily Negro districts. The Civil War did little to disturb this arrangement except, with the rush of freedmen to cities, to enlarge the black neighborhoods on the urban fringes. Dispersed in relatively small groups, blacks remained vulnerable to physical attack, and their leaders found it difficult to pull together their meager resources.

About 1880, however, a variety of factors began to reshuffle the residential distribution of both whites and blacks. With the advent of first horse-drawn and then electric mass transit systems, the five

TABLE 5-8 INDEXES OF SEGREGATION, THREE SOUTHERN CITIES, 1870–1920

	1870	1890	1900	1910	1920
RICHMOND					
Negro-Native White	3	35	43	40	20
Negro-Foreign White	8	29	37	30	12
LOUISVILLE					
Negro-Native White	28	29	30	35	41
Negro-Foreign White	33	31	27	26	34
NEW ORLEANS					
Negro-Native White	24	18	19	15	17
Negro-Foreign White	18	16	16	19	24

Wards Tending Toward Segregation[a]

	1870	1890	1900	1910	1920
NEW ORLEANS (17 Wards)					
Ward 2					
Negro	3,523 (20 %)	3,284 (20 %)	3,662 (22 %)	4,733 (27 %)	6,036 (34 %)
White	14,519	13,122	13,094	12,530	11,592
Ward 11					
Negro	2,493 (17 %)	5,271 (25 %)	6,720 (28 %)	9,986 (36 %)	12,247 (40 %)
White	12,188	15,740	17,302	17,465	18,107
Ward 15					
Negro	3,013 (44 %)	4,496 (44 %)	6,075 (41 %)	5,760 (37 %)	4,874 (29 %)
White	3,806	5,838	8,700	9,711	11,911
Ward 16					
Negro	—	1,982 (56 %)	2,442 (49 %)	3,300 (42 %)	3,154 (30 %)
White	—	1,548	2,456	4,538	7,479
LOUISVILLE (12 Wards)					
Ward 4					
Negro	1,868 (20 %)	2,982 (24 %)	3,332 (27 %)	3,261 (28 %)	2,928 (28 %)
White	7,519	9,629	8,976	8,184	7,574
Ward 9					
Negro	2,162 (28 %)	3,558 (34 %)	4,635 (42 %)	4,038 (41 %)	3,887 (45 %)
White	5,668	6,806	6,490	5,738	4,686
Ward 10					
Negro	2,255 (20 %)	4,884 (33 %)	6,587 (44 %)	7,999 (58 %)	8,385 (69 %)
White	9,161	9,896	8,648	5,746	3,784
Ward 11					
Negro	1,178 (8 %)	3,789 (15 %)	5,330 (17 %)	6,526 (20 %)	7,761 (26 %)
White	12,192	21,766	25,175	25,393	22,475
RICHMOND					
Ward—Jackson					
Negro	—	13,531 (79 %)	15,592 (83 %)	—[b]	—
White	—	3,679	3,121	—	—

[a] Selection was made on the basis of those wards which seemed to show a linear growth of blacks vs. whites, or those which had an "extreme" percentage of blacks in any one census year.
[b] It is interesting, nonetheless, that in 1910 two new wards, Henry and Washington, were 62 % and 30 % Negro respectively, and several wards had risen 10 to 20 "black-percentage" points over 1900. By 1920 Henry and Washington wards had been eliminated and the entire city was divided into but four wards, one of which was still 50 % black.

cities began to expand geographically at an unprecedented pace. At the same time there began a process of sorting out which, broadly speaking, tended to place the more successful whites on the periphery while concentrating the blacks in the central city. But the progress of this shift and the precise patterns it produced varied from place to place.

Among these five towns a central-city ghetto, or something very like it, appeared first and in its most highly articulated form in Rich-

201

mond. It then had a larger proportion of blacks in its population than any other city except Savannah and, during the late nineteenth century, when Jackson Ward took shape, its rate of population growth was steady if not spectacular. More significantly, a large segment of Richmond's black population (since before the Civil War) was employed as artisans, mechanics, and especially as factory workers. And it was, after Appomattox as before, easier for members of these occupational categories, as opposed to domestic servants, to establish residences in black districts well beyond the master's eye.

Louisville, for similar reasons, developed in a similar fashion, despite the fact that its black population was smaller than Richmond's and that its overall growth rate was slower. Here, too, it seems, occupational structure combined with the impact of transportation innovations were the critical factors. But other forces played a role in shaping the early twentieth-century configuration. In 1890, Louisville's developing ghetto was in two pieces, one on each side of the Central Business District. By 1910, the "West End" was generally recognized as the principal Negro residential sector, and, not surprisingly, it got the city's first Negro branch library.

Savannah provides an interesting variation. Its general rate of population growth exceeded that of both Richmond and Louisville, but since it started from a smaller ante-bellum base its residential rearrangement and geographic expansion after 1880 was not as dramatic. It had, moreover, from 1870 on, the largest proportion of blacks of any of the five cities, a fact which probably accounted for the early appearance (by 1870) of a large black settlement on the eastern edge of town near an area known as Yamacraw. But the economy remained heavily commercial, and the occupations open to blacks were restricted. They worked chiefly as laborers along the docks and around the railway terminals and factories which flanked the town, or as domestic servants. Consequently, here, too, as in Louisville, not one but two major centers of Negro concentration developed. They lay on either side of the city's center, but were, as late as 1910, separated from the business district by a white buffer. Thus situated, Savannah's dual ghettos provided living space within easy walking distance of the wharves, railroads, factories, and the employers of domestic servants. And both districts tended to expand on a north-south axis away from the river as the white population pushed southward.

Had Savannah, given the severe commercial and service orientation of its black occupational pattern, been larger in 1865 or a more rapidly growing city thereafter, and had the blacks constituted a smaller proportion of the total population, it is likely that in 1920 Negroes there would have been more dispersed. This is, in any case, precisely what happened in New Orleans. In 1860, New Orleans was already a big city, and it had a steadily moderate growth rate up to 1920. The proportion of blacks in the total population remained at a relatively low level, and its economy remained commercial. Here, as in Savannah, blacks worked chiefly on the docks, around the railway terminals in the front and rear of the city and up the river, and as domestics. Hence, though a central-city ghetto was taking shape before 1920, New Orleans' blacks were more dispersed than in any of the five towns.

Birmingham falls in a class entirely its own. Founded after the war, it had no opportunity to develop the residential characteristics of the slave cities. But after 1880 it grew dramatically in size and population, and its economy, compared to the other cities, was lopsidedly industrial. From almost the beginning it was residentially segregated, though a 1920 school survey map showed a black population scattered in solid but far-flung and relatively small enclaves.

This pattern was in large part a product of the great annexation of 1910. From the 1880s on, urban growth in the Birmingham district proceeded by the proliferation of satellite cities around outlying factories. In each of these places residential segregation was the rule, and their annexation produced the distinctive pattern of 1920. Nonetheless, old Birmingham by then had a black inner-city ghetto which had developed a black Central Business District serving all the metropolitan ghettos.

VII

RESIDENTIAL developments, then, as well as improved educational levels among blacks generally, the emergence of a new black bourgeoisie, and the ability of the cities to attract rural blacks on a selective basis help explain the appearance of the race-pride and civic-betterment movement among blacks in the urban south during the early twentieth century. Trapped in the growing ghettos the black bourgeoisie took the lead in seeking a way out. Those whites on the cutting edge of the expanding Negro districts responded with hostility, but a few of those living farther out sought to improve conditions by advocating a more just application of the separate-but-equal doctrine. Thomas Jackson Woofter exaggerated, perhaps, when he maintained that residential segregation and the neglect of black neighborhoods which everywhere accompanied it had brought an "intense community consciousness" among Negroes, an organized drive for "self-improvement," and eventually a city-wide commitment to ameliorate conditions.[10] But his major premise was on the mark. "Since emancipation," he asserted in 1928, "nothing more astonishing than the shift of Negroes to cities has occurred to effect the contact between the races."[11]

[10] Thomas Jackson Woofter, Jr., and associates, *Negro Problems in Cities* (Garden City: Doubleday, 1928), p. 19.
[11] *Ibid.*, p. 29.

6

Fundamentalism and Urbanization:
A Quantitative Critique of
Impressionistic Interpretations

GREGORY H. SINGLETON

I

"HEAVE an egg out of a Pullman window," wrote H. L. Mencken during the 1920s, and you will hit a fundamentalist anywhere in the United States today."[1] Social and religious historians have not quite accepted Mencken's overstatement, but it does stand as a fair summary of the current state of scholarly understanding of the religious climate of the 1920s. Norman Furniss has shown the effects of the movement on leading denominational assemblies, and Louis Gasper has suggested that fundamentalism was strong enough to rise out of the ashes of the humiliation of Dayton, Tennessee, and form new national alliances in the 1930s and 1940s.[2] No one has systematically attempted to assess the relative strength of fundamentalism in various sections of the nation, but one of the more popular interpretations holds that the movement was strongest in the rural areas of the South and Midwest.[3] More recently, fundamentalism has been seen as an "urban" movement. Paul Carter and Ernest Sandeen have pointed to the origins of fundamentalist doctrine in northeastern cities.[4] More general treatments tend to interpret fundamentalism as a major part of American religious thought and practice in the 1920s. It was,

[1] Quoted in William Manchester, *H. L. Mencken: Disturber of the Peace* (New York: Harper & Row, 1951), p. 206.

[2] Norman F. Furniss, *The Fundamentalist Controversy, 1918-1931* (New Haven: Yale University Press, 1954); Louis Gasper, *The Fundamentalist Movement* (The Hague: Mouton, 1963).

[3] See, e.g., William E. Leuchtenberg, *The Perils of Prosperity: 1914-1932* (Chicago: University of Chicago Press, 1958), pp. 205-217.

[4] Paul A. Carter, "The Fundamentalist Defense of the Faith," in *Change and Continuity in Twentieth-Century America: The 1920's*, edited by John Braeman, Robert H. Bremmer, and David Brody (Columbus: Ohio State University Press, 1968), pp. 179-214; Ernest R. Sandeen, "Towards a Historical Interpretation of the Origins of Fundamentalism," *Church History*, 36 (1967), pp. 66-83.

according to George Mowry, "a strong surge of feeling and opinion in the American Churches."[5]

Besides the controversy over the locus of fundamentalism, there is also disagreement over the constituency and intellectual vigor of the movement. Furniss has shown fundamentalist influence in the major denominations, such as the Presbyterian and the Protestant Episcopal churches. Kenneth T. Jackson, however, specifically excluded these two denominations in his discussion of the possible relations between the Ku Klux Klan and fundamentalism in Memphis.[6] A recent anthology of the fundamentalist-modernist conflict tends to indicate that the movement was characterized by the reasoned arguments of J. Gresham Machen, and John Hicks has given Billy Sunday and Aimee Semple McPherson as examples of the primitive fundamentalism of "great numbers of the Protestant clergy."[7]

All scholars of this movement, however, seem to agree that there is *some* connection between fundamentalism and urbanization. Whether that connection is seen as a response or a reaction to the growth of cities, the fact that the fundamentalists were most active during the "first decade of the urban era in America" is seen by most scholars as a fact to conjure with.[8] This is probably a function

[5] George E. Mowry, *The Urban Nation, 1920-1960* (New York: Hill and Wang, 1965), p. 29.

[6] Kenneth T. Jackson, *The Ku Klux Klan in the City, 1915-1930* (New York: Oxford University Press, 1967), pp. 45-49.

[7] *Controversy in the Twenties: Fundamentalism, Modernism, and Evolution,* edited by Willard B. Gatewood, Jr. (Nashville: Vanderbilt University Press, 1969); John Hicks, *Republican Ascendency* (New York: Harper & Row, 1960), p. 182.

[8] Aside from the works cited elsewhere, the works referred to here are: Bernard Weisberger, *They Gathered at the River* (Boston: Little, Brown and Company, 1958); Richard Hofstadter, "Fundamentalism and Status Politics on the Right," *Columbia University Forum,* 8 (Fall, 1965), pp. 18-24; Richard Hofstadter, *Anti-Intellectualism in American Life* (New York: Alfred A. Knopf, Inc., 1963); Paul A. Carter, *The Decline and Revival of the Social Gospel* (Ithaca: Cornell University Press, 1956); William G. McLaughlin, *Billy Sunday Was His Real Name* (Chicago: University of Chicago Press, 1955); William G. McLaughlin, *Modern Revivalism: Charles Grandison Finney to Billy Graham* (New York: The Ronald Press Company, 1959); William G. McLaughlin, "Is There a Third Force in Christendom?" in *Religion in America,* edited by William G. McLaughlin and Robert N. Bellah (Boston: Beacon Press, 1968), pp. 45-72; Ralph Lord Roy, *Apostles of Discord* (Boston: Beacon Press, 1953); Ray Ginger, *Six Days or Forever? Tennessee v. John Thomas Scopes* (Boston: Beacon Press, 1958); Stewart G. Cole, *The History of Fundamentalism* (New York: R. R. Smith, Inc., 1931); Robert Moats Miller, *American Protestantism and the Social Issues, 1919-1939* (Chapel Hill: University of North Carolina Press, 1958); Herbert W. Schneider, *Religion in 20th Century America* (Cambridge, Mass.: Harvard University Press, 1952); Kenneth K. Bailey, *Southern White Protestantism in the Twentieth Century* (New York: Harper & Row, 1964); Willard B. Gatewood, Jr., *Preachers, Pedagogues and Politicians: The Evolution Controversy in North*

of the perception of some types of numbers as magical by historians who are not accustomed to a systematic scrutiny of quantitative data. The report of the 1920 census that over half of the nation's population were in settlements of 2,500 or more (one of those magical numbers) seems to be the decisive piece of evidence. This study is not intended as a frontal attack on this general "urban" interpretation. It is taken as a matter of fact that fundamentalism is coincident with the rise of urban America. Rather, this study will attempt to investigate some of the ways in which fundamentalism and urbanization are connected, and to suggest areas in which the most rudimentary form of quantitative analysis could shed some light on those areas where disagreement has been more a function of the lack of clearly defined concepts than of interpretive differences.

Before proceeding to the specifics, let me state a few general assumptions based on an acquaintance with the sociology of religion, my own research, and my own involvement in church activities at various local and denominational levels between 1959 and 1964. First, American religious history has tended to be intellectual history. For example, Baptists are seen as people who believe in baptism by immersion and are insistent on the independence of the local congregation.[9] This interpretation is derived from a study of doctrinal statements which are issued by national assemblies and may be matters of indifference to a large part of the laity. Second, it may be erroneous to assume that even a majority of the membership of any given denomination includes their religious affiliation as an important part of their own self-definition. Third, attitude studies, past and present, should be used by the religious historian with care, if at all. Such studies do not tell us what a group of people believe, but what they are willing to *say* they believe. I am suggesting that a Methodist, for example, is never so aware of being a Methodist as when he is asked what he as a Methodist believes. At that moment he may recite Methodist doctrine or guess what a Methodist *should* answer.[10]

Carolina, 1920-1927 (Chapel Hill: University of North Carolina Press, 1966); Robert T. Handy, "Fundamentalism and Modernism in Perspective," *Religion in Life*, 24 (1955).

[9] This sort of interpretation is outlined and criticized by sociologist Paul M. Harrison, *Authority and Power in the Free Church Tradition: A Social Case Study of the American Baptist Convention* (Princeton: Princeton University Press, 1959).

[10] The bibliography of attitude studies is too long to be included here. Two good examples, both of which contain numerous citations of similar studies, are Rodney Stark and Charles Y. Glock, *American Piety: The Nature of Religious Commitment* (Berkeley and Los Angeles: University of California Press, 1968); and Jeffrey K. Hadden, *The Gathering Storm in the Churches* (Garden City: Doubleday & Company, Inc., 1969).

Obviously my assumptions lead me to focus on what Anthony Wallace has disdainfully called, "the scaffolding and milieu of religion rather than religion itself."[11] I think there are two excellent reasons for working within that limited context, however. First, the value of using religious groupings for social analysis has been demonstrated over the past few decades by such diverse scholars as Liston Pope, Arthur J. Vidich and Joseph Bensman, Stephan Thernstrom, and Richard Jensen.[12] Second, to state the obvious, "religion itself" is not necessarily equatable with denominational affiliation. My own work on religious affiliation in Los Angeles, for example, tells me much more about the nature of the social and political structure of that city than about the nature of religious commitment, which remains a questionable area for systematic investigation.[13]

II

I MUST apologize for the length of the following discussion over the classification of religious organizations, but definitions of fundamentalism range from "biblical literalism" to "devoutly religious." Obviously, we need more rigorous classifications which will allow us to combine various denominations into confessional groups and correlate membership with various social indices. Unfortunately, the state of religious statistics in the United States is such that most of the inferential tools that have proven most valuable in population studies cannot be used.[14] The national data from the *Year Book of American*

[11] Anthony F. C. Wallace, *Religion: An Anthropological View* (New York: Random House, 1966), p. vii.

[12] Liston Pope, *Millhands and Preachers: A Study of Gastonia* (New Haven: Yale University Press, 1942); Arthur J. Vidich and Joseph Bensman, *Small Town in Mass Society: Class, Power, and Religion in a Rural Community* (Princeton: Princeton University Press, 1958); Stephan Thernstrom, *Poverty and Progress: Social Mobility in a Nineteenth-Century City* (Cambridge, Mass.: Harvard University Press, 1964); pp. 171-180; Richard Jensen, *The Winning of the Midwest: Social and Political Conflict, 1888-1896* (Chicago: University of Chicago Press, 1971).

[13] I did make an attempt to get a general feel for religious attitudes in Los Angeles through sermon material. The problem, of course, is that the sermons are written by ministers and are therefore not very indicative. My own experience has been that ministers are given a great deal of freedom with few proscriptions, but that treading into the proscribed area usually results in the loss of a position. That is to say, there is nothing positive that can be inferred for a congregation or denomination from sermon material. On this, see Ernest Q. Campbell and Thomas Pettigrew, *Christians in Racial Crisis: A Study of Little Rock's Ministry* (Washington: Public Affairs Press, 1959).

[14] For a thorough discussion see William Petersen, "Religious Statistics in the United States," *Journal for the Scientific Study of Religion*, 1 (April, 1962), 163-179.

Churches and the Bureau of the Census volumes in *Religious Bodies* contain, at best, approximations.[15] Local materials are usually incomplete and sketchy, denying the cautious researcher anything approaching a random sample. This is especially true of short-lived denominations which have left only a record of their church locations in city directories. These denominations, as will be seen, have been important in the fundamentalist movement. We must, therefore, be quite clear about our use of the term "fundamentalism," and we must eschew the sort of hazy definition which will render the sparse available data impotent.

Norman Furniss used attitudes toward evolution and modernism as the criteria for classification of individual churchmen.[16] For denominations, this is a bit more difficult. It would be more useful to divide the various Protestant denominations into three levels of participation in the fundamentalist movement. There are two criteria for including a denomination of the "Definitely Fundamentalist" category. (See Table 6-1) One is membership in the World's Christian Fundamentals Association, founded in Chicago in 1919 to further fundamentalist doctrine and combat modernism.[17] The other is changes in doctrinal statements to conform with the five "Fundamentals": the virgin birth of Christ; the physical resurrection; the inerrancy of the Bible in every detail; the substitutionary theory of atonement; and the imminent and physical second coming of Christ.[18] This was the *summa* of the twelve volumes of *The Fundamentals: A Testimony of the Truth*, published between 1909 and 1912, financed by two wealthy Los Angeles oilmen, Milton and Lyman Stewart, and distributed without charge to religious leaders throughout the land.[19]

There were twenty-three "Definitely Fundamentalist" denominations of various Baptist, Reformed, Pentecostal, and Adventist persuasions which had changed their doctrinal statements to encompass the

[15] For a criticism of the latter source, see C. Luther Fry, *The U.S. Looks at Its Churches* (New York: Institute of Social and Religious Research, 1930), pp. 1-6.

[16] Furniss, p. vii.

[17] The general narrative can be found in Furniss or Cole. An interesting account of the activities of the most prominent member of the WCFA can be found in Lawrence W. Levine, *Defender of the Faith, William Jennings Bryan: The Last Decade 1915-1925* (London: Oxford University Press, 1965).

[18] The most useful nonpolemical brief statement of the "Fundamentals" is in Vergilius Ferm (editor), *An Encyclopedia of Religion* (New York: Philosophical Library, 1945), pp. 291-292.

[19] The role of the Stewart brothers in the conception of the project as well as its funding is greater than has been indicated by most scholars, and future work will have to give careful consideration to the Stewart Papers, Bible Institute of Los Angeles.

TABLE 6-1 NATIONAL MEMBERSHIP

	Definitely Fundamentalist	Sympathetic	Fundamentalist Influence
1916	4,121,036 (16.3)[a]	3,206,584 (12.8)	10,189,789 (40.2)
	(9.8)[b]	(7.6)	(24.3)
1926	5,380,124 (18.0)	4,612,288 (15.4)	12,924,104 (43.1)
	(9.9)	(8.4)	(23.7)
1936	5,192,386 (17.1)	4,995,405 (16.5)	13,283,694 (43.9)
	(9.3)	(9.0)	(22.0)

[a] Parentheses indicate Percentage of Total Protestant Membership.
[b] Parentheses indicate Percentage of Membership of all Religious Bodies.
SOURCE: Data from U.S. Department of Commerce, Bureau of the Census, *Religious Bodies, 1916*, pp. 20-21; *Religious Bodies, 1926*, I, pp. 82-91; *Religious Bodies, 1936*, I, pp. 86-97. Figures were compared with the data from the *Yearbook of American Churches*, published irregularly from 1916 to 1931 and biennially thereafter. Minor adjustments were made in conformity with the data in Fry, *op. cit.*, for 1926 and the *Southern Baptist Handbook* (Nashville, 1937) for 1936. Classification was determined from the following sources: *WCFA Bulletin* (1919-1928); doctrinal statements in the *Yearbook of American Churches* and *Religious Bodies;* denominational yearly reports and periodicals for the period. The sources for the "Fundamentalist Influence" categorization are Furniss and Leslie H. Buckham, "Congregational Dissension, 1915-1940: A Study of the National Council," (unpublished M.A. thesis, Claremont Graduate School and University Center, 1963). Buckham's work has convinced me that Furniss was in error in excluding the Congregationalists from the "controversy." A complete list of denominations in the "Definitely Fundamentalist" and "Sympathetic" categories will be found in an appendix in my dissertation, "Religion in the City of the Angels: A Social Analysis of Denominational Affiliation in Los Angeles, 1850-1930."

No data beyond 1936 are included because that was the last systematic compliation made by the federal government. The *Yearbook* omits too many of the smaller denominations to be useful. For the period under consideration, the data, though far from accurate, seem to be fairly complete. I found only two churches in Los Angeles city directories during this period which were not affiliated with one of the national organizations reported. The Apostolic Full-Gospel Church of Jesus, The Carpenter, was found for only one year. The Church of the First Born of the United Sons of the Almighty existed in Los Angeles for two years. In 1916, the membership of these denominations was 4,121,036: 16.3 per cent of the Protestant population and only about 4 per cent of the total population of the United States. By 1926 the number of denominations had grown to thirty-eight. Twelve of the new organizations were formed since 1919, and fifteen others had joined between 1919 and 1926, but had been disbanded. The constituency of the "Definitely Fundamentalist" denominations had grown to 18 per cent of all Protestant church membership, but had remained approximately 4 per cent of the total population. With the exception of the Southern Baptist Convention, with a membership of over 2,500,000 in 1916, all these denominations were small, with national memberships of less than 70,000. By 1936 they had suffered an absolute loss of almost 200,000 members, and a relative loss of the percentage of the Protestant and total populations. There was a relative decrease in the growth of religious organizations during the 1930s in general, but there were gains, however small, in almost all religious organizations outside the "Definitely Fundamentalist" camp.[20]

[20] It is tempting to interpret this as a "decline" in fundamentalism, but it is possible that it represents a loss of membership through southern migration during the depression.

"Fundamentals," or which had sent official delegates to the WCFA organizational meeeting in 1919.

In the "Sympathetic" category, I have included denominations which neither joined the WCFA nor changed their doctrinal statements, but which already had explicit doctrinal statements in general agreement with the "Fundamentals," primarily of the Millenarian-Adventist type. The number of such organizations remained between seventy and eighty from 1916 to 1936, but in 1926, twenty-eight of those listed in 1916 were no longer to be found, and thirty-one new organizations had replaced them.[21] The situation was similar in 1936. Some of these organizations were really federations of loosely organized denominations, and no one of them had a reported membership of over 100,000. Although their numbers, until 1936 at least, were smaller than the "Definitely Fundamentalist" denominations, their relative growth was greater. We should be careful about assigning too much significance to this "Sympathetic" group, however. The Millenarian denominations were quite unconcerned about modernism and evolution, to judge by their publications. They seemed much more concerned with the Second Coming, which most of their publications assumed would take place during that current generation.[22] Even if this group is included in our consideration, the discernible fundamentalists, until 1936, remain under one-quarter of the Protestant membership and under 10 per cent of the total population.

The final category, "Fundamentalist Influence," includes those denominations that experienced a fundamentalist "controversy" in their regional or national assemblies during the 1920s: the Congregational Churches, Northern Baptist Convention, Presbyterian Church, U.S.A. (Northern), Disciples of Christ, and the Protestant Episcopal Church.[23] These were the large "established" denominations, and rep-

[21] Newly organized denominations in this category were included on the basis of doctrinal statements that were in agreement with the "Fundamentals," but were not specific in adopting them. Obviously, the lack of confessional change could not be used as a test in these cases.

[22] This statement is based on a systematic reading of the ephemera and periodical literature in the Small Denominations Collection, Claremont Graduate School and University Center, Claremont, California. On this point, see T. Rennie Warburton, "Holiness Religion: An Anomaly of Sectarian Typologies," *Journal for the Scientific Study of Religion*, 8 (Spring, 1969), pp. 130-139.

[23] These denominations are often classified together and, indeed, my research on Los Angeles indicates that they operated in that city as an organic social and political unit. For some interesting insights on this, see H. Richard Neibuhr, *The Social Sources of Denominationalism* (New York: Henry Holt and Company, 1929); Peter L. Berger, *The Noise of Solemn Asssemblies: Christian Commitment and the Religious Establishment in America* (Garden City: Doubleday & Company, Inc., 1961); and E. Digby Baltzell, *The Protestant Establishment: Aristocracy and Caste in America* (New York: Alfred A. Knopf, Inc., 1964).

resented over 40 per cent of the Protestant church membership and a steady 10 per cent of the total population. It is impossible to assess fundamentalist strength in any one of these denominations. In each case, the "controversy" centered on clearly defined issues, such as the attempt to remove Harry Emerson Fosdick from his position at New York's First Presbyterian Church in 1923. Although there were minor victories for the fundamentalists early in the decade, by 1930 all the denominations in this category had rejected (although not *repudiated*) fundamentalism. The most dramatic example of this was the withdrawal from the Presbyterian Church, U.S.A., of J. Gresham Machen in 1930, after a three-year struggle over his proposed advancement to the rank of full professor at Princeton Theological Seminary. He subsequently formed the Orthodox Presbyterian Church in conformity to fundamentalist doctrine.[24] By 1936, that denomination numbered only 11,961.[25]

This classification obviously excludes organizations which were hostile to fundamentalism, such as the Unitarians, and denominations in which the doctrinal issues raised by the fundamentalists were superfluous, such as the Christian Scientists. It also excludes one large confessional family of denominations, the Lutherans. There are some interesting reasons why the Lutherans were not affected by the "controversy," but they need not be gone into here.[26] For our present purposes, it is enough to state that none of the indices chosen for this categorization warrants their inclusion.

The distribution of the membership of the denominations in these categories tends to reinforce the interpretation of fundamentalism as a southern and midwestern phenomenon, although its greatest relative strength was in the west—California, Oregon, Nevada, and Arizona—with 12 per cent of the "Definitely Fundamentalist" membership

[24] See Edwin Harold Rian, *The Presbyterian Conflict* (Grand Rapids, Michigan: William B. Eerdmans Publishing Co., 1940); Ned B. Stonehouse, *J. Gresham Machen, A Biographical Memoir* (Grand Rapids, Michigan: William B. Eerdmans Publishing Co., 1955); and Lefferts A. Loetscher, *The Broadening Church* (Philadelphia: University of Pennsylvania Press, 1954).

[25] U.S. Department of Commerce, Bureau of the Census, *Religious Bodies, 1936*, I, p. 96.

[26] See Paul W. Spaude, *The Lutheran Church under American Influence: A Historio-Philosophical Interpretation of the Church in Its Relation to Various Modifying Forces in the United States* (Burlington: Lutheran Universities Press, 1943); Vergilius Ferm, *The Crisis in American Lutheran Theology: A Study of the Issue Between American Lutheranism and Old Lutheranism* (New York: The Century Co., 1927); Reginald Deitz, "Eastern Lutheranism in American Society and American Christianity, 1870-1914: Darwinism, Biblical Criticism, The Social Gospel," (unpublished Ph.D. dissertation, University of Pennsylvania, 1956).

in 1926 and only 13 per cent of the total population in 1936. (See Table 6-2.) The south contained the largest "Definitely Fundamentalist" population, but with less relative strength than the west. Four midwestern states—Ohio, Illinois, Indiana, and Iowa—accounted for 12.2 per cent of this category. Although this was smaller than the percentage of the total population in these states, fundamentalist strength was much greater than throughout the rest of the midwest and the northeast. There were members of "Definitely Fundamentalist" denominations in all forty-eight states between 1916 and 1936.

TABLE 6-2 GEOGRAPHICAL DISTRIBUTION
(In Percentages)

	South[a]	Ohio, Ill., Ind., Iowa	Calif., Ore., Nev., Ariz.	All Other States
I. Total Population				
1916	31.9	16.5	4.2	47.4
1926	31.0	16.3	5.4	47.3
1936	31.0	15.8	6.0	47.2
II. Definitely Fundamentalist				
1916	38.3	11.7	10.2	39.8
1926	38.6	12.2	11.9	37.3
1936	38.8	13.1	12.5	35.6
III. Sympathetic				
1916	42.7	9.3	12.7	35.3
1926	42.3	9.8	15.6	32.3
1936	41.2	9.5	29.4	19.9

[a] South = Alabama, Arkansas, Florida, Georgia, Kentucky, Louisiana, Mississippi, Missouri, North Carolina, Oklahoma, South Carolina, Tennessee, Texas, Virginia.

SOURCES: Estimates for percentage of total population are based on a straight-line interpolation from U.S. Statistical Abstract, A 1-3. Data for denominational categories were derived from Religious Bodies, 1916, pp. 148-149; Religious Bodies, 1926, I, pp. 34, 42-47, 140-141, and passim; Religious Bodies, 1936, II and III, passim. Geographical concentration was determined by using a multi-coordinant repeating program.

Over half of the membership of "Sympathetic" denominations were located in the south and the west, and these latter four states (California, Oregon, Nevada, and Arizona) experienced an unusual growth of this group of denominations by 1936. Members of denominations in this category were found in every state except Maine and Washington. The membership of the "Fundamentalist Influence" denominations was fairly evenly distributed throughout the states, and they were, of course, found in every state.

The interpretation of fundamentalism as a rural phenomenon has some justification. Even though the number of "Definitely Fundamentalist" constituents living in urban areas (as defined by the Bureau of the Census) grew slightly between 1916 and 1936, over 60 per cent of the members of this group were still living in rural areas. (See Table 6-3.) The "Sympathetic" denominations, which had a very small urban constituency in 1916, had moved to the city by 1936. Enough data have not yet been found to draw firm conclusions, but it would seem that this can be accounted for, in part, by the success of such urban-based denominations as the Foursquare Gospel and the continued migration of blacks, who may have accounted for one-third of the membership of the "Sympathetic" denominations.[27]

TABLE 6-3 MEMBERSHIP IN
URBAN AREAS (2,500+)
(In Percentages)

	Definitely Fundamentalist	Sympathetic	Fundamentalist Influence
1916	35.3	28.7	51.9
1926	37.6	31.2	54.2
1936	38.1	56.8	58.7

SOURCES: Data derived from *Religious Bodies, 1916*, passim; *Religious Bodies, 1926*, I, pp. 82-91; *Religious Bodies, 1936*, I, pp. 86-97; U.S., *Statistical Abstract*, A 195-209.

If we limit our meaning of the term "fundamentalist" to those denominations we have called "Definitely Fundamentalist," the movement was obviously small, was concentrated in three geographical areas and spread rather thinly over the rest of the nation, and was predominantly rural in composition. If the "Sympathetic" denominations are added, we have a larger group, but one with a larger urban constituency. There is obviously no way of apportioning membership from the "Fundamentalist Influence" denominations, but the lack of success of the theological conservatives in the 1920s may indicate a lack of fundamentalist sentiment generally. This categorization is cer-

[27] For interesting insights and references to further material on this possibility, see the chapter entitled "Negro Religion in the City," in E. Franklin Frazier, *The Negro Church in America* (New York: Schocken Books, Inc., 1964), pp. 47-67.

214

tainly not a final answer in defining and isolating fundamentalism, but it is preferable to an assumed fundamentalist "spirit" permeating the religious atmosphere of the 1920s.

III

Now that we are fairly clear about what is meant by the term "fundamentalist," at least for the purpose of this paper, we may return to the original problem. In all the verbiage about fundamentalism as a rural movement or a reaction to urbanization, one fact has been overlooked: over one-third of the "Definitely Fundamentalist" membership lived in urban areas between 1916 and 1936, and a growing number of the "Sympathetic" membership was located in urban areas. Were the urban dwellers reacting to urbanization, and, if so, were they reacting in the same way as their rural brethren? What specific indices can be found that indicate such a "reaction?" Unfortunately, rural and urban fundamentalism have never been isolated in order to study common or divergent trends, and the reaction has been inferred from sermons and hymns which contained rural and agrarian references.[28] This is, at best, a shaky proposition. A survey of the hymnals of the "Fundamentalist Influence" denominations reveals many hymns, such as "Bringing in the Sheaves," with rural imagery, and their membership was predominantly urban during the entire period from 1916-1936. Urban-based Bruce Barton, certainly not a fundamentalist, gloried in the rural origins of Christ the Businessman.[29] Christianity is, after all, an agrarian religion in both origin and tradition.[30] It is still possible to observe a celebration of the Feast of Harvest Home in metropolitan churches.

The idea of a "reaction" to urbanization is dramatic—perhaps even romantic—but a contest between a body of literal believers and an impersonal force of the modern world is a proposition that goes far beyond what the available data will support. We must content ourselves, for the present, with the social indices that can be associated with membership in fundamentalist organizations in urban areas. There is a small body of literature on fundamentalism in rural areas that can be used for comparative purposes, although the data are by no means satisfactory. The general pattern that emerges is one

[28] See especially Weisberger, *op. cit.*, pp. 220-274.

[29] Bruce Barton, *The Man Nobody Knows* (New York: Bobbs-Merrill Company, Inc., 1925), esp. pp. 51-61.

[30] Two of the best treatments of Christianity as an agrarian religion are to be found in S. Reinach, *Cultes, Mythes et Religions* (Paris: E. Leroux, 1905), ii; and Homer W. Smith, *Man and His Gods* (Boston: Grosset & Dunlap, 1952), pp. 122-229.

of fundamentalist membership as a function of location. Proximity to a church building during the 1920s and 1930s seems to have been the strongest determining factor, and socioeconomic differences seem to have been negligible.[31]

Fundamentalism in urban areas—or at least in one urban area—functioned quite differently. Los Angeles has enjoyed a reputation in the popular press for harboring fundamentalism since the 1920s, and certainly there is some justification for that claim.[32] It was the home of the Bible Institute of Los Angeles (an offshoot from the Moody Bible Institute in Chicago), the Stewart brothers made Los Angeles their home, and it was the site of Aimee Semple McPherson's Angeles Temple (although her organization is listed as "Sympathetic" in the classification used here). The actual percentage of the total population in "Definitely Fundamentalist" denominations was slightly lower than that of the nation as a whole but much higher than any area outside the three major areas of concentration, and the proportion of the city's population in "Sympathetic" denomination was even larger. (See Table 6-4.)

Unfortunately, the records of most of these organizations have been

[31] Selected titles from this literature are: Roy Edwin Bowers, "The Historic Rural Church," *Ohio State Archaeological and Historical Quarterly,* 51 (1942), pp. 89-100; Garland A. Bricker, *The Church in Rural America* (Cincinnati: The Standard Publishing Co., 1919); Charles Otis Gill and Gifford Pinchot, *Six Thousand Country Churches* (New York: Macmillan Company, 1920); Hermann Nelson Morse and Edmund de S. Brunner, *The Town and Country Church as Illustrated by Data from One Hundred and Seventy-nine Counties and by Intensive Studies of Twenty-five* (New York: George H. Doran Co., 1923); C. Luther Fry, *Diagnosing the Rural Church, A Study in Method* (New York: George H. Doran Co., 1924); Elizabeth R. Hooker, *Hinterlands of the Church* (New York: Institute of Social and Religious Research, 1931); Ralph Almon Felton, *Our Templed Hills, A Study of the Church and Rural Life* (New York: Council of Women for Home Missions and Missionary Education Movement, 1926); A. John W. Myers and Edwin E. Sundt, *The Country Church As It Is; A Case Study of Rural Churches and Leaders* (New York: Revell, 1930); John William Jent, *Rural Church Problems* (Shawnee: Oklahoma Baptist University Press, 1935); and Edmund de S. Brunner and Mary V. Brunner, *Irrigation and Religion* (New York: George H. Doran Company, 1922).

There is also a body of literature on the city church for the same period. Unfortunately, even the best scholars of the urban church, such as H. Paul Douglass, were so concerned with institutional change that their data are all but useless for social historians. For a welcome exception to this generalization, see Carl Douglass Wells, "A Changing Institution in an Urban Environment: A Study of the Changing Behavior Patterns of the Disciples of Christ in Los Angeles," (unpublished Ph.D. dissertation, University of Southern California, 1931).

[32] See, e.g., Cary McWilliams, *Southern California Country: An Island on the Land* (New York: Duell, Sloan & Pearce, 1946); Christopher Rand, *Los Angeles: The Ultimate City* (New York: Oxford University Press, 1967); and Richard Gilbert, *City of the Angels* (London: Secker & Warburg, 1964).

TABLE 6-4   LOS ANGELES MEMBERSHIP

	Total L. A. Population	Definitely Fundamentalist	Sympathetic	Fundamentalist Influence
1916	494,000	9,351 (12.9)[a]	13,897 (19.1)	48,297 (64.5)
1926	974,000	19,609 (14.1)	30,024 (21.6)	80,063 (57.6)
1936	1,843,000	15,593 (9.7)	51,831 (32.3)	89,133 (55.6)

[a] Parentheses indicate percentage of total Protestant membership.

SOURCES: *Religious Bodies, 1916*, p. 125; *Religious Bodies*, 1926, I, pp. 457-459; *Religious Bodies, 1936*, I, pp. 568-570. The data were augmented by the annual "Los Angeles Religious Inventory" in the Los Angeles *Times*, which contains information on some of the smaller denominations which were consolidated in the "Other" category in the breakdown for Los Angeles in *Religious Bodies*. Estimates of total Los Angeles population are based on straightline interpolations from the United States Bureau of the Census. *Thirteenth Census of the United States: Population 1910*, I; United States Bureau of the Census, *Fourteenth Census of the United States: 1920. Population*, II; United States Bureau of the Census, *Fifteenth Census of the United States: 1930*, I; United States Bureau of the Census, *Sixteenth Census of the United States: 1940*, I.

The careful reader will notice that these denominations account for over 90 per cent of the Protestant church membership in Los Angeles between 1916 and 1936.

lost or discarded. I have been able to find directories for seven "Definitely Fundamentalist" churches, representing 627 members, and eleven "Sympathetic" churches, representing 842 members. The directories were all published between 1919 and 1926, and the churches were located primarily in the downtown and southeast section of the city. This, of course, means that this "sample" may be nowhere near representative. There are two reasons for believing that these data are worth analyzing, however. A survey of the location of churches in Los Angeles has indicated that over 60 per cent of the "Definitely Fundamentalist" and "Sympathetic" churches were located in the downtown and southeast sections of Los Angeles.[33] Furthermore, the sample of the "Fundamentalist Influence" churches with which the other two groups will be compared was taken from a listing of the complete membership of those denominations. Parish reconstructions, from a random selection process, indicate that none of the "Fundamentalist Influence" congregations had a structure comparable to that of the "Definitely Fundamentalist" and "Sympathetic" congregations. That is to say, even if the unscientific sample from the "Definitely Fundamentalist" and "Sympathetic" categories is unrepresentative, it is indicative of a pattern that is not to be found in the larger denominations.

[33] The location of churches was determined by using Los Angeles City Directories for the period covered. Detailed information is included in my dissertation.

Before comparing the social indices collected for these groups, it is necessary to make a few brief statements about the relation between religious affiliation and the political and social structure of Los Angeles in the early twentieth century. In the 1890s, the Los Angeles Federation of Churches was formed by the Congregational, Presbyterian, U.S.A., Northern Baptist, Methodist, Disciples of Christ, and Episcopal churches. Under their sponsorship, the California *Independent* was published, bearing the banner-line, "Pure Faith, Pure Morals, Pure Government." To implement the latter, prominent laymen from these six denominations ran for various city and county offices. Until the turn of the century, they were often announced as the "Protestant candidates." Between 1900 and 1919, over 90 per cent of the elective city and county offices were held by members of these six denominations. Over 80 per cent of the membership of local business and social organizations, such as the Merchants and Manufacturers Association and the Jonathan Club, were also members of these six denominations. During this period, their membership never accounted for more than 17 per cent of the population of the city. After 1919, these denominations (which are the "Fundamentalist Influence" denominations) began losing power to a growing Catholic, Jewish, and secular population, although they retained a disproportionate share.

The first distinction that must be made between these larger denominations and the smaller "Definitely Fundamentalist" and "Sympathetic" bodies is that of precedence. By the turn of the century, local churches had long been established for all the "Fundamentalist Influence" denominations, and local denominational structures had been created. With the exception of one Southern Baptist church, none of the denominations in the two more conservative categories began establishing churches in the Los Angeles area before 1913.[34] In general, they moved into areas that had either been abandoned or ignored by the major denominations.[35]

The occupational structure of the membership of the denominations in these three categories shows clearly differentiated patterns. (See Table 6-5.) The year 1922 was chosen for this comparison in order to include the greatest number of "Definitely Fundamentalist" and "Sympathetic" members. The "Fundamentalist Influence" denomina-

[34] Determined from the survey referred to in note 33, and *Directory of Churches and Religious Organizations in Los Angeles County* (Los Angeles: Southern California Historical Records Survey Project, 1940), which gives the founding date of all churches still operant at that time.

[35] From the survey referred to in note 33, and Keith Eugene Duke, "Geographical Factors in the Location of Church Sites in Urban Los Angeles" (unpublished Ph.D. dissertation, University of California at Los Angeles, 1965).

TABLE 6-5   OCCUPATION (1922)
(In Percentages)

	All Los Angeles[a]	Definitely Funda-mentalist	Sympa-thetic	Funda-mentalist Influence
Professional-Management	5.3	2.1	1.5	9.6
Proprietor	9.8	5.3	.7	14.9
Supervisor-Clerical	23.4	11.6	4.3	37.1
Skilled	18.3	8.4	16.8	11.3
Semi-skilled	27.6	42.7	31.4	16.5
Unskilled	16.4	29.9	45.3	10.6
N =	—	438	507	3,512

[a] Estimates

SOURCES: The estimates for the total Los Angeles population are derived from data in Michael Hanson, "Occupational Mobility and Persistence in Los Angeles, 1910-1930," (unpublished seminar paper, University of California, Los Angeles, 1970), and California Department of Industrial Relations, *Labor in California, 1922.* Occupation was obtained from the Los Angeles City Directory (1922). As can be seen, a majority of the "Definitely Fundamentalist" and "Sympathetic" groups were employed. The "Fundamentalist Influence" group was taken from a random sample of 8,000, and less than half of that sample was employed. This can, perhaps, be accounted for by the fact that in the first two groups about the same percentage of women as of men was employed. In the "Fundamentalist Influence" group, very few women were employed. We may assume that the same was probably true of children in each category.

tions have a configuration that is not surprising when we consider the power concentrated there. The "Definitely Fundamentalist" and "Sympathetic" denominations, on the other hand, are overwhelmingly working-class.

The apparent differences between the "Definitely Fundamentalist" and "Sympathetic" denominations are interesting, but may be misleading. If the ideology of the "Sympathetic" denominations can be considered as a greater deviation from "established" Protestantism than that of the "Definitely Fundamentalist" organizations, there may be some case for further exploration using data from other cities. The variance in this case, however, *may* be accounted for by the small and unrepresentative sample. In any event, it is clear that over half of the sample in these two denominational groupings were employed as "semi-skilled" and "unskilled" laborers. They are, therefore, differentiated not only from the higher-status "Fundamentalist Influence" membership, but also from the total population of the city. Because the majority of the residents of Los Angeles were not members of one of these denominational groupings, it would be an overstatement to say that the members of the "Definitely Fundamentalist" and "Sym-

219

pathetic" denominations worked for members of the "Fundamentalist Influence" organizations, but such an overstatement does give some idea of the functional relationship between these denominational groupings.

This class division between "established" and peripheral denominations should be no surprise. Over two decades ago, Liston Pope stated that "however much details may differ, stratification is found in all American communities, and religion is always one of its salient features."[36] The work of Pope and a host of others, such as John Dollard and E. Digby Baltzell, has left little doubt about the connection between religion and social structure.[37]

Too often, however, a discussion of class differentials between denominations or denominational groupings concentrates primarily on doctrinal and occupational variance (with little attention given to the relation between the two). One is usually left with the impression that "The Long Road from Pentescostal to Episcopal," as one popularizer has phrased it,[38] is characterized by a change in occupation and by exchanging gospel-hymns sung in a store-front church for the Apostles' creed recited in a pseudo-Gothic cathedral. Everything we know of class differentiation should make us suspicious of such narrowly conceived frameworks. Occupation is probably the most important index in an industrial social structure, but there are others which can add to our understanding of the patterns of life which further tend to differentiate classes. That is to say that to be classified as "semi-skilled" means more than stating that a man is employed as a semi-skilled laborer. Rather than concentrate on the relationship between doctrinal and occupational variances, a few other social indices which can be milked from the available data will be investigated. It may be argued that the balance of the data is perhaps a function of social class rather than religious affiliation. I can only answer, "Precisely." Because of the origins of this study, Table 6-5 may be

[36] Liston Pope, "Religion and the Class Structure," *The Annals of the American Academy of Political and Social Science,* Vol. 256 (March 1948), p. 89.

[37] John Dollard, *Caste and Class in a Southern Town* (Garden City: Doubleday & Company, Inc., 1957—third edition), pp. 220-249; E. Digby Baltzell, *Philadelphia Gentlemen: The Making of a National Upper Class* (New York: The Free Press, 1958), pp. 223-261. The classic formulation of "Castes, Estates, Classes, and Religion" is found in Max Weber, *The Sociology of Religion,* trans. Ephraim Fischoff (Boston: Beacon Press, 1963), pp. 80-94. For conceptual insight this work should be consulted, but it is of little substantive value for a consideration of religion and *industrial* social structure.

[38] Vance Packard, *The Status Seekers* (New York: David McKay Company, Inc., 1959), pp. 193-206.

misleading. I have not sought to identify laborers as fundamentalists or the "upper" and "middle" classes as members of "established" denominations—the opposite is more nearly true. Nor have I sought to make occupation a "function" of denominational membership. Rather, I would suggest that occupation and religious affiliation may be considered to be two important indices that are highly related. The fact that they are so highly related requires some exploration of other indices.[39]

IV

ONE may wonder why mobility was not traced in the comparison of occupational structure. The geographic mobility of the membership of the "Definitely Fundamentalist" and "Sympathetic" denominations was so great as to make such a study impossible. (See Table 6-6.)

TABLE 6-6 LENGTH OF RESIDENCE IN
LOS ANGELES 1920-1930
(In Percentages)

	Definitely Fundamentalist	Sympathetic	Fundamentalist Influence
One Year or Less	10.9	12.5	.7
One to Nine Years	67.8	71.9	31.0
Ten Years or More	21.3	15.6	68.3

SOURCES: Determined from Los Angeles City Directories from 1910 to 1930. A person leaving the city in 1921, who had been in the city continually from 1910, would be listed in the "Ten Years or More" category.

Of the members of the first category in Los Angeles in 1920, a little over one-fifth remained until 1930, and over 10 per cent left after staying only one year or less. The "Sympathetic" category was even more transient. Although Los Angeles was not a union town during the 1920s, it was a fairly good labor market. It is difficult to account for this low persistence rate in "market" terms in any event. During the twenty-year period from 1910 to 1930, the persistence rate for the city was 32 per cent, and for manual laborers

[39] Louis B. Perry and Richard S. Perry, *A History of the Los Angeles Labor Movement, 1911-1941* (Berkeley: University of California Press, 1963), pp. 193-236; Robert M. Fogelson, *The Fragmented Metropolis: Los Angeles 1850-1890* (Cambridge, Mass.: Harvard University Press, 1967), pp. 108-134.

it was 22 per cent.[40] By contrast, the solidly established "Fundamentalist Influence" denominations experienced remarkably low geographic mobility.

As one would expect, the membership of the more transient denominations gives evidence of less political participation than does the more stable membership of larger denominations. (See Table 6-7.) When a comparison is made of the percentage of each category registered to vote, using comparable periods of residence, it can be seen that the relative lack of political participation of the most rudimentary sort may be a function of more than transiency. Members of the

TABLE 6-7 PER CENT REGISTERED VOTERS
(Of Voting Age)

	Definitely Fundamentalist	*Sympathetic*	*Fundamentalist Influence*
1924			
Total Sample	5.6	3.1	33.7
One Year or Less	.8	.1	11.3
One to Nine Years	4.7	2.3	38.6
Ten Years or More	9.4	5.7	30.8
1934			
Of Sample Remaining	23.9	18.4	32.1

SOURCES: Determined from a programmed survey of the records of the Registrar of Voters, Hall of Records, County of Los Angeles. Estimates for total Los Angeles population from Registrar of Voters, County of Los Angeles, *Annual Report,* 1924 and 1934. It may be of interest to know that of those who were registered to vote in both 1924 and 1934, the majority of both the "Definitely Fundamentalist" and "Sympathetic" categories were Democrats, and the majority of the "Fundamentalist Influence" category were Republicans.

larger denominations who were in the city for one year or less were more likely to become registered voters than members of the "Definitely Fundamentalist" and "Sympathetic" denominations. Indeed, the one-year resident from one of the more established denominations was more likely to become a registered voter than a ten-year resident from one of the more conservative denominations. A survey of voter registration one decade later indicates an increase in political participation, but by this time the sample had dwindled to less than 400 for both the "Definitely Fundamentalist" and "Sympathetic" categories,

[40] Hanson, *op. cit.* For a discussion of the problem of geographical mobility, see Stephan Thernstrom and Peter R. Knights, "Men in Motion: Some Data and Speculations on Urban Population Mobility in Nineteenth-Century America," *Journal of Interdisciplinary History,* 1. (Fall, 1970), pp. 7-35.

and represented long-time residents. The increase, nonetheless, is significant.

One other index that has proved useful in distinguishing fundamentalists from the more established denominations has been records of arrests. During the period from 1920 to 1929, the arrest rate in Los Angeles for both misdemeanors and felonies was 14 per 1000 population per year.[41] The arrest rate for the "Definitely Fundamentalist" group in misdemeanors and for the "Sympathetic" group in felonies was higher than the average for *all* arrests for the city in general. (See Table 6-8.) The arrest rate in both categories for the

TABLE 6-8   COMPARATIVE ARREST RATES
(Per 1000)

	Definitely Fundamentalist	Sympathetic	Fundamentalist Influence
1920-1929			
Misdemeanor	18.3	15.7	3.2
Felony	12.4	21.8	2.6
1930-1939			
Misdemeanor	4.5	6.3	4.7
Felony	6.1	5.8	3.4

SOURCES: Determined from a programmed survey of the Arrest and Booking Records, Los Angeles Police Department.

"established" denominations was negligible. For the period 1930-1939, the arrest rate (misdemeanors and felonies) for the city rose to 17 per 100 per year.[42] While the rate for the "Fundamentalist Influence" churches rose slightly, the "Definitely Fundamentalist" and "Sympathetic" groups experienced a sharp reduction.

Unfortunately, as in the case of voter registration, the rate for the latter two groups was determined from a ridiculously small number of those who remained in the area through the 1930s. It is quite possible, of course, that the high arrest rates for the 1920s may be connected to the low persistence rates. The location of churches in these two groups, however, would indicate a slight shift to neighborhoods that were more homogenous than the exclusively working-class

[41] Information given by IPS Management Service division, Los Angeles Police Department. (I am indebted to Joseph G. Woods, now preparing a dissertation at the University of California, Los Angeles, on the structure and personnel of the Los Angeles Police Department in the early twentieth century, for helpful information on the police records in this city.)

[42] *Ibid.*

neighborhoods that characterized the location of these churches during the 1920s.[43] It is also instructive that it was during the 1930s that most of these churches were invited to take part in the Los Angeles Church Federation activities.[44] This is simply to suggest that both the rise in the percentage of voter registration and the lower arrest rate, while certainly not as low as indicated by the sparse data we have to work with, may have been a function of assimilation into a pattern more conformable to that of the larger established denominations.[45]

V

THIS exploratory analysis of available data at once points to the possibilities and limitations of a quantitative approach in the field of religious history. Although it is possible to say something more about the implications of denominational affiliation than can be inferred from doctrinal statements and religious literature, we are limited by the absence of the sort of plentiful data necessary for complete social analysis.

There are some valid inferences that can be made from this material, however. The fact that the membership lists for the "Definitely Fundamentalist" and "Sympathetic" denominations in Los Angeles came from the area of the greatest concentration of those churches, and the lack of *any* congregation among the "Fundamentalist Influence" denominations which approximated the configuration of the two smaller groups, does lend a sense of validity to the data. The "Definitely Fundamentalist" and "Sympathetic" denominations were differentiated from the more established denominations and the total population by lack of power, lack of political participation, working-class roots, greater transiency, and higher arrest rates.

It would, of course, be interesting to know where these people came from, but that information has eluded me except for sixteen persons—all from the rural south. I do have this information for the "established" denominations, however. The majority of the membership in these churches between 1900 and 1929 had midwestern or

---

[43] Determined from the survey referred to in note 33, and compared with Eshref Shevky and Marilyn Williams, *The Social Areas of Los Angeles: Analysis and Typology* (Berkeley: University of California Press, 1949), and property tax records (County of Los Angeles).

[44] Los Angeles *Times*, July 18, 1934, vol. 2, 3.

[45] It should be mentioned that other indices, not used in this paper, were employed. Some, such as family size, produced no significant results. Others, such as individual property-tax correlations, simply reinforced the general pattern suggested by the other data.

224

southern rural backgrounds, which would indicate that fundamentalism as a reaction to urbanization (at least insofar as this means a "confrontation" between the rural migrant and the city) is not a compelling argument for Los Angeles. A much more convincing argument can be made for considering fundamentalism in Los Angeles as a religious manifestation of alienation. Certainly there was a basis for feelings of alienation. It must be again emphasized that the "Definitely Fundamentalist" and "Sympathetic" membership was disadvantageously differentiated not only from their more affluent and stable Protestant brethren, but from the total population. This is further supported by the analysis of Protestants from the "established" denominations who changed their affiliation during the 1920s to either a "Definitely Fundamentalist" or "Sympathetic" church. They were primarily manual laborers, political nonparticipants, and short-term residents in Los Angeles.[46]

Obviously my criticism of impressionistic interpretations is not so much that they are incorrect, but that they tell too little about fundamentalism as a *social* movement. Like so much in religious history, the concerns of the laity have been inferred from the words of the leadership. It may strike some readers as ironic that a paper that began with a denunciation of the overemphasis on doctrinal statements as a means for "understanding" the nature of religious affiliations should have relied so heavily on such statements to establish categories for social analysis. First, I would point out that the data seem to have justified such a categorization. Second, there is no attempt to deny the possibility that doctrinal statements may be of some use to the social historian of religion. We need not fall into the "either/or" argument that characterizes the division between two extremely capable scholars of seventeenth-century England. According to Michael Walzer, his basic disagreement with Christopher Hill is that Hill interprets Puritanism as the social religion of merchants and artisans and Walzer considers it as the political religion of ministers.[47]

Surely it can be both. In fact, we should expect some distinction between the composition and motivations of the leadership and membership of any movement or organization. Recent works in American

[46] From my dissertation. It should be noted that the Stewart brothers, although ideologically in the "Definitely Fundamentalist" camp, remained members of Immanuel Presbyterian Church.

[47] Michael Walzer, *The Revolution of the Saints: A Study in the Origins of Radical Politics* (Cambridge, Mass.: Harvard University Press, 1965), p. 328. See Christopher Hill, *Puritanism and Revolution* (London: Secker & Warburg, 1958), and *Society and Puritanism in Pre-Revolutionary England* (London: Schocken Books, 1964).

colonial history, especially those of Emery Battis and Gary B. Nash, have successfully handled religious movements by carefully analyzing both the personal lives and motivations of the leaders and the social composition of the followers.[48] It is possible to see fundamentalism as a theologically sophisticated system of thought which recognized the implications of modern science better than liberal theology did. It is also possible to see it as the simplistic religion of Mencken's classic "boob" on a farm somewhere in Tennessee.

To raise a suggestion—not a conclusion—about the possible relation between the ideology and social basis of fundamentalism in one city, it may be argued that the adoption of a defensive theology which defined the "official" ideology of the more "established" Protestant membership as apostate and surrendering Biblical faith to modern science was a sublimated ideological reaction to alienation. I would further suggest that it is not surprising to find an increased emphasis on the saving grace of faith alone and a de-emphasis of the social and ethical implications of the New Testament among those who had a lower incidence of political participation and a higher arrest rate than did the population as a whole.

If we can allow a variety of intellectual sophistication under the rubric "fundamentalism," then certainly it can be suggested that we might stop thinking of fundamentalism along a "rural-urban" axis and begin to think of it as a movement that may have performed different functions in the country and in the city. To hazard a generalization, rural fundamentalism seems to have been an expression of a cohesive community while urban fundamentalism was an expression of social fragmentation. I would suggest that Bernard Weisberger's *They Gathered at the River* or Sinclair Lewis' *Elmer Gantry* may be a good point of departure for understanding rural fundamentalism, but Vittorio Lanternari's *The Religions of the Oppressed* or E. J. Hobsbawm's *Primitive Rebels* may provide a better framework for understanding urban fundamentalism than the standard approaches taken by religious historians.[49] If the indices which tend to imply

[48] Emery Battis, *Saints and Sectaries: Anne Hutchinson and the Antinomian Controversy in the Massachusetts Bay Colony* (Chapel Hill: University of North Carolina Press, 1962); Gary B. Nash, *Quakers and Politics: Pennsylvania, 1681-1726* (Princeton: Princeton University Press, 1968), esp. pp. 241-305.

[49] Sinclair Lewis, *Elmer Gantry* (New York: Harcourt, Brace and Company, 1927), presents a comprehensive view of religious practice in America in the 1920s, of which rural fundamentalism is only a part. The more I study religion during this period, the more I am impressed with Lewis's knowledge and insight. Vittorio Lanternari, *The Religions of the Oppressed*, trans. Lisa Sergio (New York: Alfred A. Knopf, Inc., 1963), and E. J. Hobsbawm, *Primitive Rebels* (London: Frederick A. Praeger, Inc., 1959), both provide excellent frameworks for the

226

a degree of assimilation in the 1930s in Los Angeles can be supported by data from other cities, it may be worthwhile to compare the urban fundamentalists to immigrant populations in the city.[50] The data for filling in these frameworks will be meager, and the important questions that I have scrupulously avoided (e.g., the origins and dynamics of the movement) are exasperatingly difficult. The caution that most quantitative historians wish to exercise may have to be abandoned on occasion, but it is worth both the risk and the irritation to apply the rigor of this method to areas that are "data-poor."

---

study of movements whose composition deviates significantly from the norm, or at least the "establishment." Interesting ideas are also found in Weber, *The Sociology of Religion*, pp. 95-117; A. Leland Jamison, "Religions on the Christian Perimeter," in *The Shaping of American Religion*, vol. 1 of *Religion in American Life*, edited by James Ward Smith and A. Leland Jamison (Princeton: Princeton University Press, 1961), pp. 162-231; and Elmer T. Clark, *The Small Sects in America*, revised edition (New York: Abingdon Press, 1949). Unfortunately, even the best works in urban religious history—e.g., Aaron I. Abell, *The Urban Impact on American Protestantism* (Cambridge, Mass.: Harvard University Press, 1943); Henry May, *Protestant Churches and Industrial America* (New York: Harper & Row, 1949); and the introduction to Robert D. Cross (editor), *The Church and the City: 1865-1910* (Indianapolis: The Bobbs-Merrill Company, Inc., 1967)— have not provided a good basis for grasping the social implications of religion in the city.

[50] I have in mind, of course, the sort of comparative study initiated by Oscar Handlin, *Boston's Immigrants: A Study in Acculturation* (Cambridge, Mass.: Harvard University Press, 1941; revised edition, Cambridge, Mass: Harvard University Press, 1959), and further perfected in studies such as Richard J. Hopkins, "Occupational and Geographical Mobility in Atlanta, 1870-1896," *Journal of Southern History*, 34 (May 1968), pp. 200-213; and Stephan Thernstrom and Elizabeth H. Pleck, "The Last of the Immigrants? A Comparative Analysis of Immigrant and Black Social Mobility in Late-Nineteenth Century Boston," paper delivered at the 1970 annual meeting of the Organization of American Historians. The matter is discussed in more detail in Ms. Pleck's forthcoming Harvard University doctoral dissertation on "The Black Community of Boston, 1870-1900."

7

Urbanization and Slavery: The Issue of Compatibility*

CLAUDIA DALE GOLDIN

I THE PROBLEM

THE American plantation slave population grew steadily from its inception until its forced demise with the close of the Civil War. But its urban counterpart reached a peak in its growth sometime between 1830 and 1850 and declined during its last decade. Some cities showed a weakening in their slave populations earlier, and a few declined throughout the forty-year period, 1820 to 1860. Many historians and students of the ante-bellum period have tried to discover the cause for this decline and, in general, their answers have been quite similar. It seemed obvious to them that slavery could flourish only in the production of agricultural staples and that it was incompatible with city and industrial life. Some stressed the fact that profitability from slaves was closely connected to the plantation system, but most agreed that slavery did not gain substantial inroads into urban and industrial life because of some inherent incompatibility.

One of the earliest to state the proposition that slavery could not survive in an urban environment was John Elliott Cairnes, whose book *The Slave Power* attempted to influence British foreign policy during the Civil War. Cairnes believed that slavery was an economic system "unsuited to the functions of commerce; for the soul of commerce is the spirit of enterprise . . . found wanting in communities where slavery exists." Slavery was excluded from manufacturing industry and urban areas because it "could only be carried on at a constant risk of insurrection . . . effectually [preventing] . . . such societies from ever attaining any considerable growth." Thus, Cairnes concluded, "excluded by these causes from the field of manufactures and commerce, slavery finds its natural career in agriculture."[1]

* The author thanks her doctoral committee, Robert W. Fogel, H. Gregg Lewis, and Donald McCloskey, all of the University of Chicago, for assistance in completing "The Economics of Urban Slavery" (unpublished Ph.D. dissertation, University of Chicago, 1972) of which this paper is but a part. *Urban Slavery*, forthcoming, will be an expanded version of this dissertation.

[1] John Elliott Cairnes, *The Slave Power* (Torchbook Edition, 1969; originally published London: London, Parker, Son and Bourn, 1862, p. 71.

Some writers, with more than slightly racist overtones, believed that slaves could not be trained and that this fact accounted for the inability of the cities to support an ever-growing slave population. Especially prominent among these writers was Ulrich B. Phillips, whose opinion of the Negro led him to believe that slavery "failed to gain strength in the North because there was no work which [N]egro slaves could perform with notable profit to their masters. . . . [But] in certain parts of the South the system flourished because the work required was simple, the returns were large and the short-comings of [N]egro slave labor were partially offset by the ease with which it could be organized."[2] Another historian to hold similar views on this matter was Lewis Cecil Gray, who questioned "the tendency for the slave to displace free labor where conditions were favorable to producing and marketing the staples." He concluded that a major cause of this tendency was that "the rewards and punishments of the plantation system were more powerful stimuli . . . [to] the primi-tive Negro . . . than the rewards of industry."[3]

The contention that slavery would never be profitable in urban areas was implicit in Charles W. Ramsdell's natural-limit thesis. Slav-ery was "a cumbersome and expensive system [which] . . . could show profits only as long as it could find plenty of rich lands to cultivate."[4] Therefore, it could survive only in the production of agri-cultural staples, and as land became more scarce slavery would eventu-ally decline.

More recently, the issue of urban slavery has been raised by Richard C. Wade in his *Slavery in the Cities.*[5] His general thesis, that slavery declined in the cities because it was incompatible with urban life, goes back to earlier theories, especially Cairnes's. The urban slave, according to Wade, had far more freedom than his rural brother because of various institutional changes in the nature of slavery when it came in contact with an urban area.

The trouble with urban slavery, to Wade, was not that slaves were not trainable, as had been assumed by earlier students of the period. Instead, crucial problems arose because, in fact, they were trained

[2] Ulrich B. Phillips, "The Economic Cost of Slaveholding in the Cotton Belt," *Political Science Quarterly*, xx (June, 1905), pp. 257-275.
[3] Lewis Cecil Gray, *History of Agriculture in the Southern United States to 1860* (Washington: Carnegie Institute of Washington, 1933), p. 470.
[4] Charles W. Ramsdell, "The Natural Limits of Slavery Expansion," *Mississippi Valley Historical Review*, 26, No. 2 (September, 1929), pp. 151-171.
[5] Richard C. Wade, *Slavery in the Cities, The South 1820-1860* (New York: Oxford University Press, 1964).

and educated to be profitable investments in their urban and industrial settings. Many slaves were apprenticed to learn a trade; others acquired some form of literacy through the Church or through work necessitated by their jobs. Slaves lived apart from their masters in large numbers in the Southern cities, and although this arrangement proved to be acceptable to the individual owners, it created social problems for the urban centers as a whole. In addition, many slaves were given permission from their masters to hire out their own time, an arrangement under which the slave periodically paid his owner a specified sum of money and managed to find jobs himself. In general, the urban environment gave the slave more freedom and more education, and these contributed to the institution's decline. According to Wade, with the white masters no longer having control over their bondsmen and the white citizenry constantly fearing insurrections, city slaves were sold to the plantations. Thus, the root of the decline of slavery in the cities was the inherent incompatibility between slavery and urban life.

Most of the above explanations of why slavery did not flourish in urban areas conclude that it was not profitable in cities and in industry. Many reasons have been given. Some rely on a discredited belief that the Negro was naturally inferior, and some are based on the assumption that the slave could more easily create problems in the cities than on plantations. But, in general, the belief was that slaves were pushed out of the cities—in other words, that the demand for slaves was declining in these areas. However, if this were true one would expect a decline in city slave prices, possibly an absolute one, but at least a decline relative to plantation prices. Much of the city slave labor force had skills specific to urban areas, but the selling price to plantations of these slaves would be equal to that paid for any other prime field hand. If the city demand were declining, city slave prices should then fall absolutely from their previous levels. In addition, transfer costs, within limits, would put a wedge between the price of a slave in a growing area and one in a declining city area. The puzzling feature about an explanation which relies on a declining demand for city slaves is that urban slave wages continued to rise during the period 1820-1860 and "more than matched the general increase."[6]

---

[6] *Ibid.*, p. 244. Wade also states that "hiring rates continued to rise throughout the last ante-bellum decades," which is exactly when many of the cities' slave populations showed the greatest weakening in numbers. Data collected from archival probate records support this statement of Wade's and

An explanation which hinges on a generally declining demand for city slaves fails to come to grips with the fact that the rates of change for the slave population in the various cities fluctuated in magnitude and even in sign over the four decades. While some urban areas had large decreases, others had large increases in their slave populations. The declining-demand theory does not enable us to predict these differences. In fact, the most heavily industrial city, Richmond, showed increases in its slave population throughout the forty-year period 1820 to 1860. Wade's analysis of urban slavery would lead us to predict just the opposite. Richmond should have lost slaves as time wore on, since it contained an unusually high proportion of skilled slave labor. This concentration should have created more severe problems for Richmond than for other cities.

Moreover, the exodus of slaves from cities was greater among the unskilled than the skilled. As 1860 approached, the cities were left with a more highly skilled male slave labor force than they had in earlier periods. Unskilled male slaves were sold to the plantations, but the skilled remained in the cities. This, again, is inconsistent with a "push" theory for the decline in urban slaves. That is, if demand for all types of urban slaves were declining we would not expect any change in the skill-composition of those remaining. Furthermore, if Wade's thesis is correct, if urban masters sold their bondsmen because they no longer felt that they had control over them, we again would not expect a change in the male skill-mix of the type indicated. Presumably the educated and skilled slaves were more hostile to slavery, and hence constituted a greater threat than the uneducated slaves.

Not only were the cities left with a more highly skilled male slave population, but they had more females and fewer children by the eve of the Civil War than previously. Thus, if the cities pushed their slaves out, they did so with much discrimination. While we might be inclined to rationalize the greater exodus of unskilled males and children on the grounds that they constituted a more acute threat to safety than did skilled males and women, no evidence to support such a view has yet been marshalled.

These facts may lead us to doubt the thesis that slaves were pushed from the cities by a declining demand for them in urban areas. The balance of this paper explores the alternative hypothesis that slaves

---

show that the rate of change in wages for slaves in Richmond, Fredericksburg, and Lynchburg averaged 6.8% per year for 1850-1860. Those for more rural areas were about 4-5% annually. See C. Goldin, "The Economics of Urban Slavery" (unpublished Ph.D. dissertation, Chicago, 1972).

were pulled from the cities. I will argue that the urban demand for slaves was probably increasing over time, accounting for the evidence we have on city slave prices and wages. In general rural demand was also increasing, perhaps at an accelerating rate. Nevertheless, there is evidence to suggest that many city demand functions were increasing at a rate even greater than was that of the overall supply of slaves. It may seem contradictory to argue that the urban slave population was declining even though the demand for urban slaves increased more rapidly than the aggregate slave population. The contradiction is only apparent. It can be resolved by considering the difference between the elasticity of demand in rural and in urban areas. Differences in these elasticities may also explain changes in the rate of change in the quantity of urban slaves. The alternative hypothesis is consistent with the facts observed previously, that unskilled male slaves were sold to the plantations during periods when the price of slaves was very high, and that male slaves with skills more specific to the cities, and females, were retained there.

II The Data

TABLE 7-1 presents data on the slave and free populations for the ten major Southern cities and the rate of change in population for these cities for four decades, 1820 to 1860. In most of these cities the slave population increased from 1820 to approximately 1850 and then declined during the last decade. This slave population peak occurred earlier for these cities as a whole because New Orleans dominates the aggregate figures. But when we observe the percentage changes in the slave population for the four decades the picture becomes clearer. Every city, with the exception of Mobile and New Orleans, shows a cyclical pattern in the percentage rate of change of slaves over the four decades. The percentage increase in slaves for the ten-year periods 1820 to 1830 and 1840 to 1850 is greater (or equivalently the decrease, as in the case of Baltimore, is smaller) than for the other two decennial periods. In addition, the swings of these cycles are very large. Many cities experienced large increases in slaves during the first and third decades and decreases during the other two decades. Other cities—for example, Richmond—experienced increases in their slave populations throughout this forty-year period, but, despite this, the increases were cyclical in rate of change. Therefore, it seems clear that a theory which attempts to explain why slavery did not take root in the cities must be consistent with these large cycles in slave population change.

235

TABLE 7-1 PART A: SLAVE AND FREE[a] POPULATIONS FOR 10 CITIES, 1820-1860

Cities	1820 Slave	1820 Free	1830 Slave	1830 Free	1840 Slave	1840 Free	1850 Slave	1850 Free	1860 Slave	1860 Free
Baltimore, Md.	4357	58381	4120	76500	3199	99114	2946	166108	2218	210100
Charleston, S.C.	12652	12128	15354	14935	14673	14588	19532	23453	13909	26613
Louisville, Ky.	1031	2979	2406	7935	3430	17780	5432	37762	4903	63130
Mobile, Ala.[b]	836	1836	1175	2019	3869	8803	6803	13712	7587	21671
New Orleans, La.	7355	19821	9397	20340	23448	78745	17011	99364	13385	155290
Norfolk, Va.	3261	5217	3756	6058	3709	7211	4295	10031	3284	11336
Richmond, Va.	4387	7680	6345	9715	7509	12644	9927	17643	11699	26211
St. Louis, Mo.[c]	1810	8210	2796	11419	1531	14938	2656	75204	1542	159231
Savannah, Ga.[d]	3075	4448	4000	n.a.[e]	4694	6520	6231	9081	7712	14580
Washington, D.C.	1945	11302	2330	16496	1713	21651	2113	37888	1774	59348

[a] Free white and free black
[b] 1820 Mobile returns are for Mobile County
[c] 1820 and 1830 St. Louis returns are for St. Louis County
[d] No Census population data were given for Savannah for 1830. The 1830 slave figure is an approximation based on the manuscript census figures.
[e] n.a. = not available.
SOURCE: United States Census Office, 4th, 5th, 6th, 7th and 8th Censuses.

PART B: DECENNIAL RATES OF CHANGE, SLAVE AND FREE POPULATIONS FOR 10 CITIES FOR 4 DECADES

Cities	1820-1830 Slave	1820-1830 Free	1830-1840 Slave	1830-1840 Free	1840-1850 Slave	1840-1850 Free	1850-1860 Slave	1850-1860 Free
Baltimore, Md.	−5 %	31 %	−22 %	30 %	−8 %	68 %	−25 %	26 %
Charleston, S.C.	21	23	−4	−2	33	61	−29	13
Louisville, Ky.	133	166	43	124	58	112	−10	67
Mobile, Ala.	41	10	229	336	76	56	12	58
New Orleans, La.	28	3	150	287	−27	26	−21	56
Norfolk, Va.	15	16	−1	19	16	39	−24	13
Richmond, Va.	45	26	18	30	32	40	18	49
St. Louis, Mo.	54	39	−45	31	73	403	−42	112
Savannah, Ga.	30	n.a.	17	n.a.	33	39	24	61
Washington, D.C.	20	46	−26	31	23	75	−16	57

The ten cities in Table 7-1 were chosen because they were the largest Southern cities whose population statistics could be collected for the period 1820 to 1860. Statistics for the period 1850 to 1860 for twelve other cities having total populations which exceeded 5000 in 1860 can be found in Table 7-2.

These data are useful because they show that there is a small bias in using only the original ten cities' slave populations for the last decade; that is, the percentage decrease in the total urban slave population is lessened by the addition of these cities (see Table 7-2). Data for these and other Southern cities are practially nonexistent for the earlier time period, 1820 to 1840. But, since cities other than the original ten were very small prior to 1850, and were questionably

236

urban in nature, no extensive bias is expected from using the data in Table 7-1.

Tables 7-1 and 7-2 would be more pertinent if they reported the labor force, or at least slaves who were of working age. The five censuses, 1820 to 1860, give age breakdowns for slaves, but the age limits they report are not comparable among all decades. That is, the censuses of 1830 and 1840 had different age breakdowns than

TABLE 7-2 SLAVE POPULATIONS FOR
12 ADDITIONAL CITIES, 1850-1860

Cities	1850	1860
Augusta, Ga.	4718	3663
Alexandria, Va.	1061	1386
Fredericksburg, Va.	1174	1291
Lynchburg, Va.	3424	2694
Memphis, Tenn.	2360	3684
Montgomery, Ala.	2119	4400
Nashville, Tenn.	2028	3226
Natchez, Miss.	3031	2138
Newbern, N.C.	1927	2383
Portsmouth, Va.	1751	934
Petersburg, Va.	4729	5680
Wilmington, N.C.	3031	3777

AGGREGATE URBAN SLAVE POPULATION,
1850-1860, FOR TEN ORIGINAL
CITIES AND TWENTY CITIES

	1850	1860
10 Original Cities	76,900	68,000
22 Cities	108,275	104,228

DECENNIAL RATE OF CHANGE, URBAN
SLAVE POPULATION 1850-1860

	1850-1860
10 Original Cities	−9%
22 Cities	−3%

SOURCE: United States Census Office, 7th Census, 1850 (Washington, 1853). United States Census Office, 8th Census, 1860 (Washington, 1864).

TABLE 7-3 AVERAGE ANNUAL RATES OF CHANGE OF SLAVE POPULATIONS
AND LABOR FORCES FOR TEN CITIES, THREE REGIONS,
AND THE UNITED STATES

| | Total Population | | | | Labor Force[d] | | | |
	1820-30	30-40	40-50	50-60	1820-30	30-40	40-50	50-60
Baltimore	− .006	− .025	− .008	− .028	+ .004	− .023	− .006	− .031
Charleston	+ .019	− .005	+ .029	− .034	+ .018	.000	+ .036	− .035
Louisville	+ .085	+ .035	+ .046	− .010	+ .098	+ .031	+ .054	− .018
Mobile	+ .034	+ .119	+ .056	+ .011	+ .037	+ .122	+ .062	− .001
New Orleans	+ .025	+ .091	− .032	− .024	+ .015	+ .097	− .028	− .028
Norfolk	+ .014	− .001	+ .015	− .027	+ .014	.000	+ .016	− .017
Richmond	+ .037	+ .017	+ .028	+ .016	+ .044	+ .025	+ .031	+ .020
St. Louis	+ .043	− .060	+ .055	− .054	+ .045	− .052	+ .055	− .060
Savannah	+ .026	+ .016	+ .028	+ .021	+ .028	+ .017	+ .033	+ .016
Washington, D.C.	+ .018	− .031	+ .021	− .017	+ .026	− .028	+ .021	− .029
Total U.S.	+ .027	+ .021	+ .025	+ .021	+ .025	+ .023	+ .029	+ .021
[a]New South	+ .026	+ .095	− .014	− .013	+ .017	+ .100	− .009	− .019
[b]Old South	+ .030	− .003	+ .027	− .009	+ .024	+ .009	+ .032	− .008
[c]Border States	+ .024	− .017	+ .029	− .023	+ .032	− .014	+ .032	− .030

[a] Mobile, New Orleans
[b] Richmond, Savannah, Charleston, Norfolk
[c] Louisville, Baltimore, Washington, D.C., St. Louis
[d] Defined as that portion of the population between the ages of 10 and 55.

those for 1850 and 1860, and those for 1820 are rather poor. Computation of the labor force figures required these to be reworked. Table 7-3 presents such a reformulation of the data and gives the average annual rate of change[7] for slave populations and slave labor forces for the cities studied. These data will be used in section III to compute the rate of change in the demand for urban versus rural slaves. In this way we can discover why urban slavery appears to have declined during the period immediately preceding the Civil War.

Table 7-4 shows the aggregate slave figures for the United States, and the decennial rates of increase for the four decades. The rate of increase for slaves is again not constant but has small cycles, with greater rates of increase for the first and third than for the second and fourth decades. These cycles have been attributed to the cycles in the importation of mature Negroes prior to the embargo placed on slave importations.[8] That is, the two larger rates of increase are

[7] Average annual rates computed using the formula: $X_{(t+10)} = X_t e^{r(10)}$.
[8] See Alfred H. Conrad and John R. Meyer, "The Economics of Slavery in the Ante-Bellum South," reprinted in Conrad and Meyer, *The Economics of Slavery and Other Studies in Econometric History* (Chicago: Aldine Press, 1964), p. 69. Price data for male and female slaves during the period 1796 to 1810 support this hypohesis. In addition, chlorea epidemics in the 1830s and 1850s served to diminish the slave population for those periods.

then a result of the two generations following that of these adult slaves. The other two decades are the periods in the intergenerational cycle. Therefore, the aggregate slave population had cycles of population change that were not as violent as those of the cities. It can be shown that a difference in demand elasticities is a sufficient explanation for these large differences in population change.

TABLE 7-4   TOTAL SLAVE
POPULATION FOR THE UNITED
STATES, 1820-1860
(to nearest thousand)

1820	1,538,000
1830	2,009,000
1840	2,487,000
1850	3,205,000
1860	3,954,000

DECENNIAL RATE OF INCREASE
FOR TOTAL SLAVE POPULATION,
1820-1860

1820-1830	30.6%
1830-1840	23.8
1840-1850	28.8
1850-1860	23.4

SOURCE: United States Census Office, 4th, 5th, 6th, 7th and 8th Censuses.

Section III will test the hypothesis that the demand for urban slave labor, rather than declining during the period 1820 to 1860, was increasing. Critical to the empirical work in that section is a set of urban slave prices. The only slave price data available to previous researchers were those compiled by U. B. Phillips.[9] Phillips used prices for prime male field hands, and these prices in average annual rate-of-change form for four trading areas are given in Table 7-5. They are also presented in deflated form, with the Warren and Pearson

[9] These data are appraised prices and are about 20% lower than actual selling prices. Because they include prices for all slaves appraised they are not absolutely comparable to Phillips' data which are only for prime field hands. A more comprehensive discussion of these price data can be found in C. Goldin, "The Economics of Urban Slavery" (unpublished Ph.D. dissertation, Chicago, 1972) and R. W. Fogel and S. L. Engerman, *Time on the Cross: The Economics of American Negro Slavery* (Boston: Little, Brown and Co., 1974.)

TABLE 7-5   PRICE DATA FOR SLAVES IN AVERAGE
ANNUAL RATE OF CHANGE FORM

(1) Four Trading Areas, Phillips and Virginia Cities[a]

	Richmond	Charleston	Mid-Georgia	New Orleans	Virginia Cities
1820-1830	− .050	− .047	− .031	− .032	− .015
1830-1840	+ .057	+ .044	+ .025	+ .022	+ .044
1840-1850	− .007	+ .003	+ .011	+ .010	+ .003
1850-1860	+ .054	+ .043	+ .059	+ .049	+ .053

[a] Richmond, Fredericksburg, and Lynchburg.
SOURCES: U. B. Phillips, *American Negro Slavery* (Baton Rouge: Louisiana State University, 1966). Virginia city prices were collected from probate records, slave sales and inventories, Genealogical Society, Salt Lake City.

(2) Phillips and Virginia City Prices Deflated by the Warren and Pearson Wholesale Price Index for All Commodities

1820-1830	− .035	− .032	− .016	− .017	.000
1830-1840	+ .053	+ .040	+ .021	+ .018	+ .040
1840-1850	+ .002	+ .012	+ .020	+ .019	+ .012
1850-1860	+ .043	+ .032	+ .048	+ .038	+ .042

SOURCE: Warren and Pearson Wholesale Price Index, *Historical Statistics of the U.S. Colonial Times to 1957* (Washington: GPO, 1960), p. 115.

wholesale commodity index as the deflator. It is clear that in those decades for which the rate of change of the aggregate slave population was the lowest, the price increase was the greatest. Price data have recently been collected from probate records and other archival sources. Prices for one group of Virginia cities are currently available and are also presented in rate-of-change form in Table 7-5. The rate of change in prices for urban slaves is very similar to that for rural slaves in the same region.

Since the price data for almost all the regions[10] show cyclical changes and the population data for the aggregate United States and the cities show similar oscillations, a hypothesis can be advanced to explain the relative decline of urban slavery. If the demand for urban slaves were more elastic than the demand for rural slaves,[11]

[10] The New Orleans price data do not show the same cyclical pattern that the other data show. In addition, the New South cities, Mobile and New Orleans, also show a pattern of change different from that of the other Southern cities. This is because the period 1830 to 1840 was one of rapid growth for these areas. That is, the 1830 price for the New South was much higher than that for other areas.

[11] This appears to have been the case since substitutes for slave labor in the cities were more readily available and appear to have been closer substitutes

then the shifts in the supply function which caused the cyclical changes in price could easily have resulted in the cities' undergoing violent population swings. The larger the difference in these demand elasticities, the more pronounced would be the population cycles in the cities than those for the aggregate.

Furthermore, the demand for urban slaves need not have been declining during any of the decades studied for the equilibrium population or labor force to have been diminishing. The larger the difference in the elasticity of demand between urban and rural slave labor, the greater would be the cycles in the cities versus those for the aggregate. In addition, the larger the elasticity of demand for urban slave labor the greater the shift term in the demand function could have been during a period of rising prices and falling urban slave quantities. That is, the decline of urban slavery during the 1850s could have been the result of urban slave owners' cashing in on their capital gains. The cities may have lost slaves even though their demand functions were moving to the right at a rate faster than that for the aggregate.

The 1850s can be viewed as merely part of an over-all forty-year picture. The two decades 1820 to 1830 and 1840 to 1850 were periods of gains in urban slavery or periods during which cities lost very few slaves. But 1830 to 1840 and 1850 to 1860 were decades during which slavery declined or increased very slowly in the cities. The changes which occurred during these periods need not require diverse explanations. The slave-price data and intuitive reasoning about elasticity differences suggest the more integrative hypothesis put forth above. The entire era in this context was marked by the great flexibility of the urban slave institution. Periods of overall rising prices led to the selling of slaves from the cities (or the hiring out of these slaves), and periods of falling prices led to the reverse situation. The last decade of urban slavery may have represented not the decline of the institution but its very ability to survive in a changing economy. Had emancipation not occurred and had the prices of slaves declined, urban slave quantities might have again increased.

III THE DEMAND FOR URBAN SLAVES

I HAVE suggested above that the demand for urban slaves need not have declined during the period 1820 to 1860 even though the equilibrium quantities of urban slaves changed radically. In this sec-

---

than those for agricultural slave labor. In addition, the price elasticity of demand for those goods which used urban slave labor in production was probably greater than the price elasticity of demand for agricultural commodities.

tion I will demonstrate that, with a very simple economic model, reasonable elasticity values yield surprisingly strong annual growth rates for urban slave demand.

I will assume that each city or region has a demand schedule for slaves which takes the form:

$$Q_i = D_i P_i^{-e_i}, \tag{1}$$

where Q_i is the quantity of slaves in city or region i, P_i is the price for slaves, D_i is the shift term, and e_i is the (constant) price elasticity of demand. It was this price elasticity of demand which I postulated to be larger for urban than for rural slaves, thus accounting for the strange population and labor force cycles experienced in the cities. In this section I will assign various values to e_i to test the hypothesis which Wade and others stressed that D_i, or the shift term, declined over time. To accomplish this, equation (1) must first be expressed in rate-of-change form. Differentiating totally the logarithmic transform of (1) yields:

$$\overset{*}{Q_i} = \overset{*}{D_i} - e_i \overset{*}{P_i}, \tag{2}$$

where an asterisk (*) over any variable indicates the rate of change in that variable.

Solving for $\overset{*}{D_i}$ gives:

$$\overset{*}{D_i} = \overset{*}{Q_i} + e_i \overset{*}{P_i}, \tag{3}$$

which will aid in determining $\overset{*}{D_i}$ for various values of e_i.

Let us assume for the moment that the statistical work to follow demonstrates that $\overset{*}{D_i}$ was positive. This would mean that the demand for urban slaves was increasing. What, though, does this imply about the underlying economic and social forces in these cities? A positive $\overset{*}{D_i}$ need not indicate that all citizens felt secure in the cities and that urban slave owners were not taxed in many ways. That is, we cannot infer that the costs of using slaves in the cities did not rise relative to those of the rural areas as 1860 approached. But we can state unequivocally that these costs were outweighed by other forces such as increases in real income or rising wage rates for alternative labor sources.

The issue of increased taxation on slaves is very interesting and deserves further comment. Many have viewed taxes, jail fees, and badge costs as methods of discouraging urban owners and hirers of slaves from using this form of labor in the cities. That is, many see these fees as internalizing the apparent externalities which slaves imposed on the community. Whether these fees did increase over time has not yet been completely resolved,[12] but the relative value of the fines was small in comparison with yearly slave-hire rates. More importantly, a positive $\overset{*}{D}_i$ shows that even if fines increased they were dwarfed by demand increases stemming from other factors.

To determine whether the demand for urban slaves did increase during the forty-year period 1820 to 1860 on a decadal basis, I have used equation (3) to construct Table 7-6. For each city or group of cities we have data on $\overset{*}{Q}_i$ (in Table 7-3) and $\overset{*}{P}_i$ (in Table 7-5), but not on e_i. Therefore, I have selected three values for e_i (.5, 1, 1.5) to see how sensitive the $\overset{*}{D}_i$ results are to the choice of this parameter. Additional research I have done indicates that these bounds are correct.[13]

The results for the cities are quite impressive. For almost all decades, for almost all cities or urban aggregates, the demand for slaves increased—that is, $\overset{*}{D}_i$ was positive. The only cities for which demand may have declined during the controversial decade 1850 to 1860 are Baltimore, Charleston, New Orleans, and St. Louis. Elasticity values greater than .5 reverse this result for Baltimore and New Orleans, and values greater than 1 yield positive $\overset{*}{D}_i$ for all cities.

One very interesting result is that the decade which appears the weakest in terms of the size of $\overset{*}{D}_i$ is not 1850 to 1860 but 1820 to 1830. This finding is not at all obvious from viewing slave-quantity data alone. In fact, the conclusion that urban slavery was "an institution which had been an integral part of urban life in Dixie in 1820" but which "was languishing everywhere in 1860"[14] is typical. My model, though, suggests that the cities should have been gaining even more slaves during 1820 to 1830 to have shown the demand strength they did during 1850 to 1860, when prices rose tremendously. Although many cities lost slaves during 1850-1860, demand strength in that

---

[12] More recent work I have done shows that these fees probably did not increase from 1850 to 1860. See C. Goldin, *Urban Slavery: 1820 to 1860*, forthcoming.

[13] I have run regressions on a more complete model, and my estimates of e_i range between .10 and 2.8, with the majority of the cities having an elasticity around 1. These estimates are biased downward because there are no data on the wage rate for free whites and blacks. See Goldin, "The Economics of Urban Slavery" (unpublished Ph.D. dissertation, Chicago, 1972).

[14] R. C. Wade, *op. cit.*, p. 243.

Decades	Old South[b,c]			New South[c,f]			Border States[d,e]			United States Aggregate[h]		
	e = .5	e = 1	e = 1.5	.5	1	1.5	.5	1	1.5	.25	.5	1
1850–1860	+.013	+.034	+.055	.000	+.019	+.038	−.009	+.012	+.033	+.032	+.043	+.064
1840–1850	+.038	+.044	+.050	.000	+.010	+.017	+.038	+.044	+.050	+.030	+.030	+.031
1830–1840	+.029	+.049	+.069	+.109	+.118	+.127	+.006	+.026	+.046	+.037	+.050	+.076
1820–1830	+.024	+.024	+.024	+.009	.000	−.008	+.032	+.032	+.032	+.014	+.007	−.010

Decades	Baltimore[e]			Charleston[g]			Louisville[e]			Mobile[f]		
	.5	1	1.5	.5	1	1.5	.5	1	1.5	.5	1	1.5
1850–1860	−.010	+.009	+.032	−.019	−.003	+.013	+.003	+.024	+.045	+.018	+.037	+.056
1840–1850	.000	+.006	+.012	+.042	+.048	+.054	+.060	+.066	+.072	+.071	+.080	+.089
1830–1840	−.003	+.017	+.037	+.020	+.040	+.060	+.051	+.071	+.091	+.131	+.140	+.142
1820–1830	+.004	+.004	+.004	+.002	−.014	−.030	+.098	+.098	+.098	+.029	+.020	+.019

Decades	New Orleans[f]			Norfolk[e]			Richmond[e]		
	.5	1	1.5	.5	1	1.5	.5	1	1.5
1850–1860	−.009	+.010	+.029	+.004	+.025	+.046	+.041	+.062	+.083
1840–1850	−.019	−.009	.000	+.022	+.028	+.034	+.037	+.043	+.049
1830–1840	+.106	+.115	+.124	+.020	+.040	+.060	+.045	+.065	+.085
1820–1830	+.007	−.002	−.010	+.014	+.014	+.014	+.044	+.044	+.044

Decades	St. Louis[c]			Savannah[g]			Washington[e]		
	.5	1	1.5	.5	1	1.5	.5	1	1.5
1850-1860	−.039	−.018	+.003	+.032	+.048	+.064	−.008	+.013	+.034
1840-1850	+.061	+.067	+.073	+.039	+.045	+.051	+.027	+.033	+.039
1830-1840	−.032	−.012	+.008	+.037	+.057	+.077	−.008	+.012	+.032
1820-1830	+.045	+.045	+.045	+.012	−.004	−.020	+.026	+.026	+.026

[a] $\overset{*}{D} = \overset{*}{Q} + e\overset{*}{P}$, where $\overset{*}{Q}$ = average annual rate of slave labor force; see Table 7-3.

[b] Richmond, Savannah, Charleston.

[c] Mobile, New Orleans.

[d] Louisville, St. Louis, Washington, D.C., Baltimore.

[e] $\overset{*}{P}$ = Virginia city price average annual rates of change, deflated by Warren and Pearson Wholesale Commodity Index, see Table 7-5.

[f] $\overset{*}{P}$ = Phillips' New Orleans price average annual rate of change, deflated by the Warren and Pearson Index, see Table 7-5.

[g] $\overset{*}{P}$ = Phillips' Charleston price average annual rate of change, deflated by the Warren and Pearson Index, see Table 7-5.

[h] $\overset{*}{P}$ = Phillips' Richmond price average annual rate of change, deflated by the Warren and Pearson Index, see Table 7-5.

decade was considerable. The decline of urban slavery did not show any inherent weakness in the institution as many have previously believed. On the contrary, it had developed into a very flexible labor source which responded to economic changes in the entire society.

In many cases the increases in the demand for urban slaves more than matched the increases in the supply of slaves. This implies that the cities were contributing to the increase in the price of slaves or, alternatively, were slowing down any price increases during certain decades.

The shift term for the aggregate demand curve has also been estimated. Consistent with prior reasoning, the e_i values for this exercise are somewhat lower than those for the cities. The computed $\overset{*}{D}_i$ can be compared to those for the cities to see how they fared with respect to rural demand.[15] In general, using low e_i values for the aggregate and large e_i values for the cities yields larger $\overset{*}{D}_i$ for the latter than the former.

IV   CONCLUDING REMARKS

STUDENTS of American history have long questioned whether or not slavery would have survived into the twentieth century in the absence of the Civil War. A great majority of them would reply that, as the South urbanized, slavery would have disappeared because slavery and urbanization are incompatible. This paper demonstrates that, at least for the period 1820 to 1860, urban slavery was a vigorous institution and that slavery was flexible enough to be compatible with urban sprawl.

This paper suggests an economic model which rationalizes the ups and downs of city slave populations. It integrates the apparently weak decade of the fifties into a whole picture, resting its explanation on elasticity differences coupled with general price movements for slaves. It then tests the hypothesis put forth by many that the demand for urban slaves declined toward 1860. This appears to be erroneous. In fact, the cities showed strength in almost all decades. Slaves appear not to have been pushed out of the cities by some inner force, such as the citizens' fear of insurrections. Instead, urban slavery responded to economic changes and slaves were pulled out of cities in the 1850s. Urban slavery appears to have been a vigorous and flexible institution as late as 1860.

[15] Actually, the aggregate shift term is estimated, but this can be shown to be equal to $\lambda \overset{*}{D}_r + (1 - \lambda)\overset{*}{D}_c$, where $\lambda = [Qr/Qr + Qc]$ and $r = $ rural and $c = $ city. If λ is large, $\overset{*}{D}_r$ is a close approximation to the aggregate shift term.

8

Urbanization and Inventiveness in the United States, 1870–1920

ROBERT HIGGS

I

THIS chapter seeks to illuminate the causes of invention in the United States during the half century after 1870. In recent years economists have attempted to explain invention by reviving and elaborating upon the idea that inventive activity is essentially an *economic* endeavor which varies directly with its expected rate of return. The present analysis extends the expected-profitability model in a new direction by taking into account the costs of information and by relating those costs to the locational distribution of the population between the countryside and the cities. The major empirical finding is that urbanization and inventiveness (inventions per capita) were closely associated during the 1870-1920 period. This finding may well be significant for the explanation of economic growth as a self-sustaining process.

II

THREE HYPOTHESES CONCERNING INVENTIVENESS

In this discussion, some crucial background conditions are taken for granted: the American people during the 1870-1920 period were mostly literate and highly motivated by economic incentives; American inventors benefited from the existence of a patent system and from laws that provided strong protection for private property in any form. Obviously such conditions do not prevail over all times or places.

Our fundamental assumption is that inventive activity is an *economic* endeavor: the quantity of resources devoted to inventive activity varies directly with the expected rate of return on inventive activity. This assumption has been the foundation of much fruitful investigation in recent years,[1] but it is hardly a modern notion. The writers of

[1] R. R. Nelson, "The Economics of Invention: A Survey of the Literature," *Journal of Business,* 32 (April 1959), pp. 101-127; *idem,* editor, *The Rate and Direction of Inventive Activity* (Princeton: Princeton University Press, 1962);

247

the United States Constitution subscribed to it when they gave Congress the power to establish a patent system, "To promote the Progress of Science and useful Arts, by securing for limited Times to Authors and Inventors the exclusive Right to their respective Writings and Discoveries." In fact, it is difficult to find anyone who is really informed about the process of invention denying that inventors are economic men. Patent Commissioner W. E. Simonds remarked in 1891 that "perhaps no idea was ever so much opposed to reason and to evidence as the notion that inventors are not actuated by the motives common to the human race, and that if the incentive to invention be destroyed inventors will continue to invent from motives of pure benevolence."[2] And four years later Commissioner J. S. Seymour, anticipating Jacob Schmookler's model by more than a half century, said: "The relation which exists between industrial demand and inventive activity is very close. Each may be said to be dependent upon the other. In any line in which there is little or no call there will be but little inventive effort. On the other hand, should any change or advance in industrial conditions cause a sudden increased demand for some article, means for producing that article or its equivalent will be created very rapidly in the brains of ambitious inventors."[3]

There exists, we assume, a production function relating inputs of resources to outputs of inventions. This production function is not completely deterministic, since creative efforts are always surrounded by a good deal of uncertainty. Still, *ceteris paribus*, a hundred men working to develop an idea have a higher probability of succeeding than fifty men so occupied. We might say that the production function relates quantities of inputs to *expected values* of outputs, but this is merely an analytical flourish. Following Schmookler, we define an invention as a new combination of previously existing knowledge which satisfies some want.[4] Inventive activity, then, is nothing more than the process of creating new *information*. From this definition it is only a short step to formulating a production function with just two inputs: inventive talent and prior information.

I. Feller, "Inventive Activity in Agriculture, 1837-1890," *Journal of Economic History*, 22 (December 1962), pp. 560-577; Jacob Schmookler, *Invention and Economic Growth* (Cambridge, Mass.: Harvard University Press, 1966); and G. H. Daniels, "The Big Questions in the History of American Technology," *Technology and Culture*, 11 (January 1970), pp. 1-21.

[2] *Annual Report of the Commissioner of Patents for 1891* (Washington: Government Printing Office, 1892), p. vi.

[3] *Annual Report of the Commissioner of Patents for 1895* (Washington: Government Printing Office, 1896), p. xiii.

[4] Schmookler, *op. cit.*, p. 10.

To proceed, we assume that inventive talent is randomly distributed throughout the population. If this is so, then differences in inventive activity among regions or places must depend upon variations in the expected costs of acquiring information. Since rates of return depend upon both revenues and costs, two kinds of information are relevant. The first is information about opportunities for profitable invention, that is, about the extent of the market for invention; the second is information that can serve as inputs into the production of inventions. The former determines the potential inventor's expectation of the revenue-stream his invention will generate, and the latter determines his expectation of the initial cost of producing the invention. Together these imply an expected rate of return, which serves as a signal encouraging him either to devote his energies to inventive activity or to use his talents and time in an alternative manner.

Within this framework of analysis is an implication that the inventiveness of urban people will exceed that of rural people. This can be shown as follows. The expected rate of return depends upon the expected stream of revenue from invention. Under conditions preceding mass communication, when most reliable information was acquired by direct observation or by word of mouth, the average search-cost of information about potential markets for inventions was an increasing function of market distance; therefore, the market *as perceived by the average potential inventor* was largely restricted to nearby locations. Assuming that the locational distribution of actual inventive opportunities coincided with that of the population, the probability that an opportunity would be perceived was then much higher for urban than for rural persons. Given the assumed relation between market distance and the average search-cost of information, this proposition follows from the definition of a city as an area of spatially agglomerated population and economic activity. Moreover, if the reasonable assumption be made that, in relation to population, actual inventive opportunities were disproportionately concentrated in the cities, there are even stronger grounds for postulating that the expected stream of revenue from invention was larger for urban than for rural persons.

The expected rate of return depends also upon the expected costs of inventing; here an inverse relation with urbanization can be proposed. "In a pre-mass-communications context, such as the relatively compact cities of the late nineteenth century, where diffusion of technical knowledge [was] highly reliant upon personal interaction, the possibilities for invention ought to [have been] enhanced by the . . . network of interpersonal communications and confrontations."[5] In the absence of well-developed means of mass communication, the costs of acquiring information were heavily dependent upon *spatial proximity*. The expected costs of acquiring informational inputs were lower for the potential urban inventor than for his rural counterpart simply because of the enormously greater proximity of urban information carriers to one another. The greatest handicap of rural persons was their spatial isolation from one another.

Combining the assumptions about the expected revenue stream and the expected total costs of inventing, it follows that the expected rate of return on inventive activity was higher in the city than in the countryside. It is now easy to derive the testable hypothesis that, *ceteris paribus*, an increasing linear relation existed between inventiveness and the proportion of the population in cities (Hypothesis 1).[6]

Adam Smith and many others have maintained a different view of the causes of invention. This view is not inconsistent with the urbanization hypothesis; rather, the two are complementary. According to Smith,

> The invention of all those machines by which labour is so much facilitated and abridged, seems to have been originally owing to the division of labour. . . . A great part of the machines made use of in those manufactures in which labour is most subdivided, were originally the inventions of common workmen, who, being each of them employed in some very simple operation, naturally turned their thoughts towards finding out easier and readier methods of performing it.[7]

If one assumes, as Smith did, that the division of labor was more extensive in manufacturing than in other activities, then it is easy

---

[5] Allan R. Pred, *The Spatial Dynamics of U.S. Urban-Industrial Growth, 1800-1914* (Cambridge, Mass.: M.I.T. Press, 1966), p. 96.

[6] By definition, the total number of inventions, I, is the sum of those made by urban people, Iu, and those made by rural people, Ir: $I = Iu + Ir$. Iu is proportional to the urban population, Pu, and Ir is proportional to the rural population, Pr; but because of differences in the actual distribution of inventive opportunities, in information costs, and therefore in the expected profitability of invention, the urban proportionality factor, α, is greater than the rural proportionality factor, β: $Iu = \alpha Pu$, and $Ir = \beta Pr$, where $\alpha > \beta > 0$. Substituting these equations into the definition of I and dividing both sides of the equation by the total population, P, give an expression for inventiveness:

$$I/P = \alpha Pu/P + \beta Pr/P.$$

Since $Pr/P = (1 - Pu/P)$, it follows that $I/P = \beta + (\alpha - \beta) Pu/P$, where $(\alpha - \beta) > 0$.

[7] Adam Smith, *The Wealth of Nations* (New York: Modern Library, 1937), p. 9.

to derive the testable hypothesis that, *ceteris paribus*, an increasing linear relation existed between inventiveness and the proportion of the labor force in manufacturing (Hypothesis 2).[8]

In many instances the economic historian is compelled to treat the south as a special case, and for a study of inventiveness such a possibility ought to be considered. Hypotheses 1 and 2 relate inventiveness to urbanization and to employment structure, but other factors also influence inventiveness. One suspects that the south, with its concentration of racially oppressed people, its rigid class structure, and its relatively low level of educational attainment, might have been uninventive even in comparison with non-southern areas having similar patterns of urbanization and employment structure. To test for this possibility (Hypothesis 3), the regression equations include a dummy variable to distinguish southern states.

III

TESTS OF THE HYPOTHESES

Since the three hypotheses are complementary and the *ceteris paribus* qualification applies to each of them, a properly specified framework for testing them is a multiple regression equation. The dependent variable is inventions per capita, and the explanatory variables are (1) the proportion of the population in cities, (2) the proportion of the labor force in manufacturing, and (3) a dummy variable to distinguish southern states.

---

[8] By definition, the total number of inventions, I, is the sum of those made by manufacturing workers, Im, and those made by nonmanufacturing workers, In: $I = Im + In$. Im is proportional to the manufacturing labor force, Lm, and In is proportional to the nonmanufacturing labor force, Ln; but because the division of labor is more extensive in manufacturing the opportunities for invention are greater there, and the manufacturing proportionality factor, α°, is greater than the nonmanufacturing proportionality factor, β°: $Im = \alpha^\circ Lm$, and $In = \beta^\circ Ln$, where $\alpha^\circ > \beta^\circ > 0$. Substituting these equations into the definition of I and dividing both sides of the equation by the total population, P, give an expression for inventiveness: $I/P = \alpha^\circ Lm/P + \beta^\circ Ln/P$. The ratio of population to total labor force, L, is assumed the same everywhere: $\sigma = P/L$. The last equation can therefore be rewritten as $I/P = \alpha' Lm/L + \beta' Ln/L$, where $\alpha' = \alpha^\circ/\sigma$ and $\beta' = \beta^\circ/\sigma$. Since $Ln/L = (1 - Lm/L)$, it follows that $I/P = \beta' + (\alpha' - \beta') Lm/L$, where $(\alpha' - \beta') > 0$.

Adam Smith's views on invention are actually rather more complicated than the quotation in the text indicates. See Nathan Rosenberg, "Adam Smith on the Division of Labour: Two Views or One?" *Economica*, 32 (May 1965), pp. 127-139. But whatever the precise origin of the hypothesis developed here, it is still an interesting and widely held view. Pred, for example, heavily emphasizes the connection between invention and manufacturing. See Pred, *op. cit.*, pp. 86-142.

Patent data are used to measure the number of inventions for a cross section of American states. The many defects of these data must be faced: not all inventions are patented; patented inventions vary greatly in importance; and the propensity to patent inventions varies from one industry to another. Still, it seems clear that patent statistics can be fruitfully used and that they constitute the main resource for the historical study of invention.[9] Many of the most damaging criticisms of patent statistics apply only with much-reduced force to the nineteenth and early twentieth centuries, when, "independent inventors were overwhelmingly the source of inventions, and whatever the legal hazards, they usually had to have patents to make much from their inventions."[10] Moreover, patent data are more appropriate for cross-sectional than for time-series studies.[11] All things considered, one can hardly improve upon Schmookler's appraisal: "We have a choice of using patent statistics cautiously and learning what we can from them, or not using them and learning nothing about what they alone can teach us."[12]

To eliminate some of the randomness in the data, three-year centered averages are used (e.g., the patent value for 1870 is an average of 1869, 1870, and 1871). The urban population is defined conventionally as persons living in incorporated places of 2,500 or more.

With one exception, the data include every state which had achieved statehood prior to the three-year averaging period for patents. The single exception is Connecticut, which is excluded from the sample throughout the period. Connecticut was consistently the nation's most inventive state, and its inventiveness far exceeded the prediction of the model. So great was its deviation that should it be left in the regressions it alone would account for about half of the unexplained variance. It does not seem useful to permit a single observation to influence the results to this extent, and the exclusion does not affect the outcome of any hypothesis tested. In a later section we shall return to Connecticut for a closer look.

---

[9] On the adequacy of patent data and the problems of using them, see Simon Kuznets, "Inventive Activity: Problems of Definition and Measurement," and B. S. Sanders, "Some Difficulties in Measuring Inventive Activity," both in Nelson (editor), *Rate and Direction;* Schmookler, *op. cit.,* pp. 18-56; D. C. Mueller, Patents, Research and Development, and the Measurement of Inventive Activity," *Journal of Industrial Economics,* 15 (November 1966), p. 36; and John Jewkes, David Sawers, and Richard Stillerman, *The Sources of Invention* (second ed., New York: W. W. Norton, 1969), pp. 88-91, 198.

[10] J. Schmookler, "Comment," in Nelson, *op. cit.,* p. 79.

[11] Mueller, *op. cit.,* p. 36.

[12] Schmookler, *Invention and Economic Growth,* p. 56.

Table 8-1 shows the regression results.[13] The coefficients of multiple determination, ranging from 80 to 92 per cent, indicate that the equations provide a remarkably close fit to the data, especially remarkable when it is recalled that these data are cross-sectional.

TABLE 8-1 ORDINARY LEAST-SQUARES
REGRESSION ESTIMATES

Date	Proportion of Population in Cities	Proportion of Labor Force in Manufacturing	Southern Dummy	
1870	0.558	0.899	−3.423	$R^2 = 0.893$
	(0.174)	(0.261)	(3.614)	$N = 36$
1880	0.753	0.355	−0.251	$R^2 = 0.921$
	(0.125)	(0.182)	(2.639)	$N = 37$
1890	0.939	0.176	−1.956	$R^2 = 0.923$
	(0.122)	(0.183)	(3.044)	$N = 37$
1900	0.756	−0.208	−7.370	$R^2 = 0.885$
	(0.102)	(0.166)	(2.304)	$N = 44$
1910	0.783	−0.598	−14.234	$R^2 = 0.802$
	(0.126)	(0.214)	(3.059)	$N = 45$
1920	0.794	−0.535	−13.386	$R^2 = 0.816$
	(0.118)	(0.190)	(2.814)	$N = 47$

SOURCE: Patent data are from the annual reports of the U.S. Commissioner of Patents. Urbanization data are from the Census. Labor-force data are from H. S. Perloff *et al.*, *Regions, Resources and Economic Growth* (Baltimore: The Johns Hopkins Press, 1960), Appendix Tables A-1 and A-6.

NOTE: The dependent variable is patents per 100,000 population. Standard errors are in parentheses. States considered "southern" are Virginia, North Carolina, South Carolina, Georgia, Florida, Alabama, Mississippi, Louisiana, Texas, Oklahoma, Arkansas, Tennessee, Kentucky, and West Virginia.

Surprisingly, the regression coefficient for the dummy variable is insignificant for the pre-1900 cross sections but highly significant for the later ones. This indicates that although southern uninventiveness can be explained in the nineteenth century by the region's paucity

[13] Because the proportion of the population in cities and the proportion of the labor force in manufacturing are rather highly correlated, the specter of multicollinearity is raised. To determine whether this is actually a problem the regression equations have been estimated in a stepwise manner; and the behavior of the sampling variation of the coefficients indicates that multicollinearity is not a problem. Specifically, parameter magnitudes do not change dramatically, no sign changes occur, and *t*-values that are initially significant remain so as additional variables are added. The standard hypothesis tests can therefore be taken at face value.

of cities and manufacturing, some additional influence became important during 1900-1920. A variety of explanations, all necessarily conjectural, might be offered for this development: the southern class system, racial segregation, educational backwardness, and various traditions have been suggested as areas deserving study.[14] But why these should become significant only beginning in 1900 seems a mystery.

Smith's division-of-labor hypothesis (Hypothesis 2) fares rather badly: two tests (1870 and 1880) support it; two (1890 and 1900) find it insignificant; and two (1910 and 1920) show that its inverse was the case. These findings may, however, simply indicate that the proportion of the labor force in manufacturing is a progressively poorer index of the extent of the division of labor.

Finally, the most outstanding aspect of these results is the consistent support shown for Hypothesis 1. In every case the regression coefficient for the urbanization variable is positive and highly significant. Perhaps the question should be raised: Why does the coefficient of the urbanization variable not decline over time, as one would expect in view of the improvements in communications during this period? At the moment no answer is apparent. One might conjecture that actual inventive opportunities were shifting into the cities fast enough to offset the advantage rural persons were gaining through reduced information costs; or perhaps the telephone, better mail service, technical journals, and other forms of improved communications—all of which benefited urban as well as rural people—reduced information costs for rural people no faster than they did for city dwellers, thus preserving the urban advantage.

IV

THE SPECIAL CASE OF CONNECTICUT

From the data shown in Table 8-2 it can be seen that the level of inventiveness in Connecticut was not only two to four times the U.S. average, but it was also 22 to 39 per cent above the level of the next-ranking state, usually Massachusetts. (The five states listed in Table 8-2 were the leading ones at every date except 1910, when California [6.2], Illinois [5.8], and Colorado [5.8] ranked above some of them.) And not only was Connecticut's level of inventiveness high in comparison with the levels of other states; it also stood well above the level predicted on the basis of its urbanization, its labor-force concentration in manufacturing, and its northern location, as shown below. This exceptional behavior suggests several questions, only one

[14] Pred, *op. cit.*, pp. 120-127.

254

of which is examined here: namely, did the relation between urbanization and inventiveness, already confirmed for the cross section of
American states, also exist within Connecticut?

The data examined here have been obtained as a random sample
from the *Annual Report of the Commissioner of Patents* for the years
indicated. A sample of 200 inventions issued to Connecticut residents
was drawn at quinquennial intervals for the period 1870-1915. Altogether these ten samples contain 2,000 inventions, which, in view
of the fact that they have been randomly drawn, would appear to
be a sufficient number to support some generalizations. The sampling
design called for collecting the name and residence of the inventor
and a brief description of the invention. This procedure permitted
a distinction to be drawn between the number of inventions and
the number of inventors, but generally the correspondence between
the two sets of data is so close that any statement about the one
applies as well to the other.

TABLE 8-2   THREE-YEAR CENTERED AVERAGES OF
PATENTS ISSUED PER 10,000 POPULATION,
SELECTED STATES AND UNITED STATES,
1870-1910

	1870	1880	1890	1900	1910
Connecticut	12.8	10.0	11.4	8.5	8.6
Massachusetts	9.5	7.9	9.3	6.5	6.0
Rhode Island	8.9	8.1	7.8	6.3	5.5
New York	6.7	5.6	7.1	5.4	5.5
New Jersey	5.1	5.7	7.2	5.7	5.8
United States	3.1	2.7	3.7	3.2	3.8

SOURCE: Calculated from patent data in the *Annual Report of the
Commissioner of Patents*, various years, and population data in
U.S. Bureau of the Census, *Historical Statistics of the United States,
Colonial Times to 1957* (Washington: U.S. Government Printing
Office, 1960).

To test the hypothesis that inventiveness and urbanization were
directly related, the data have been classified according to the residence of the inventor. It is apparent that the data fall into three
groups: Group I cities (Bridgeport, Hartford, New Haven, Waterbury, Meriden, and New Britain); Group II cities (New London,
Stamford, Middletown, Norwich, Danbury, and Norwalk); and Group
III, which includes all other residences, whether urban or rural. Except for 1870, every sample shows the six Group I cities accounting

TABLE 8-3   DISTRIBUTION BY LOCATIONAL ORIGIN OF RANDOMLY SAMPLED
PATENTED INVENTIONS, CONNECTICUT, 1870-1915

	1870	1875	1880	1885	1890	1895	1900	1905	1910	1915
Group I										
Bridgeport	11	30	24	42	21	32	35	28	24	29
Hartford	12	18	10	24	28	23	40	38	39	35
New Haven	33	29	55	26	22	19	31	21	27	20
Waterbury	7	11	15	12	25	15	5	8	10	25
Meriden	11	15	11	8	14	7	6	9	6	5
New Britain	3	6	9	4	24	11	5	11	27	12
Group I Aggregate	77	109	124	116	134	107	122	115	133	126
Group II										
New London	2	5	2	9	2	8	1	2	2	5
Stamford	2	4	5	5	4	7	17	10	9	2
Middletown	4	7	5	3	6	2	3	13	5	2
Norwich	10	6	5	6	6	6	1	1	0	3
Danbury	3	2	1	8	7	6	2	5	4	0
Norwalk	3	4	0	1	6	4	6	4	2	5
Group II Aggregate	24	28	18	32	31	33	30	35	22	17
Groups I and II										
Aggregate	101	137	142	148	165	140	152	150	155	143
Group III	99	63	58	52	35	60	48	50	45	57

SOURCE: Randomly drawn from the *Annual Report of the Commissioner of Patents* for the
years indicated.

for well over half of the state's inventions. The six Group II cities
provided 9 to 18 per cent and Group III residences (again excluding 1870) were the source of 17 to 31 per cent. The leading twelve
cities (Groups I and II) generally provided about three-fourths of
all the sampled inventions (Table 8-3).

To obtain an estimate of the total number of patented inventions
in each location, we proceed as follows. First, determine the proportion that the sample size (which is always 200) constitutes in the
total for the state at the date in question. Then multiply the reciprocal
of this proportion by the number of sampled inventions for a particular place; the product is the estimated total number of patented inventions for that place. For example, in 1910 the state had 990 patents.
The sample of 200 therefore constitutes approximately one-fifth of
the total. In that year Waterbury inventors contributed ten inventions
to the sample. The estimated total number of Waterbury inventions
is therefore $10 \times 5 = 50$.

Having obtained estimates of the total number of patented inventions in various locations, we can divide them by the population
figures for each place to obtain estimates of inventiveness. Table 8-4

shows these estimates. (Those who are uncomfortable with small samples but believe in the central-limit theorem may wish to focus on the figures for the group aggregates and ignore the estimates for individual cities.) As Table 8-4 shows, Group I cities were the most inventive, though their advantage over Group II cities was on two occasions negligible.[15] The inventiveness of Group III places, which include some small cities as well as all rural locations, was much lower; for 1890-1910 the level of Group III inventiveness was approximately equal to the U.S. average, as shown in Table 8-2. Manifesting a great urban-rural inventiveness differential, these data are strikingly consistent with Hypothesis 1.

TABLE 8-4   ESTIMATED LEVELS OF PATENTED INVENTIONS PER 10,000 POPULATION, CONNECTICUT LOCATIONS, 1870-1910

	1870	1880	1890	1900	1910
Group I					
Bridgeport	21.6	26.1	20.2	18.7	11.8
Hartford	11.8	7.1	24.8	19.0	19.7
New Haven	24.0	18.3	12.7	10.9	10.1
Waterbury	24.1	25.3	40.9	4.1	6.8
Meriden	39.0	21.3	30.4	9.5	11.0
New Britain	11.6	22.9	68.5	7.3	30.8
Group I Aggregate	17.7	18.1	25.2	13.1	13.9
Group II					
New London	7.3	5.7	6.5	2.3	5.1
Stamford	70.0	60.0	30.2	40.6	17.9
Middletown	21.7	22.1	31.1	11.5	21.0
Norwich	22.2	9.9	17.3	2.3	0.0
Danbury	12.5	2.6	19.9	4.8	9.9
Norwalk	13.9	0.0	27.7	18.1	6.3
Group II Aggregate	17.3	9.7	20.1	12.8	9.7
Groups I and II Aggregate	17.6	16.1	24.1	13.0	13.1
Group III	11.7	6.0	3.8	3.8	4.1

SOURCE: Estimated by a procedure described in the text.

Not only were Connecticut's twelve largest cities highly inventive in comparison with other locations within the state, but their inventiveness also greatly exceeded the levels attained by the major American cities outside Connecticut. Data which permit such comparisons have

[15] The estimates of inventiveness for Stamford are remarkably high. One might conjecture that Stamford's proximity to the New York metropolitan area had something to do with this; but, if so, it is odd that Norwalk did not also benefit to the same degree.

been compiled by Irwin Feller. His sample contains data for thirty-five of the largest and most important cities in the United States for the period 1860-1910.[16] The inventiveness of Group I cities considered as an aggregate was exceeded in 1870 by only two cities in Feller's sample (Lowell, with 17.8, and Worcester, with 24.3). In 1880, 1900, and 1910 no city in Feller's sample reached the level of inventiveness attained by the six Group I cities, and in 1890 only one did (Lynn, with 38.2). If the estimates for individual Connecticut cities be credited, it appears that at least two of them exceeded the highest city of Feller's sample at every date.

It is clear that urbanization and inventiveness were closely associated in Connecticut. No major city failed to generate a large output of inventions. The Group I cities were leaders both in population and in number of inventions, and Group II cities were the next-ranking places according to population. Since the state's urban-size ranking was quite stable throughout the post-Civil War era, a measure of the association between city-size and invention at any time during the period applies about equally well to other times. Taking the mid-point year 1890 as an example, we find that Spearman's rank-order correlation coefficient between city population and the number of inventions for the twelve largest cities is 0.84, a figure that could have been obtained by chance less than one time in a hundred. Interestingly, the rank-order correlation coefficient between city population and inventions per capita for the twelve largest cities is -0.05, which indicates that no rank-order relation exists between these variables.[17]

We conclude that the information required to stimulate a high level of inventiveness could apparently be acquired about as cheaply in a city of ten to twenty thousand as in cities several times larger. If by "urbanization" we mean the shift of a region's population out of the countryside into urban places of some minimum size, then it is probably true that urbanization promoted inventiveness; but if by "urban-

[16] Feller's sample includes "the twenty-five largest cities as of 1910, those cities not in the top twenty-five according to population but within that ranking according to either value-added in manufacturing (Paterson, Peoria, Lawrence, Dayton, and Worcester, Mass.) [or] in average number of employees (Lowell, Fall River, and Lynn), and Albany and Omaha." Feller's figures are enumerations, not estimates. I am grateful to Professor Feller for providing me with these data in advance of their publication. See his article, "The Urban Location of United States Invention, 1860-1910," *Explorations in Economic History*, 8 (Spring 1971.

[17] Feller fails to find a significant simple correlation between city size and inventiveness for the thirty-five cities of his sample. Moreover, a significant relation fails to appear even when labor-force concentration in manufacturing, recent growth rates, and regional location are controlled, as I found by performing a multiple regression analysis using Feller's data.

ization" we mean simply the growth of individual cities, this statement cannot be supported by our cross-sectional evidence.[18]

V

URBANIZATION, INVENTION, AND ECONOMIC GROWTH

Cross-sectional evidence for American states and for Connecticut cities strongly supports a hypothesis which links inventiveness to urbanization. If we are willing to accept a time-series interpretation of this finding, it may well be significant for the explanation of economic growth as a *self-sustaining* process in the period before research and development had become institutionalized. To oversimplify vastly, urbanization was a response to changes in the relative profitability of agricultural and nonagricultural activities, which in turn were the result of changes in expenditure patterns as per capita incomes rose (e.g., Engel's law). Therefore, in a setting where peculiarities of comparative advantage in international trade or of sectoral increases in productivity did not strongly intervene, economic growth gave rise to urbanization.[19] But because urbanization encouraged greater inventiveness, it produced a *feedback effect* on growth by promoting more rapid technological progress. In this way it was a cause as well as a consequence of economic growth, and the circle of a self-sustaining process was closed. Though the existence of this feedback mechanism be granted, however, the magnitude of its influence on growth remains open to conjecture.

[18] The question remains: Why were Connecticut's urban people so inventive? To deal with this question I have elsewhere developed a hypothesis which asserts that, *ceteris paribus*, the extensive use of a complex mechanical technology should be associated with high inventiveness under the prevailing technological conditions of the nineteenth century. There is much evidence that Connecticut's industrial composition was indeed heavily concentrated in activities using such methods: corsets, cutlery and edge tools, hardware, needles and pins, plated and britannia ware, sewing machines, tools, firearms, ammunition, rolled brass and brassware, clocks, and textiles can be cited. All these industries used highly mechanized, interchangeable-parts techniques of mass production. And it was in these very industries that many of the most fruitful technological ideas of the nineteenth century were first used, as shown by Nathan Rosenberg, "Technological Change in the Machine Tool Industry, 1840-1910," *Journal of Economic History,* 23 (December 1963). There is, therefore, some basis for believing that a learning process was engendered by the presence of these activities and that the skills and aptitudes acquired there carried over as a generalized problem-solving ability. In this light, Connecticut's long-hailed "Yankee ingenuity" is seen to be an important *external economy* accruing as a result of learning from experience to those closely involved in the operation and maintenance of complex mechanical techniques.

[19] Herbert A. Simon, "Effects of Increased Productivity upon the Ratio of Urban to Rural Population," *Econometrica,* 15 (January 1947), pp. 31-42.

9

Firm Location and Optimal City Size in American History

JOSEPH A. SWANSON AND

JEFFREY G. WILLIAMSON

I INTRODUCTION

OUR purpose in this section is to construct a theory of plant location which may be used to explain city growth patterns over long historical time periods. This interest stems from our earlier work on nineteenth-century urbanization in the American northeast.[1] The analytical framework developed here is meant to apply to economic systems which have already experienced extensive industrialization, where labor mobility is sufficient to satisfy the usual neoclassical assumptions of approximate real-wage equalization, and where urban systems are sufficiently large and complex to require firms to purchase significant inputs of energy, transport, warehousing, education, etc., services. Thus, the model should be most relevant in its application to American northeastern and midwestern experience since the Civil War.

The technique is to ascertain those factors which determine location decision for *new plants*. Since we begin our discussion by abstracting from the transport-cost aspects of the problem, the model breaks sharply with traditional location theory. Our premises hold that a central element of the location decision is the systematic relation of input prices to characteristics of particular sites—in particular, to population densities. In what follows, we employ the symbol c as representative of the population density of a particular site. (If we postulate that all *cities* must have the same land area, the c can represent population of the city and density of the site simultaneously.)

The goal of this work, then, is threefold: (1) characterize the criterion for optimal plant location, (2) describe the solution of the problem, and (3) evaluate the relation between the optimal solution and

---

[1] J. G. Williamson and J. A. Swanson, "The Growth of Cities in the American Northeast, 1820-1870," *Explorations in Entrepreneurial History*, 2nd Series, 4, No. 1 (1967) supplement. Also J. A. Swanson and J. G. Williamson, "A Model of Urban Capital Formation and the Growth of Cities in History," *Explorations in Economic History*, 8, No. 2 (1970), pp. 213-222.

260

the postulated representation of cost variability. When we have done so, the implications for urban *employment* growth, and thus the growth pattern of cities as measured by population, become straightforward.

II The Optimal Location Decision: U-Shaped Cost Functions in the Municipal Service Sector

ii.1 the model

We focus on the "footloose" firm with reference to the optimal plant location in a particular region (e.g., the northeast). Firms are assumed to produce a single homogeneous commodity. Transport costs (of the final product) from any site in the region to any distribution center are assumed to be equal. Thus, the net price exclusive of transport costs, $p(t)$, is constant across all urban locations. Further, all urban sites are characterized by equal delivered prices for new capital goods.[2] To the extent that capital goods are imported from outside the region, this assumption is reasonable since it applies equally to all cities in the importing region. The early nineteenth century, when the import content of investment was fairly high, may fulfill these requirements with respect to equipment, but nowhere after the Civil War is the assumption satisfied with respect to plant. Labor inputs bulk large in plant construction, and thus low-wage cities would have had an advantage over high-wage ones, if efficiency in construction was fairly constant across cities. In the last analysis, however, it is our historical ignorance which dictates the following assumption: the price of investment goods does not vary over plant sites.

We admit with some haste that $p(t)$ will also vary from city to city: buyer's price differs from seller's price by transport costs. However, we see no reason to hypothesize a systematic relationship between $p(t)$, and the city's size. While asserting that the net price of a firm's output is independent of city-size, it should be emphasized that we deal here only with export products. The location theorists have focused attention on the spatial distribution of cities, and thus have placed primary emphasis on unit transport costs as the key variable in the location decision. Quite naturally, the secular behavior of such costs has stimulated research activity by urban historians, the most colorful of which has been that relating to city rivalries. Breaking with this tradition in the hope that fruitful new hypotheses can be developed, we have chosen to assume that unit transport costs do not vary over cities in the region.

[2] The following two paragraphs are taken from Swanson and Williamson, "A Model. . . ," pp. 215-216.

Finally, we shall hold that the firm perfectly anticipates future prices of outputs and inputs, and that the price of the firm's final product is assumed invariant with respect to time.

The isoquant map of the plant is well approximated by the (concave) function

$$[1a] \qquad Q = \Phi(J, K, L),$$

where J is the flow of municipal services employed in the production of Q, K is the stock of capital assets employed as a surrogate for capital services (via the traditional assumption of proportionality of service flow and stock), and L is a measure of labor services. Municipal services are employed in constant proportion to capital services:

$$[1b] \qquad J = \alpha K,$$

so that

$$[1c] \qquad F(K, L) = \Phi(J, K, L).$$

Now J *can* be interpreted as an intermediate (raw material) input. In traditional location theory, however, the delivered price of J is determined by some finite transport costs. In our model, J is *not* a traded good and as such transport costs are infinite.

We hold that F is *strictly concave* such that

$$[2a] \qquad F_K = \alpha\Phi_J + \Phi_K > 0$$
$$[2b] \qquad F_L = \Phi_L > 0$$

and the Hessian of F is negative definite; *viz.*,

$$[2c] \qquad \begin{vmatrix} F_{KK} & F_{KL} \\ F_{LK} & F_{LL} \end{vmatrix} = \begin{vmatrix} \alpha^2\Phi_{JJ} + \Phi_{KK} & \Phi_{KL} \\ \Phi_{LK} & \Phi_{LL} \end{vmatrix} > 0$$

We require that the second partial derivatives be continuous functions of K and L, and further that the service flows of capital goods be proportional (by a factor of unity) to the stock of capital goods.

Define the instantaneous *net receipts* (or cash flows), $Z(t)$, of the plant at time t as revenue $R(t)$ less the sum of outlay on current account and capital expenditures, $q(t)I(t)$. Net receipts are defined as

$$[3] \quad Z(t) = R(t) - [u(t)J(t) + w(t)L(t)] - q(t)I(t)$$

where

$$R(t) = p(t)Q(t),$$

and,

> u: the price of public services,
> w: the money wage rate,
> q: the price of new capital goods (assumed temporally constant),
> I: the quantity of new capital goods.

We postulate below that the prices of the "current inputs" vary system-atically with c (to ensure the concavity of Z).

The optimal location of the plant will be at a site with characteristic c^*, which in *equilibrium* represents the optimal city size. (Since the average size of cities has grown consistently since 1860, there is some suggestion that c^* rises through time. We wish to ascertain why.) For the representative firm, c^* is found by maximizing the present value of the plant:

$$[4] \qquad V(0) = \int_0^\infty \exp\left[- \int_0^t \rho(\theta)\, d\theta \right] Z(t)\, dt$$

subject to [2] and the net investment identity

$$[5] \qquad\qquad\qquad I(t) = K(t) + \delta K(t).$$

(We assume that depreciation occurs at the constant rate, δ.) The maximization is with respect to I, J, L, and c given $K(0) = 0$.

The problem, as stated above, is equivalent to the maximization of discounted future profits over the same horizon, or to the maximization of profits, $P(t)$, for all t, where

$$[6] \qquad P(t) = R(t) - u(t)J(t) - v(t)K(t) - w(t)L(t)$$

and

$$[7] \qquad\qquad\qquad v(t) = q(t)[\rho(t) + \delta]$$

where $\rho(t)$ is the short-term rate at which the firm may borrow or lend.

Thus far we consider "J goods" as only intermediate inputs to firms rather than as public goods consumed by households. There are two dichotomous cases of financing we could consider: (1) full-cost pric-ing of municipal services with the total charge to the firm, $u(t)J(t)$, varying with intensity of use, or (2) zero price with costs financed wholly by property taxes. We consider case (2) in the present paper, but given the assumption of J used in fixed proportion with K the results should not be greatly different from case (1). Thus public services are purchased by the payment of property taxes at a rate θ:

$$[8] \qquad\qquad\qquad uJ = \theta qK$$

where, from [1b], $[\theta q]u^{-1} = \alpha$. Since α is a parameter from the production function and assumed constant, and since q is also invariant to city-size, then $[\theta u^{-1}]$ is also a constant. Thus, variations in u over c are equivalent variations in tax rates, θ. Quality variations in municipal service output are not admitted into the model, but they present no interpretive difficulties. With a constant θ over all cities, then the "quality" of J varies across cities instead of u (and thus θ). Further, the combined effect of technical change and rising factor costs on the cost of J, can be captured by variations in θ. Note that if the model were expanded to include nonhomogeneous urban products, then only firms producing products characterized by production processes with small α would locate in "small" cities, e.g., $c < c^{\circ}$.

We hypothesize U-shaped cost-functions in the supply of municipal services, though the issue on the configuration of these cost-curves is hardly settled even on contemporary evidence.[3] Property tax rates can be written as

$$[9] \qquad\qquad \theta = f(c) \cdot \phi(t)$$

where $f(c)$ represents the cost function and the output of municipal services is directly proportional to c. Since historically technical change has been generally slow in the service sector[4] and since this sector is relatively labor intensive, we expect with rising wages over time that θ will shift upward. Thus, $\phi(t)$ is assumed to fall through time.

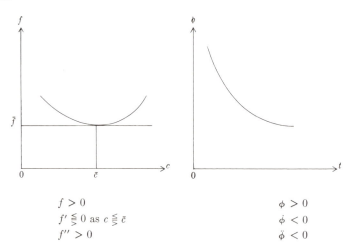

$f > 0$	$\phi > 0$
$f' \lessgtr 0$ as $c \lessgtr \bar{c}$	$\dot{\phi} < 0$
$f'' > 0$	$\ddot{\phi} < 0$

[3] Werner Z. Hirsch, "The Supply of Urban Public Services," in Harvey S. Perloff and Lowden Wingo (editors), *Issues in Urban Economics* (Baltimore: Johns Hopkins Press, 1968).

[4] See W. J. Baumol, "Macroeconomics and Unbalanced Growth: The Anatomy of Urban Crisis," *American Economic Review* (1967), pp. 415-426; and V. R. Fuchs, *The Service Economy* (New York: Columbia University Press, 1968).

Next consider interest rates facing the firm. Capital-market imperfections during nineteenth-century American development have always been of interest to economic historians. Recent work[5] documents that financing was available at lower interest rates in the larger metropolis than in the smaller cities of the hinterlands. Further, there is considerably evidence of national capital-market integration by World War I. In section II.2 and III.2 we explore the possible impact of capital-market integration on city growth and plant location. For the present, we hypothesize declining interest rates with increased urban concentration (attributable to scale economies in the financial sector and to high spatial transaction costs).[6] Furthermore, we postulate a historical decline in the interest rate structure over time. This follows from the tradition of growth theory which suggests that $\rho(t)$ declines with capital accumulation and also given high capital intensity in the capital goods sector their relative price, $q(t)$, should decline over time with development. Thus,

$$[10] \qquad \rho = g(c) \cdot \gamma(t)$$

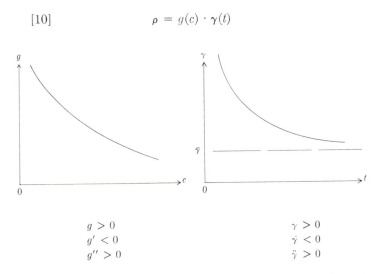

$$g > 0 \qquad\qquad \gamma > 0$$
$$g' < 0 \qquad\qquad \dot{\gamma} < 0$$
$$g'' > 0 \qquad\qquad \ddot{\gamma} > 0$$

[5] R. E. Cameron, et al., Banking in the Early Stages of Industrialization (London: Oxford University Press, 1967). L. E. Davis, "Capital Mobilities and Finance Capitalism: A Study of Economic Evolution in the U.S., 1820-1920," Explorations in Entrepreneurial History, 1, No. 1 (1963), pp. 88-105; and "The Investment Market, 1870-1914: The Evolution of a National Market," Journal of Economic History, 25, No. 3 (1965), pp. 355-399. R. Sylla, "Federal Policy, Banking Market Structure, and Capital Mobilization in the U.S., 1863-1913," Journal of Economic History, 29, No. 4 (1969), pp. 657-686. H. T. Patrick, "Financial Development and Economic Growth in Underdeveloped Countries," Economic Development and Cultural Change, 14, No. 2 (1966), pp. 174-189.

[6] Cf. J. G. Williamson, "Land Augmenting Extensive Development Under Conditions of Factor Immobility: The Development of the American West, 1870-1910," mimeo., Madison, Wisconsin (May, 1970).

Finally, we specify rising per unit labor costs with increased city size. This appears to be well supported by the historical record, and a theoretical explanation can be readily formalized. Assume that labor mobility is sufficient to insure an equalization of real wages, ω, across all urban sites. The cost of living, however, rises with city size. In the nineteenth century, a major component of household budgets was foodstuffs,[7] and these wage goods were produced in agricultural regions outside the constellation of city sites considered in optimal plant location decision in this paper. With increased transportation and distribution costs, the prices of these wage goods increased with urban concentration. Thus, we formally state

$$
[11] \quad
\begin{cases}
W = \Pi\omega \text{ [money wage]} \\
\Pi = h(c) \text{ [price of wage goods]} \\
\omega = \omega(t) \text{ [real wage]}
\end{cases}
$$

where the real wage rises over time in the course of development and capital accumulation. The rise in real wages over time is obviously well documented in American historical experience, but even if real wages did not rise—as in the labor-surplus models—*money* wages would rise over time. The latter follows since the relative price of wage goods should rise over time as long as consumption (agricultural) goods are labor-intensive and no factor reversal takes place.

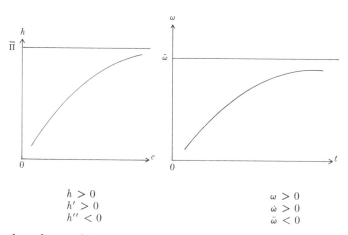

$$
\begin{array}{cc}
h > 0 & \omega > 0 \\
h' > 0 & \dot{\omega} > 0 \\
h'' < 0 & \ddot{\omega} < 0
\end{array}
$$

Note that the model can be made more realistic by adding a third wage good to the system. Thus far, this paper has focused *only* on the supply of municipal services to *firms*. How about the consumption

[7] J. G. Williamson, "Consumer Behavior in the Nineteenth Century: Carroll D. Wright's Massachusetts Workers in 1875," *Explorations in Entrepreneurial History*, 4 (1967), pp. 98-135.

of "public goods" by households? If we accept Paul Samuelson's definition of collective-consumption goods[8] such that each household's consumption of such goods leads to no subtraction from any other household's consumption of that good, then the size of the lump-sum tax per household would be independent of city site (given common preferences for the *amount* of such goods). No change in our set of wage-cost assumptions would be required under the Samuelson definition. When we expand the public-good definition to include medical care and education, for example, and recognize the economies of size in their production (or, for a fixed expenditure, a rise in the quality of such "urban goods" with city size) then we have a far more difficult system to analyze. With increases in real wages over time (e.g., $\dot{\omega} > 0$), the share of such "urban services" increases in the household budget and the share of foodstuffs declines. The implication is that $h(c)$ becomes less steep over time. We will analyze in section II.3 and II.4 the impact on plant location of reductions in $h'(c)$.

Total costs for the firm are

[12]
$$\begin{aligned} S &= uJ + vK + wL \\ &= \theta qK + q(\rho + \delta)K + wL \\ &= q[f \cdot \phi + g \cdot \gamma + \delta]K + hwL. \end{aligned}$$

We will find it convenient in the analysis which follows to define

[13] $\qquad G(c) = q[f(c) \cdot \phi + g(c) \cdot \gamma + \delta]$
[14] $\qquad H(c) = h(c) \cdot \omega$

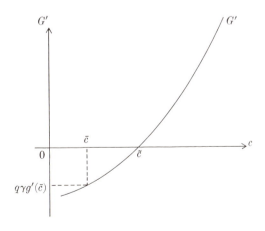

[8] P. A. Samuelson, "The Pure Theory of Public Expenditures," *Review of Economics and Statistics*, 36 (1954), pp. 387-389.

where $f'(\tilde{c}) = -g'(\tilde{c})$ and

$G'(c) = q[f'(c) \cdot \phi + g'(c) \cdot \gamma] \lessgtr 0$ as $c \lessgtr \tilde{c}$,
$G''(c) = q[f''(c) \cdot \phi + g''(c) \cdot \gamma] > 0$, as $f'' > 0$ and $g'' > 0$ for all c,
$H'(c) = h'(c) \cdot \omega > 0$, as $h'(c) > 0$ for all c,
$H''(c) = h''(c) \cdot \omega < 0$, as $h''(c) < 0$ for all c.

The profit function for the firm, P, is defined as

[6a] $\quad P(K, L, c) = pF(K, L) - G(c)K - H(c)L$

and the first-order conditions for profit maximization

[6b] $\quad \begin{cases} 0 = pF_K(K^*, L^*) - G(c^*), \\ 0 = pF_L(K^*, L^*) - H(c^*), \\ 0 = -G'(c^*)K^* - H'(c^*)L^*. \end{cases}$

Consider the third of the above conditions. By assumption $H'(\tilde{c}) > 0$, then since

$$G'(c^*)K^* = -H'(c^*)L^*$$

$G'(c)$ *must* be negative for a solution to exist (i.e., $c^* < c$). Note further that the third condition can be restated as

$$\frac{K^*}{L^*} = -\left[\frac{H'(c^*)}{G'(c^*)}\right].$$

With increasing c, the capital intensity increases. For homogeneous industry groups, we should observe historically that firms located in small urban centers should use more labor-intensive techniques.

When P is *strictly concave*, the vector (K^*, L^*, c^*) yields a maximum. Conditions of concavity require that

$pF_{KK} < 0$
$pF_{LL} < 0$
$p(F_{KK}F_{LL} - F_{KL}^2) > 0$
$pF_{KK}(G''K + H''L) + (G')^2 < 0$
$pF_{LL}(G''K + H''L) + (H')^2 < 0$
$-G''(c)K - H''(c)L < 0$
$p(F_{KK}F_{LL} - F_{KL}^2)(G''K + H''L) >$
$\qquad -[F_{LL}(-G')^2 + F_{KK}(-H)^2 - 2F_{KL}(-G')(-H')].$

II.2. COMPARATIVE STATICS OF LOCATION AND CITY GROWTH
IN HISTORY

The growth of urban labor forces and thus populations is a result of the rate of urban capital formation. Capital formation, or investment, reflects firms' adjustment to new optimal capital stocks. Thus the pattern of city growth which we observe historically can be viewed as the aggregate of individual firm's attempts to adjust their stocks of inputs to a new vector of (K^*, L^*, c^*). This section explores the implications of systematic historical changes in prices exogenous to the urban-industrial firm on their location of new plant and thus on patterns of city growth. We consider five sources of shift in (K^*, L^*, c^*). (1) What is the effect of rising regional real wages on firm location by city size? (2) What is the effect of a decline in $h'(c)$ associated with the increased importance of "urban services" in the household's budget? That is, the effect of rising costs of living associated with rising food costs as population density increases is offset as share of food expenditures in the household budget declines and that for urban services increases. How does this inevitable development affect city growth? (3) What was the probable impact of the integration of national capital markets observed between the Civil War and the First World War on city growth? (4) The rental price on capital services, $v(t)$, at least when adjusted for quality, has declined over time.[9] How would this decline have affected city growth in nineteenth- and twentieth-century American history? (5) Finally, the twentieth-century evidence suggests continual increases in the costs of urban services of all types over time.[10] What impact might this have had on American experience with city growth since the Civil War?

Restating the first-order conditions,[11] we have

$$pF_K[K(p, G, H), L(p, G, H)] - G[c(p, G, H)] = 0$$
$$pF_L[K(p, G, H), L(p, G, H)] - H[c(p, G, H)] = 0$$
$$-G'[c(p, G, H)]K(p, G, H) - H'[c(p, G, H)]L(p, G, H) = 0$$

or, on the definitions of G and H,

$$pF_K[K, L] - q[f(c)\phi + g(c)\gamma + \delta] = 0$$
$$pF_L[K, L] - h(c)\omega = 0$$
$$-q[f'(c)\phi + g'(c)\gamma]K - h'(c)\omega L = 0.$$

[9] Cf. the twentieth-century evidence reported in D. W. Jorgenson, "The Embodiment Hypothesis," *Journal of Political Economy*, 76 (1966), pp. 1-17.

[10] Fuchs, *The Service Economies*, and Baumol, "Macroeconomics of Unbalanced Growth."

[11] While the expressions which follow do not include the asterisk indicating that the values of K, L, and c are indeed optimal levels of the arguments of the profit function, it should be noted that the absence of these indicators is intended only to simplify the notation.

Consider first the impact on (K^*, L^*, c^*) or an increase in real wages, e.g., the first-order conditions differentiated w.r.t. ω:

$$pF_{KK}\left(\frac{\partial K}{\partial \omega}\right) + pF_{KL}\left(\frac{\partial L}{\partial \omega}\right) - q[f'\phi + g'\gamma]\left(\frac{\partial c}{\partial \omega}\right) = 0,$$

$$pF_{LK}\left(\frac{\partial K}{\partial \omega}\right) + pF_{LL}\left(\frac{\partial L}{\partial \omega}\right) - h'\omega\left(\frac{\partial c}{\partial \omega}\right) - h = 0,$$

$$\{-q[f'\phi + g''\gamma]K - h''\omega L\}\left(\frac{\partial c}{\partial \omega}\right) - q[f'\phi + g'\gamma]\left(\frac{\partial K}{\partial \omega}\right)$$
$$- h'\omega\left(\frac{\partial L}{\partial \omega}\right) - h'L = 0,$$

$$\frac{\partial c^*}{\partial \omega} = \frac{\begin{vmatrix} pF_{KK} & pF_{KL} & 0 \\ pF_{LK} & pF_{LL} & h \\ -G' & -H' & h'L \end{vmatrix}}{\begin{vmatrix} pF_{KK} & pF_{KL} & -G' \\ pF_{LK} & pF_{LL} & -H' \\ -G' & -H' & -G''K - H'L \end{vmatrix}}.$$

In order to determine sign of $\dfrac{\partial c^*}{\partial \omega}$ we need to evaluate the determinant in the numerator. Performing the necessary operations, we get

$$p^2[F_{KK}F_{LL} - F_{KL}^2](h'L) + pF_{KL}(-G')h - pF_{KK}h(-h'\omega) \gtreqless 0,$$

since all terms in this expression are positive. Thus the impact of real wages on city size is indeterminate.

$$\frac{\partial c^*}{\partial \omega} > 0 \text{ if } \{p[F_{KK}F_{LL} - F_{KL}^2](h'L) + F_{KL}(-G')h\} < F_{KK}h(-h'\omega)$$

$$\frac{\partial c^*}{\partial \omega} < 0 \text{ if } \{p[F_{KK}F_{LL} - F_{KL}^2](h'L) + F_{KL}(-G')h\} > F_{KK}h(-h'\omega)$$

Unfortunately, similar indeterminacies result in the other four cases we wish to consider. If we retain the assumptions of this model of optimal city size, then it clearly should alert the new urban historian to fruitful research topics. In order adequately to understand the forces of city growth, we need far more empirical evidence relating to these "price-functions"—e.g., $f(c)$, $g(c)$, $h(c)$—facing firms considering location at city sites. Yet by making some reasonable simplifying assumptions, unambiguous predictions on patterns of city growth are still possible.

270

II.3. THE MODEL WITH CONSTANT MONEY WAGES

In Section II.1 we noted that the model could be made considerably more appealing by adding a third wage good to the system. We now consider explicitly the effect of allowing households to consume urban services, such as medical care and education. Assume these services to exhibit full-cost pricing, assume further that decreasing costs prevail throughout the relevant range of city sizes, and finally, assume these wage goods to be consumed in constant shares of total wage income. Let $Z = Z(c)$ be the price of such urban services, then if $h' = -Z'$ we would have, graphically the following:

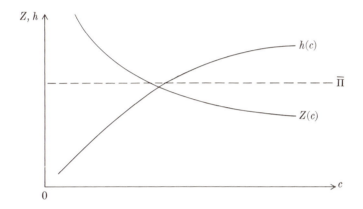

(Alternatively we could assume Z constant across cities and allow the *quality* of urban services to vary instead.) All this suggests that the premise of spatially invariant cost of living may be a condition of interest. In any case, in an effort to get unambiguous results, we now assume $h' = 0$. It then follows that

$$H = h \cdot \omega > 0$$
$$H' = h' \cdot \omega = 0$$

and (from the first-order conditions for profit maximization in this context) that

$$G'(c^*) = q[f'(c^*)\phi + g'(c^*)\gamma] = 0$$
$$f'(c^*) = \frac{-g'(c^*)\gamma}{\phi} > 0$$

This last result indicates that firms will *always* locate in city sites in excess of $\bar{c}$, that is the rising portion of $f(c)$.

271

II.4. COMPARATIVE STATICS OF LOCATION AND CITY GROWTH
IN HISTORY: SOME ANALYTICAL RESULTS

Restating the (first-order) equilibrium conditions with money wage
rates constant across city sites ($H' = 0$), we have

$$0 = pF_K(K^*, L^*) - G(c^*),$$
$$0 = pF_L(K^*, L^*) - W$$
$$0 = -G'(c^*)K^*$$

The third of these conditions (in conjunction with [1c]) implies
$G'(c^*) = 0$. We now wish to determine in turn the impact of rising
real wages, falling borrowing rates, and rising costs of municipal services on optimal city sites, c^*, and thus on city growth patterns. Differentiating each of these with respect to W, γ, and ϕ produces the
following comparative static derivatives:

$$\frac{\partial c^*}{\partial W} = 0,$$

$$\frac{\partial c^*}{\partial \gamma} = \frac{g'}{-G''} > 0,$$

$$\frac{\partial c^*}{\partial \phi} = \frac{f'}{-G''} < 0.$$

Since we will always find $c^* > \bar{c}$, the impact (on the equilibrium
solution) of an increase in property tax rates will cause the equilib-
rium-site characteristic (c) to move toward $\bar{c}$, while a decrease in
the level of interest rates will have the same effect. That is, the combination of rising costs of municipal services and the general fall in
economy-wide borrowing rates both should contribute to a lowering
in optimal city sizes. Given lags in adjustment, we should observe
greater relative growth rates in cities of intermediate size, not unlike
recent twentieth-century American experience.

III   SUGGESTIONS FOR EMPIRICAL RESEARCH BY NEW URBAN
       HISTORIANS

THE particular theory of location at hand suggests several fruitful
lines of inquiry. Attention is called to further evidence in support
of the "empirical premises" which we have invoked with respect to
input price patterns. Our analysis suggests the usefulness of empirical
studies of several areas. First, the discussion of money wage variability
over nineteenth- and early twentieth-century cities is brought to light
as a topic of concern. The existence of such variations, the rate of

their disappearance, and their sources should be established. Such investigations should include analyses of patterns of urban consumption and the pricing of "staple goods" as well as pricing patterns in the urban service sector. Our work also suggests the import of the structural characteristics of the service sector in early urban economies. In this regard we are concerned with the analysis of urban-services pricing, taxation of urban properties, the availability of these "goods," technological developments, and the scale (or engineering) characteristics of production processes in this sector. (We have recently begun an extended investigation of several of these phenomena.)

It is interesting to note that the empirical research suggested in this report is not of the type that would have been outlined by extant theories of plant location. We have, of course, broken sharply with such theories by abstracting from transportation costs. We would suggest that such theories, bound (as they commonly are) to "fixed coefficient" representations of the production process and wholly innocent of recent developments in the neoclassical theory of optimal capital accumulation, are doomed to limited future use. On the other hand, the special location theory outlined above may serve as a guide for future studies of location decisions. Let us hope that, by the nature of its design, this theory will encourage more historical inquiry along lines which will usefully advance our ability to provide explanations of the growth pattern of American cities during the nineteenth and early twentieth centuries.[12]

[12] This report is a revision of the discussion offered at the Madison conference. We acknowledge the helpful comments of Raymond Dacey, Cliff Lloyd, Roy Ruffin, and Thomas Weiss. Partial financial support from the National Science Foundation (Grants No. 3238 and 3239) is also acknowledged.

The Contributors

Martyn J. Bowden is associate professor of geography in the Graduate School of Geography, Clark University, where he has taught since 1964. He studied geography at University College, London, and the University of Nebraska, and received his Ph.D. in historical geography at the University of California (Berkeley) in 1967. He taught previously at Dartmouth College. He was founding editor and later co-editor of the *Historical Geography Newsletter* to 1973, and he is founding secretary of the *Eastern Historical Geography Association.* Related publications include "Downtown Through Time," *Economic Geography* (1971) and "Reconstruction Following Catastrophe: The Laissez-faire Rebuilding of Downtown San Francisco After the Earthquake and Fire of 1906," *Proceedings of the Association of American Geographers* (1970).

Kathleen Neils Conzen is assistant professor of history at Wellesley College. She received her Ph.D. in history from the University of Wisconsin (Madison) in 1972. Her dissertation, *"The German Athens": Milwaukee and the Accommodation of Its Immigrants, 1836-1860,* will be published by Harvard University Press.

Claudia Dale Goldin is currently assistant professor of economics at Princeton University, on leave from the University of Wisconsin (Madison). She received her doctorate in economics from the University of Chicago in 1972. She has published "The Economics of Emancipation" in the *Journal of Economic History* (1973) and is completing a monograph entitled *Urban Slavery.*

Robert Higgs is associate professor of economics at the University of Washington. He received his Ph.D. in economics from Johns Hopkins University in 1968. His publications include *The Transformation of the American Economy, 1865-1914: An Essay in Interpretation* (1971).

Kenneth T. Jackson is associate professor of history and director of the College Urban Studies Program at Columbia University. A native of Memphis, he received his Ph.D. in history and economics at the University of Chicago in 1966 and has taught at Antioch College, the Air Force Institute of Technology, and New York University. He has written *The Ku Klux Klan in the City, 1915-1930* (1967) and co-edited *American Vistas* (1971) and *Cities in American History* (1972). A Fellow of the Society of American Historians, Professor

274

Jackson is currently working on a history of the process of suburbanization in the United States, 1850-1950.

Eric E. Lampard graduated from the London School of Economics and the University of Wisconsin (Madison) where he studied economic history and land economics. Formerly professor of economic history and adjunct professor of urban and regional planning at Wisconsin, he now teaches at the State University of New York at Stony Brook. Author of *Industrial Revolution* (1957), *The Rise of the Dairy Industry* (1963), and co-author of *Regions, Resources, and Economic Growth* (1960), he has contributed to many professional journals and symposia. His most recent publication is the 1972 Prothero Lecture of the Royal Historical Society: "The Pursuit of Happiness in the City," appearing in the society's *Transactions*, 1973. He was a member of the Social Science Research Council's Committee on Urbanization, the Committee on Urban Economics (CUE), and of the National Research Council's Social Science Advisory Panel to the U.S. Department of Housing and Urban Development.

Zane L. Miller received his Ph.D. in history at the University of Chicago in 1966. He held a post-doctoral research fellowship in the Center for Urban Studies at the University of Chicago (1970-1971) and is currently associate professor of history at the University of Cincinnati. He is the author of *Boss Cox's Cincinnati* (1968) and *The Urbanization of Modern America* (1973), and co-editor of *Physician to the West: Selected Writings of Daniel Drake on Science and Society* (1970).

Allan R. Pred is professor of geography at the University of California (Berkeley). He obtained his A.B. from Antioch College, his M.S. from Pennsylvania State University, and his Ph.D. from the University of Chicago. His published works include *The Spatial Dynamics of U. S. Urban-Industrial Growth, 1800-1914* (1966), *Urban Growth and the Circulation of Information: The United States System of Cities, 1790-1840* (1973), and *The Growth and Development of Systems of Cities in Advanced Economics* (Lund Studies in Geography, Series B, No. 38, 1973, pp. 1-82). Professor Pred is currently carrying out further work on the process of city-system development.

Leo F. Schnore is professor of sociology at the University of Wisconsin (Madison), where he has taught since 1959. He received his Ph.D. from the University of Michigan in 1955, and has subsequently published some eighty-odd articles and reviews in journals of demography, economics, geography, political science, urban transportation, and urban planning, as well as in sociological periodicals. He received an unrestricted research award from the Social Science Research Coun-

275

cil in 1962, and was a Fellow at the Center for Advanced Study in the Behavioral Sciences in 1971-1972. He is a member of the editorial board of the new *Journal of Urban History;* co-editor of *The Study of Urbanization* (1965) and *Urban Research and Policy Planning* (1967); editor of *Social Science and the City* (1968); and author of *The Urban Scene: Human Ecology and Demography* (1965) and *Class and Race in Cities and Suburbs* (1972). His current research, supported by the National Science Foundation, deals with "The Ecology of American Cities: Some Quantitative Studies in Urban History."

Gregory H. Singleton is assistant professor of history at Northeastern Illinois University. He completed his Ph.D. in history from the University of California (Los Angeles) in 1972. His publications include "The Genesis of Suburbia: A Complex of Historical Trends," in *The Urbanization of the Suburbs,* Louis H. Masotti and Jeffrey K. Hadden (editors) (1973), and "'Mere Middle-class Institution': Urban Protestantism in Nineteenth Century America," *Journal of Social History* (1973). He is coeditor of *The Great Lakes Review.*

Joseph A. Swanson is associate professor of economics at the University of Iowa (Iowa City). He received his Ph.D. in economics from the University of Wisconsin (Madison) and has taught at Purdue University. His previous research work was in the area of microeconomic models of urban growth. Swanson's current research is on patterns of municipal spending in the twentieth century and the stochastic structure of the U.S. quarterly income and product accounts.

Jeffrey G. Williamson is professor of economics at the University of Wisconsin (Madison). He received his Ph.D. in economics from Stanford University in 1961. He is currently editor of *Explorations in Economic History* and serves as a member of the editorial boards of *Economic Development and Cultural Change* and *The Review of Economics and Statistics.* Awarded the Cole Prize in 1972, he has since 1970 assumed main responsibility for the annual Cliometric Conference. His papers in economic history have appeared in the *Journal of Political Economy, Journal of Economic History, American Economic Review,* and *Explorations in Economic History.* His books include *American Growth and the Balance of Payments, 1820-1913* (1964), *Dualistic Economic Development: Theory and History* (1972), *Lessons from Japanese Development: An Analytical History* (1974), and a forthcoming volume, *Late Nineteenth Century American Development: A General Equilibrium History.*

Index of Names and Places*

Abell, Aaron, I., 227n
Abilene, Texas, 128n
Abramovitz, Moses, 44n
Alameda, California, 131
Albany, New York, 72, 113, 258n
Albion, Robert G., 58n, 59n, 60n, 61n, 84n, 85n
Alexander, John K., 128n
Alexandria, Virginia, 237
Allen, R.G.D., 18n
Alonso, William, 147n
Amory, Cleveland, 131n
Amsterdam, 86
Anderson, Harry H., 182n
Antwerp, Belgium, 86
Aristotle, 47
Armroyd, George, 61n
Atlanta, 31, 32, 34, 146n, 227n
Augusta, Georgia, 73, 237

Bacon, E. H., 184n
Bailey, Kenneth K., 206n
Bailyn, Bernard, 86
Baltimore, Maryland, 52, 57, 58, 59, 60, 61, 70, 71, 72, 73, 113, 116, 123, 124, 235, 236, 238, 243, 244, 245n
Baltzell, E. Digby, 211n, 220
Balzac, 13n
Banfield, Edward, 126
Barton, Bruce, 215
Barton, E. E., 180n
Barton's Point, Massachusetts, 111
Battis, Emery, 226
Baumol, W. J., 264n
Baylies, A., 152n
Bedarida, François, 26n
Bellah, Robert N., 206n
Bensman, Joseph, 208
Berger, Bennett M., 111
Berger, Peter L., 211n
Berkeley, E. C., 16n
Berkhofer, R. F., 41n
Berry, Brian J. L., 17n, 62, 75n, 147n
Bickenbach, Irene, 10

Birmingham, Alabama, 34, 123n, 185, 188, 190, 192, 194, 195, 197, 199, 203
Birmingham, England, 108
Blair, Pat, 10
Blake, Nelson Manfred, 117n
Blau, Peter M., 9n, 35n
Blumenfeld, Hans, 117n, 123n
Blumin, Stuart, 129, 146n
Bogue, Allan G., 26n, 31n
Bogue, Donald J., 121n, 191, 193
Bombay, India, 120n
Bordentown, New Jersey, 61
Boston, Massachusetts, 6, 27, 28, 30n, 31n, 57, 58, 59, 60, 61, 62, 70, 72, 73, 78, 83–84, 85, 86, 88, 111, 113, 114, 115n, 116, 123, 131, 133, 134, 146n, 157n, 227n
Botero, Giovanni, 79
Boulding, Kenneth, 47
Bowden, Martyn J., 75–109, 7, 9, 27, 28, 32, 77n, 78n, 84n, 86n, 89n, 104n, 274
Bowen, Daniel, 130n
Bowers, Roy Edwin, 216n
Bradford, Sheila Kaplan, 152n
Braeman, John, 205n
Bremner, Robert H., 205n
Brett-James, N. G., 79n, 80n, 82n, 85n, 105n
Bricker, Garland A., 216n
Bridenbaugh, Carl, 5, 24n, 83n, 111
Bridgeport, Connecticut, 255, 256, 257
Brighton, Massachusetts, 115n, 134
Brody, David, 205n
Bronx, 114, 120n, 135, 136, 139
Brookline, Massachusetts, 115n
Brooklyn, New York, 57, 114, 115n, 131, 138, 139
Brown, A. Theodore, 9, 13n
Brown, Lawrence, 56n
Bruce, William G., 145n
Bruges, Belgium, 86
Brunner, Edmund de S., 216n
Brunner, Mary V., 216n

* In view of the detailed summaries provided in Professor Lampard's Foreward, a subject index was deemed unnecessary.

Library of Congress Cataloging in Publication Data

Schnore, Leo Francis, 1927-
  The new urban history: quantitative explorations by
American historians.

  (Quantitative studies in history)
    1. Cities and towns—United States—History—Ad-
dresses, essays, lectures. I. Bowden, Martyn J.
II. Title. III. Series.
HT123.S32   301.36'3'0973   73-2474
ISBN 0-691-10026-8